Alabama *now & then*

a contemporary look

By Donald B. Dodd

Published in the United States by The Advertiser Company,
200 Washington Avenue, Montgomery, Alabama 36104.

International Standard Book Number 1-882616-06-5
Library of Congress Catalog Card Number 94-073159

Photo/caption courtesy of Ned Jenkins, Linda Derry and Greg Rhinehart, Alabama Historical Commission

Living History Reenactors pose for the 1994 Alabama Archaelogy Week Poster: L-R, top to bottom; coal miner Jack Bergstresser, Spanish explorer Richard Cobb, British frontiersman Lee Lehman, African-American woman Evelyn Cox, Creek warrior Butch Fuller, French frontiersman Ned Jenkins, Creek girl Amanda Sexton, Creek wife "Rising Fawn" Ginger Sexton, French frontiersboy Chase Jenkins.

Introduction

Alabama has contrasting images. Consider these: Mobile's Mardi Gras and Winfield's Mule Day; Sheffield and Slapout; Birmingham and Bayou La Batre; the Shakespeare Festival and the Rattlesnake Rodeo; Nat King Cole and Bocephus; Vulcan and the Boll Weevil Monument; 16th Street Baptist Church and the Little White House of the Confederacy; De Soto Falls gorge and Gulf Shores beaches; the Coon Dog Cemetery and Anniston's Museum of Natural History; Samford Hall and Denny Chimes; Coretta Scott King and Bull Connor; and Mount Cheaha and Bellingrath Gardens. All make up our collective mosaic of Alabama. Ours is a diverse state.

Alabama's geography and history also suggest diversity, conflict, and connecting links. In the pre-statehood era, Alabama served as a buffer between French and English, Spanish and English, Spanish and American and, as an American territory, between Indians and Americans. A constant theme is sectionalism between "South Alabama" and "North Alabama," particularly during the secession crisis. After the Civil War, a political conflict was added between the forces of conservatism ("Bourbons") and reform (Populists, Progressives, New Dealers, etc.). The state has evolved from a rural agricultural state centered on cotton to an urban industrial state with diversified agriculture.

Preface

Alabama Now and Then is the culmination of a lifelong trip through the multi-faceted history of Alabama. Admittedly, it is a broad stroke of the brush not intended for those wishing an in-depth study of a single facet or a comprehensive survey of our history. But perhaps it will be welcomed by those who wish for the big picture with a few side trips to little-known places. Though a selective and popular history for a general audience, it should serve as a good introduction for more thorough study. Topics are included that are just generally fun to read about (and often neglected in state history books) in an effort to give an understanding of the fullness of our history as a people and a state.

As a history, the "then" part of the title is the central theme, but as a contemporary look the "now" is always in mind. Therefore, the reader will find the De Soto Expedition map depicts contemporary locations near de Soto's approximate route and Fort Conde's location is tied to the Mobile Tunnel and I-10. A general objective is to connect an Alabama reader's knowledge of the present — from geographic locations to our practice of driving on the right side of the road — to the past.

Those who enjoyed Michael Shaara's **Killer Angels** (and its hero, the 20th Maine's Joshua Chamberlain,) which Ted Turner had made into the movie "Gettysburg," will find of interest the gallant repeated Confederate attacks against Chamberlain's formidable natural defenses (including the charges of the 15th Alabama regiment commanded by Henry County's William C. Oates, a post-Civil War governor of Alabama). Oates at Little Round Top, John B. Gordon and the 6th Alabama at Antietam and Menewa at Horseshoe Bend a half-century earlier, are all stories herein of the "Chamberlain" variety. Equally moving are the events of the civil rights movement — Jo Ann Robinson's experiences in the bus boycott, Floyd Mann heroics upon the arrival of the freedom riders in Montgomery, and the tragedy at the 16th Street Baptist Church in Birmingham.

A number of authors add variety and spice in the form of short, special interest articles and present history in a broader context than just politics and economic development. Literature, architecture and preservation, folklore, music, education, and football are all addressed. Nonbylined sidebars are by the author. Although the narrative uses some "I was there" materials such as the reminiscences of Oates and Gordon, the bulk of the narrative synthesizes books and articles on Alabama history.

In Alabama and Southern history courses at Auburn University at Montgomery (AUM) students have a wide choice of reading and writing assignments to respond to individual needs. They nearly always read the most interesting and entertaining books first. In a Civil War course the progression has been Shaara's **Killer Angels,** Stephen Sears, **Landscape Turned Red** (Antietam), and Bruce Catton's **Civil War.** The five most popular books in Alabama and New South classes have been Paul Gaston's **Women of Fair Hope,** Jo Ann Robinson's **Montgomery Bus Boycott,** Bob Ingram's **That's The Way I Saw It, II,** Carl Elliott's **Cost of Courage,** and Howell Raines' **My Soul Is Rested.** Civil War in Alabama enthusiasts like

Malcolm McMillan's collection of original sources in **The Alabama Confederate Reader,** and James Pickett Jones' **Yankee Blitzkrieg.** Selected materials from all of these books are synthesized in **Now and Then** to present them to a broader audience and to produce an interesting summary of Alabama history.

For the same purposes, the names of authors and books are likewise sprinkled throughout the narrative — and to acknowledge specific debts of documentation. Authors also are listed in the index. Full citations of all these sources and several thousand more, with annotations, will be published in the near future by Greenwood Press as a **Bibliography of Alabama History.** Complete citations and the addresses of publishers are also available in most libraries and book stores in the volumes of **Books in Print.** The best source for a steady dose of popularly presented Alabama history is the "Alabama Heritage" magazine published at the University of Alabama (as is the more academic "Alabama Review"). The single most comprehensive source of Alabama history books is the University of Alabama Press (UAP). Two recent UAP publications of great value to **Now and Then** were **From Civil War to Civil Rights: Alabama, 1850-1960,** a collection of Alabama Review articles by the editor Sarah Woolfolk Wiggins, and **Alabama: The History of a Deep South State,** a mammoth 735-page history in three sections — part one (to 1865) by Leah Rawls Atkins of Auburn University, part two (1865-1920) by William Warren Rogers of Florida State University and Robert David Ward of Georgia Southern University, and part three (1920-1990s) by Wayne Flynt, Auburn University. Also useful were Ben Williams' **Literary History of Alabama in the 19th Century,** Al Head's MLA thesis at AUM (on the Tuscaloosa Bards), Malcolm McMillan's **The Disintegration of a Confederate State** on the three Civil War governors of Alabama, Taylor Branch's **Parting the Waters,** and Juan Williams' **Eyes on the Prize** on the civil rights movement, and the general Alabama histories by Albert Burton Moore, Charles Summersell, Malcolm McMillan, and Virginia Hamilton.

Particularly in the early drafts I pulled on former work ... **Historical Atlas of Alabama** for general direction and as a capsule summary of Alabama history focused on economics, demography, geography, and politics; an unpublished "Indian Trails to Interstates" manuscript (which died in a Highway Department file cabinet) for travel and transportation history; my master's thesis at Auburn under Frank L. Owsley, Jr. for 1832-1861 sectionalism (heavily based on antebellum Alabama newspapers); newspaper columns in the 1970s done for the *Daily Northwest Alabamian* (Haleyville) and *Daily Mountain Eagle* (Jasper); and two recent Alabama history textbooks collaborated with Clairmont Press co-authors — **Alabama: Its History and Geography** and **Twentieth Century Alabama: History and Geography.** The statistics and the graphs in the last chapter were based on the Alabama material in **Historical Statistics of the States of the United States: Two Centuries of the Census, 1790-1990** (Westport, CT: Greenwood Press, 1993).

Phil Coley constructed the computer-generated maps and charts. The

Advertiser's Coke Ellington, as the copy editor and production editor, expertly manipulated a new computer system to place and size all of the illustrations with narrative and sidebars into the final product. AUM photographer Frank Williams contributed the original Montgomery photographs.

Without the help of three people, **Now and Then** would not have been possible. Mr. Allen Phillips, community affairs director, the *Montgomery Advertiser*, the senior editor, provided constant guidance and effective editorial assistance. Millie Weaver, secretary to the dean of Liberal Arts at AUM, cheerfully and punctually word processed numerous revisions. Amelia Bartlett-Dodd, my wife and mother of our very energetic 7-year-old, Loren, did everything — edited incessantly and skillfully, wrote two sidebars, completed the index, and kept me humble, but gratefully so.

Several AUM colleagues read major sections of the manuscript — Phil Coley, Art Department, John Fair, head of the History Department, and Marion Michael, dean of Liberal Arts — as did Lynda Brown, Betsy Coley, Lloyd Cornett, Pamela Tyler, and Millie Weaver. Readers of one chapter or more include Tom Bartlett, Elizabeth Dunn, Martha Jane Ellington, Mindy Reynolds, and Craig Sheldon. All made comments which were incorporated into revisions or probably should have been.

Finding available photographs and illustrations was time-consuming. Three major sources were the *Advertiser* files, Bureau of Tourism and Travel, and Alabama Archives. Peggy Ross retrieved folders of photographs from the *Advertiser* files. Wayne Greenhaw made Tourism and Travel files accessible and Dan Brothers ably expedited the collection process. Mark Bonner, Ami Simpson, and Frances Smiley also assisted. Director Ed Bridges and the entire staff of Alabama Archives was equally helpful — especially Tonya Zanish, Bob Cason, Mark Palmer, and Norwood Kerr.

Billy Joe Camp, director, Alabama Development Office, introduced me to appropriate ADO staffers who made every effort to meet our needs. Robert Sutton, Mark Worsham, and Steven Prince each shared information on recent Alabama economic activity. Courtney Parker Murphy coordinated Alabama Film Commission photography with Dan Brothers.

Mrs. Billie Richey, librarian, Alabama Department of Transportation, expedited use of the department's files and retrieved the "Indian Trails to Interstate" manuscript on several occasions. Jerome Ennels, the Air University historian, provided Maxwell AFB photographs, and Joe Caver, AF Historical Agency, Maxwell AFB, located a sharp photo of B.O. Davis, Jr. The Birmingham Chamber of Commerce's Don Newton, Jr., contributed Birmingham skyline shots. Ed Davis sent a package of Space Center photos and Bill Tharpe photos from Alabama Power Company files. Other individuals who generously shared photographs and literature on some aspect of Alabama history included Dick Cooper, Alabama Music Hall of Fame, Ned and Pat Jenkins (Fort Toulouse materials), Bill Legg, Alabama Sports Hall of Fame, and Greg Rhinehart, Alabama Historical Commission.

AUM Library personnel were helpful as usual, particularly, on this project, Debbie West, the interlibrary loan librarian, and Rickey Best, the special collections librarian. I can truthfully say that every single person contacted assisted in some way.

Most of all, the inspiration for producing an Alabama history for the state's 175th Anniversary was Richard H. Amberg, Jr., publisher of the *Montgomery Advertiser.* I am especially grateful to him for giving me the opportunity to work on this project and the support to see it through. His congenial and able leadership permeates the entire *Advertiser* environs to yield a professional and productive, yet wholesome and friendly workplace. **Alabama Now and Then** was a rewarding project.

Table of Contents

List of Sidebars

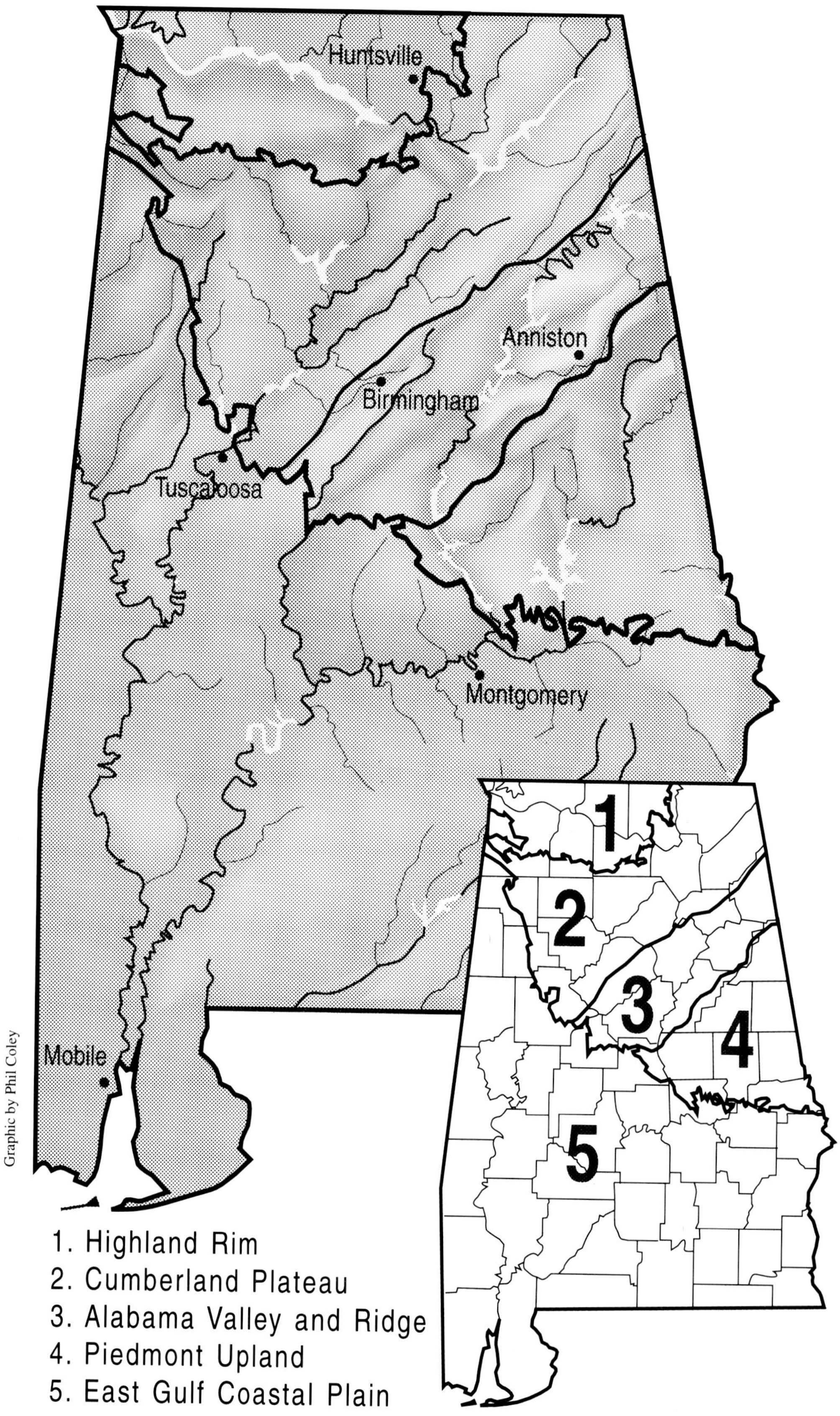

Physiographic Regions of Alabama

I

Mosaic Alabamas:

The Geographic Setting

Alabama is named for the Alabama River which, in turn, received its name from the Alabamas, an Indian tribe which once lived near the present site of Montgomery. "Alabama" is a Choctaw word meaning "thicket clearers" or "vegetation gatherers."

Alabama is unusual in having all five of the physiographical provinces existing east of the Mississippi River: the Highland Rim, the Cumberland Plateau, the Ridge and Valley, the Piedmont, and the Coastal Plain. Each has distinct physical characteristics contributing to the evolution of diverse cultures. This geographical diversity is further fragmented within a province, for example, Coastal Plain cultural differences between residents of the Black Belt, the Wiregrass, Mobile proper, and the Gulf Shores beaches.

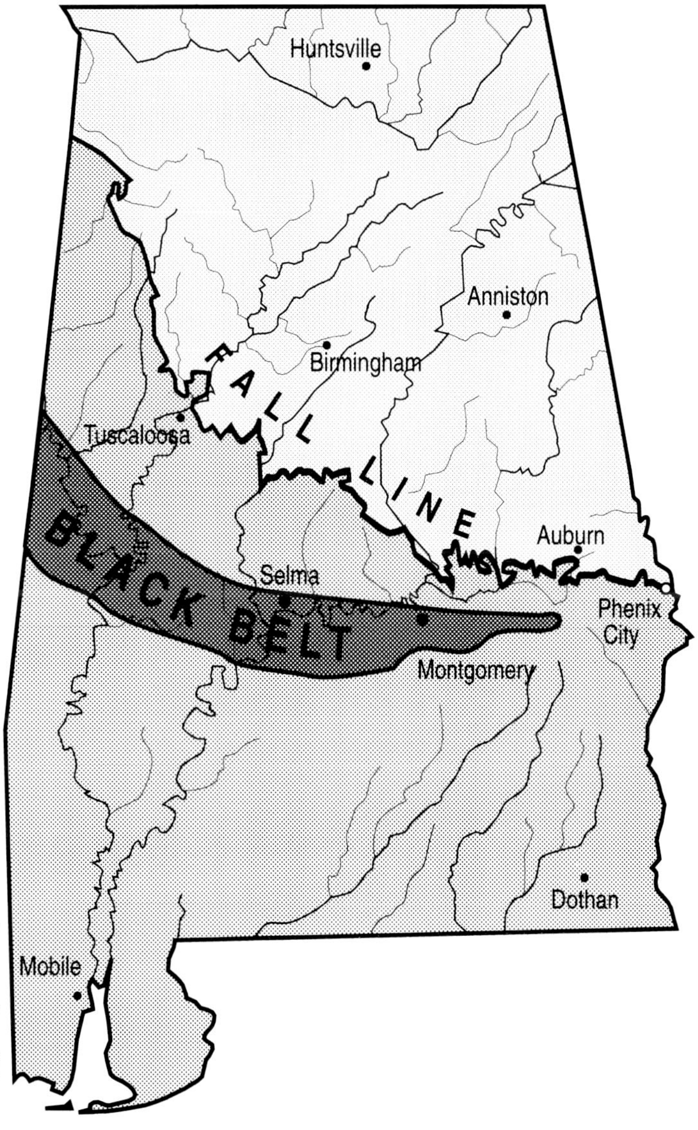

Graphic by Phil Coley

These provinces now cut across state lines and often cause Alabamians to have more in common, from a physical landscape perspective, with residents of other states in the same settings. The Highland Rim in the northwest is more like central Tennessee to the north. In the crises of 1861 many Tennessee Valley residents wanted to delay Alabama's secession to follow the lead of Tennessee. And after Alabama's secession, North Alabamians talked of joining with Tennesseans to form the separate state of "Nickajack." The Cumberland plateau shares a mountainous terrain with the Appalachian Highlands. Riding the Blue Ridge from Front Royal,

Photo by Dan Brothers, Alabama Bureau of Tourism and Travel

Rock Bridge Canyon waterfalls near Hodges

Virginia, to Cherokee, North Carolina, then crossing the Smokies to visit Cades' Cove, one can see much in common with the Mentone, De Soto Falls, and Little River Canyon areas of northeastern Alabama. The Ridge and Valley parallels the Plateau northeasterly to the Great Valley of the Shenandoah. Linking I-59 and I-81 to survey northeastern Alabama and western Virginia before moving east is a picturesque route to Washington, D.C., that will reveal the Ridge and Valley continuity.

Other classification schemes often encompass more than one physical province. The Piedmont shares a "mineral belt" classification with the Ridge and Valley area and a hydroelectric capacity with the Highland Rim. The Coastal Plain, covering two-thirds of the state, has been, historically, both a "Timber Belt" and an agricultural area and includes the "Black Belt" — named for its dark soil, although the presence of large numbers of blacks has led some social scientists to refer to "Black Belt" as a predominantly black cultural area.

TVA hydroelectric power has been a major stimulant to the industrial growth of the Tennessee Valley, especially industries which require large amounts of water and power such as chemical, textile, and aluminum. Industrialization has spurred the urbanization of the Valley from the quad cities of Florence, Sheffield, Tuscumbia, and Muscle Shoals in the west to Athens, Decatur, and Huntsville in the east.

Alabama's resources include a network of navigable rivers, a temperate climate, extensive forests, and minerals. The Tennessee River is now connected to the Tombigbee by the Tenn-Tom Canal and both rivers are navigable for their entire lengths, as is the Warrior, to Birmingham Port; the Alabama, to Wetumpka; and the Chattahoochee, to Columbus, Georgia. The fertile river valleys were centers of Indian and later European civilizations, and the waterways were main transportation routes prior to railroads and paved roads. The climate, interacting with the natural vegetation and an adequate drainage system, has produced generally fertile soils, and contributes to the state's having been agriculturally focused for much of its history. The predominant cash crops are cotton, corn, soybeans, wheat, and peanuts. The land under the soil is likewise productive; a significant part of the total labor force of several northwest Alabama counties is engaged in mining, particularly within a 75-mile radius of Walker County.

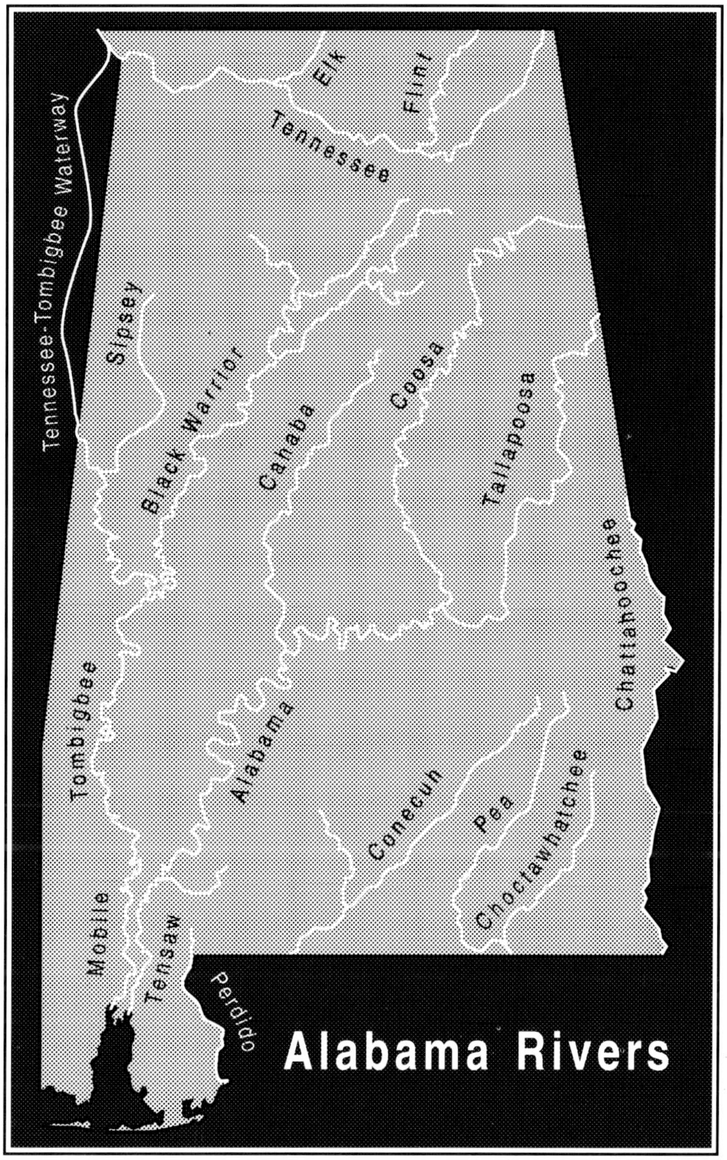

Graphic by Phil Coley

European Invaders

Five flags have flown over Alabama: the French (1702-1763); the British (1763- 1780); the Spanish (1780-1813); the United States (1813-1861; 1865-present); and the Confederate (1861-1865). The Spanish were the first to explore the coast and interior of Alabama, but the French made the first permanent settlement.

Although the Alabama coastline was accurately portrayed on European maps as early as 1507, the first known Spanish explorer of the Alabama coast was Alonzo de Pineda, who entered Mobile Bay in 1519. Pineda named Mobile Bay Bahia Espiritu Santo — the Bay of the Holy Ghost. He explored the Bay and the Mobile River north of it for a month before re-entering the Gulf.

A decade after Pineda, Panfilo Narvaez's expedition came to the Gulf area. After becoming separated from his fleet, Narvaez built five horsehide boats

Photo by Dan Brothers, Alabama Bureau of Tourism and Travel

The Mobile skyline from the U.S.S. Alabama's east side.

to traverse the Gulf coast to Mexico, which he thought was a short distance away. His troops landed near Mobile Bay before proceeding westward to the mouth of the Mississippi River, where they were swept to sea. Two members of Narvaez's party lived to become a significant part of the more comprehensive de Soto expedition to follow: Juan Ortiz, who was captured by the Indians but survived to learn their languages and be rescued by de Soto and serve as his interpreter; and Cabeza de Vaca, who eventually found his way to Mexico. De Vaca's account of his wanderings later prompted de Soto to outfit his expedition to the Southeast.

Hernando de Soto was a veteran of the Pizarro expedition to Peru. His share of Inca spoils netted him a small fortune which financed his ill-fated expedition to the southeastern United States.

De Soto's expedition landed at Tampa Bay in 1539 and explored north and east through Florida, Georgia, the western edge of the Carolinas, and Tennessee before entering northeastern Alabama June 28, 1540. The Spanish conquistadors came into the southeastern United States to find gold and silver — anticipating the exploitation of existing Indian civilizations such as the Aztecs in Mexico and the Inca in Peru. They came in the name of God, country, and personal greed — not necessarily in that order.

Mounted on powerful horses, they took what they wanted by force, through superior shields, swords, lances, and muskets. Their routine needs included corn and other supplies, guides, bearers, and chiefs for hostage. They were brutal and ruthless, on occasion using large war dogs to tear apart those who opposed them.

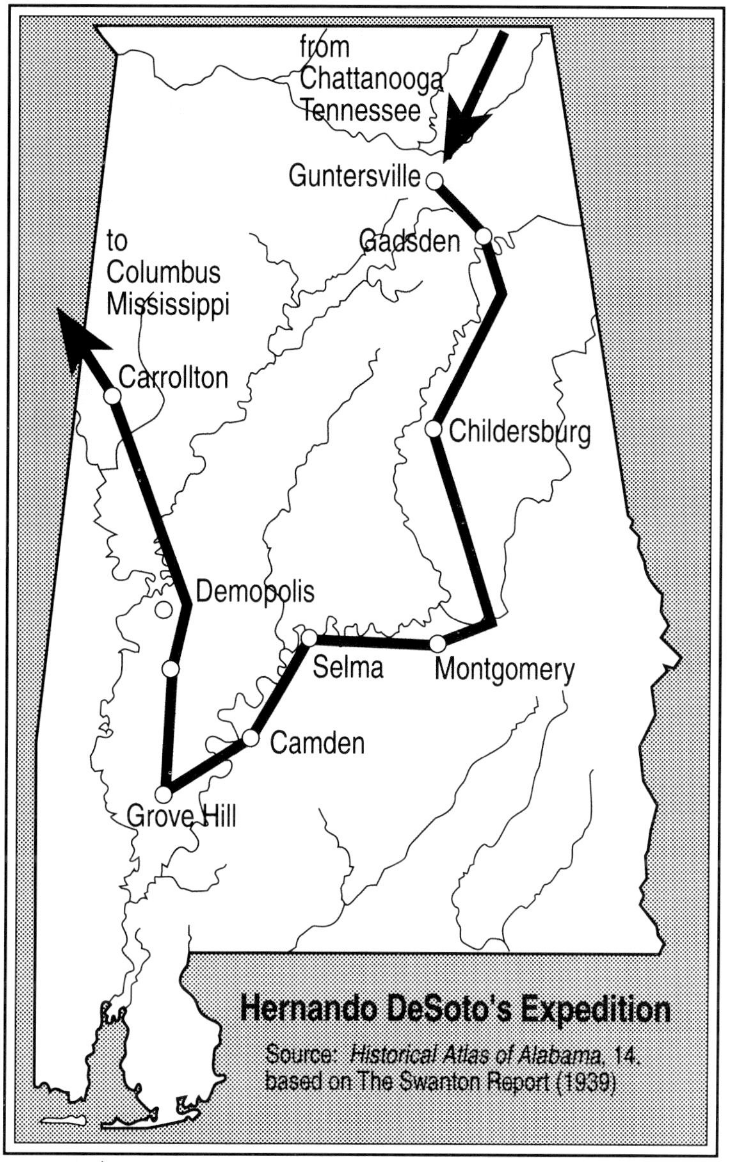

Hernando DeSoto's Expedition

Source: *Historical Atlas of Alabama*, 14, based on The Swanton Report (1939)

Graphic by Phil Coley

De Soto was looking for gold and he stayed in a village until he got answers about where to find it. One innovative tribe in the Alabama-Florida border area told of Indians in Guale (Georgia) who had so much gold they wore hats made of it. De Soto's methods preceded him to the land of Tuscaloosa, the Black Warrior, in lower Alabama. Tuscaloosa, the toughest chief de Soto encountered, was also the largest. When he was mounted on the expedition's largest horse his feet still came close to the ground. A fearless leader of a brave tribe, Tuscaloosa led de Soto to his log-stockaded fortress of Maubila, where one of the bloodiest battles ever fought between whites and Indians in North America followed. Six hundred well-armed Spaniards fought 10,000 Indians armed with bows and arrows and stone weapons for nine hours. More than 20 Spaniards died and most of the 600 were wounded. Spanish estimates of Maubilian casualties and eyewitness testimonials vary from 2,500 to 10,000. Forty-five horses were slain and most of the expedition's supplies were lost.

The power of the Maubilian was destroyed, although the tribe gave its name to Alabama's port city and its chief's name to the city of Tuscaloosa and the Black Warrior River. On the Spanish side, the wounded required a month to recuperate, and most of the pearls and other ornaments looted from other tribes had been lost. After the reversal, de Soto's expedition proceeded northwest thus initiating the recorded history of Mississippi, Arkansas, Texas, and Louisiana. De Soto died of a fever and, to bolster his claim of immortality, was buried by his men in the Mississippi River, the inland portion of which he is recorded as being the discoverer.

Having four diaries to compare for specific locations and time, distance, and direction of travel, the United States De Soto Commission in 1939 published an approximate route of the Spaniard's sojourn (and in some

Photo by Dan Brothers, Alabama Bureau of Tourism and Travel

"DeSoto's First Encounter with the Wiregrass Natives" mural, Wiregrass Festival of Murals in Dothan

cases one or more possible routes). The accompanying map hypothesizes where de Soto traveled in relationship to contemporary locations; Guntersville to Carrollton by way of Gadsden, Childersburg, Montgomery, Selma, Camden, Grove Hill, Linden, and Eutaw.

De Soto's visit to the Southeast was the most significant of the Spanish expeditions as it was larger and traversed more terrain. It was especially important to Alabama history because the Spanish records constitute our main source of information on the geography and Indian life of "Alabama" in the 16th century. In fact, other than the limited records of a couple of minor Spanish return visits, the de Soto records remain the standard reference point of Alabama history until the arrival of the French a century and a half later.

Two Spanish conquistadors who followed de Soto were Guido de las Bazares and Tristan de Luna. Bazares visited Mobile Bay in late 1558; de Luna arrived in the same locale the following fall. The Spanish wished to establish a base to protect gold and silver shipments passing through the Florida straits enroute from Mexico and Peru (after an overland passage at the Isthmus of Panama) to Spain. Bazares was impressed with Mobile Bay because of its harbor, timber for shipbuilding, food grown by the Indians, game, fishing, and good pottery clay on the eastern shore. Bazares' stay was brief but de Luna brought 500 soldiers and 1,000 civilians with the aim of establishing a Gulf Coast colony. When eight of his 13 ships were destroyed by a hurricane soon after landing, de Luna's colony subsisted on supplies sent by Velasco, the Viceroy of Mexico, game and fish, and whatever they could coerce from the local Indians. When the Indians fled, de Luna sent a party to the Indian village of "Coosa" (near Childersburg in Talladega County). They successfully acquired provisions from the Coosas after fighting with them against enemies to the west. The "Coosa" party rejoined the main body and, in 1561, returned to Spain. Their two-year visit had been eventful, but not profitable.

The first permanent settlement in Alabama was made by the French at Mobile in 1702 by the Le Moyne brothers, Iberville and Bienville. The first site of Mobile was at Twenty-Seven Mile Bluff and was named "Fort Louis de la Mobile" in honor of Louis XIV and nearby Indians. In 1709, the original town of Mobile was flooded and the colonists moved downriver where they established a second Fort Louis de la Mobile. It was around this fort that the city of Mobile grew.

Mobile was the capital of French Louisiana from 1711 to 1720 when the capital was moved to a more central location — first in Biloxi, then to New Orleans two years later — but Mobile remained an important French possession. Construction began on a stone and brick fort in 1717 to replace the original log stockade. The name of the fort changed from Fort Louis de la Mobile to Fort Conde in 1724 and by this time construction was very near completion.

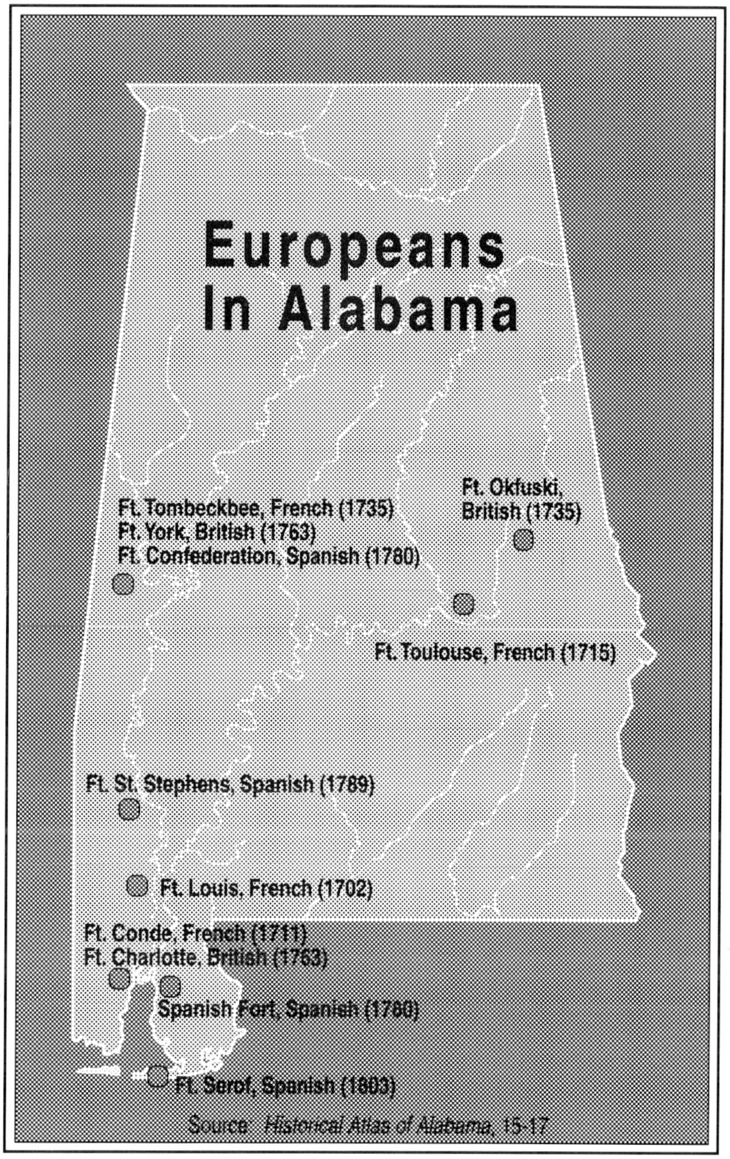

Graphic by Phil Coley

The original site of Fort Conde is now on top of one of the most outstanding features of the Interstate System in Alabama — the Mobile Tunnel on Interstate 10. The twin tube tunnel was built beneath the Mobile River, about 400 feet south of the Bankhead Tunnel. Relics of the Fort Conde era were discovered during the excavation when the equipment encountered obstructions which halted the operation. The area was filled with bulkheads and wharves with all of the old timber piling and decking still in place. Some of the bulkheads ran perpendicular to the river and others at a 45-degree angle to it. A 1711 map indicated two unnamed wharves and an almost illegible 1815 map seems to bear the names "Kings Wharf" and "Montuce Wharf."

Several hand-hewn 12 by 12 timbers with square drift pins were uncovered in the same general area. Maps of Old Mobile suggested this was the site of Fort Conde. Subsequent archaeological excavations supported the roadbuilders' theory and proved that progress can have some culturally enhancing by-products.

During their 1702-1763 tenure, the French also built log stockade forts at Tombeckbee on the Tombigbee River and Toulouse on the Alabama.

Photo courtesy of Alabama Bureau of Tourism and Travel

Periodic living history encampments are held at the Fort Toulouse-Fort Jackson site southeast of Wetumpka. Ned Jenkins, the curator, is in period garb on the extreme right.

Tombeckbee, on White Bluff (Jones's Bluff) overlooking the Tombigbee near present-day Epes in Sumter County, was a base against the pro-English Chickasaws. Toulouse, located four miles below Wetumpka, served as a trading post and military outpost against the British. The Treaty of Paris (1763), ending the French and Indian War, ceded all of French Louisiana east of New Orleans to England, including the French forts in Alabama.

The British occupied Mobile from 1763 until its conquest by the Spanish Governor of Louisiana, Don Bernardo de Galvez, in 1780. Proving again that the nation that conquers a territory and occupies it at war's end often retains it in the post-war era, Galvez's gains were consolidated into post-war Spanish control of Florida. The Spanish also became the major bottleneck for American southwestern trade because they occupied the oceanic outlets for the Mississippi, Tombigbee-Alabama, and Chattahoochee rivers.

The Spanish era was marked by U.S.-Spanish competition for trade and allies among the Southern Indians. Indians, supplied from Spanish Florida, attacked American frontier settlements, and the rivalry spilled over into the Creek Indian War, 1813-1814. Young America, however, became too much for distant Spain. The Americans claimed the Louisiana Purchase territory extended eastward to the Perdido River thus embracing Mobile. When it was known the Spanish allowed English vessels to use their ports during the War of 1812, President James Madison, supported by an act of Congress,

Florida Panhandle Could Have Been Part of Alabama

Plans to make the Florida panhandle a part of Alabama have been proposed several times. Perhaps the most serious step was made in December of 1868 when the Alabama Legislature negotiated to buy the part of Florida west of the Chattahoochee River. Florida offered the land to Alabama for $1 million, to be paid with interest in 30 years. (The cost to the United States to acquire all of Florida from Spain was $5 million.) People in west Florida were generally in favor of the deal, but opinion among Alabamians was divided. The people of Mobile were accused of opposing the purchase because Pensacola would provide port competition. Influential Alabama newspapers openly ridiculed the plan. One said the price was far too high for a "sand bank and gopher region." The state Legislature voted no.

In 1873, another plan was proposed, but Florida was no longer interested in selling. Other discussions were held in the 1960s and later, but a change in Alabama's borders seems unlikely today.

Source: Patricia Klein, Donald B. Dodd and W. Stuart Harris, **Twentieth Century Alabama: Its History and Geography** (Montgomery: Clairmont Press, 1993), 44.

ordered General James Wilkinson, at New Orleans, to take Mobile. By April 1813 the garrison was isolated by sea and land and the outnumbered Spanish commander surrendered without firing a shot. Within a decade Florida was ceded to the United States by the Adams-Onis Treaty. As Alabama became a state before the treaty completed the Florida purchase, the Gulf area directly south and naturally contiguous to Alabama was destined to be the "Panhandle" of the future state of Florida. And the United States flag flew over all of the land now called Alabama.

Native Americans: Trails, Trade, and the Creek Indian War

Indians roamed this country long before the white man dreamed of its existence. But even before they came, creatures of the wilderness etched distinctive traces between their shelters and available natural supplies of food and water. A frontier lobbyist and Missouri senator of 30 years, Thomas Hart Benton, observed that the animal trails found:

> *the lowest passes in the mountains, the shallowest fords in the rivers, the richest pastures in the forests, the best salt springs, and the shortest practicable lines between remote points.*

The Indians often followed these paths as they yielded plentiful game and water and presented the least resistance to travel. Trails on the plains avoided rough, stony ground, briars, and undergrowth; traces in the hills usually followed the ridges where the undergrowth was not so dense nor the streams so numerous.

Except for the Cherokees in the northeastern corner of Alabama, Alabama Indians by the early 1800s spoke a common Muskhogean language, but the similarities pretty well ended there. The far-ranging and aggressive

Chickasaw of northwest Alabama were bitter enemies of the close-mouthed, stay-at-home, agriculture-focused Choctaws of the southwest. The dominant Alabama tribe, the Creeks, were further split into the warlike upper towns and the more peaceful lower towns. In fact, the famed Creek Indian War of 1813-1814 began as a Creek Civil War between the two factions.

Indian trails promoted communication and commerce between tribes. Whether friendly or hostile, the natives met along the waterways and the time-worn paths through the forest. In times of war they sought alternate routes to avoid detection by their enemies. Peaceful communications enabled the Indians to barter their goods along established routes with even the most distant tribes and settlers.

Long before this territory was settled, several frontiersmen, often of mixed European parentage and many of whom married native Americans, expedited the Indian trade. Living among the Indians and adopting their customs, these "Indian countrymen" were some of the most colorful characters ever to inhabit the frontier. They included Benjamin Durant, Abraham Mordecai, John Haigue, Charles Weatherford, and James McGirth. As early as 1786 Benjamin Durant farmed the fertile land along the Alabama River west of Montgomery. His wife Sophia commanded respect as the sister of Alexander McGillivray, the leader of the Creek Confederation, but Durant also gained recognition from the Creeks for his superior fighting skills. Abraham Mordecai, who traded near the Indian village of Econchate ("Red Bluff," apparently near the powder magazine off Bell Street in current west Montgomery), was spared his life but lost his ears when caught on intimate terms with a married squaw. John Haigue, the notorious "Savannah Jack," was known as the "most blood-thirsty, fiendish and cruel" of the lot and led raids against the isolated settlers in south Alabama. He claimed to have killed enough women and children to form a pool of blood large enough for swimming. Charles Weatherford laid out the first horse race track eight miles north of current Montgomery near Parker Island. James McGirth of Macon County operated the first distillery.

The well-defined Indian routes often became roads or improved highways. The Federal Road, which opened in 1805, followed the Alamuchee-Creek Trail from Montgomery to the crossing of the Tombigbee River in Marengo County. Hobuckintopa was an old Choctaw village that later became St. Stephens, the first territorial capital of Alabama. It was connected to Mobile by a path later generally followed by U.S. 43. Alabama Highway 14 between Wetumpka and Tallassee is approximately the same route as the Fort Toulouse-Lower Creek path. The trail from Walnut Hills on the Mississippi River to Nashville became the Natchez Trace Parkway.

By the latter part of the 18th century, Mobile and Pensacola had developed a lively trade with the Indians, especially in deerskins. Both had excellent ports to service large ships. The favorable geographic position of Mobile Bay at the mouth of the Alabama and Tombigbee River systems was recognized as early as 1763. The Alabama River extended into the Creek Nation and the Tombigbee into the Choctaw. Boats drawing three feet or less of water would serve the hinterland year around.

The westward movement into Alabama and British and Spanish intrigue led to the Creek Indian War, 1813-1814. American settlers expanded the

The Montgomery Advertiser

Fort Mims Massacre. On August 30, 1813, more than 1,000 "Red Stick" warriors under Red Eagle, Peter McQueen, and High-head Jim entered the fort commanded by the unprepared Major Daniel Beasley and killed the majority of the men, women and children refuged there.

bridle paths through the Creek Nation to major highways of migration and the Creeks faced the prospect of being hemmed in between Georgians and the settlers along the Tombigbee River. British- American grievances leading into the War of 1812 influenced British agents in Canada to send the Shawnee Chief Tecumseh south for allies among other tribes. Tecumseh's oratory was effectively countered by the Choctaw Chief Pushmataha among the Choctaws and Chickasaws, but a war party of "Red Sticks" (Creek symbol of war) formed among the Creeks. Other Creeks opposed war and the conflict between Creeks carrying the red club of war and the "White Stick" Creeks developed into a tribal civil war.

The Alabama settlers followed the Indian developments closely and learned an upper Creek force was securing arms in Pensacola and returning to central Alabama via the Wolf Trail. A body of Mississippi Territory militiamen ambushed the party in a bend of Burnt Corn Creek. After an initial success, the militia became occupied with spoils and were routed by an Indian counterattack.

Terrified by the Creek success at Burnt Corn Creek, the Alabama pioneers left their cabins for refuge in the nearest frontier fort. Approximately 500 settlers, including 100 children and 175 soldiers, gathered at Fort Mims, a hastily erected one-acre stockade around the home of Samuel Mims near Lake Tensas north of Mobile. Despite repeated warnings that a number of Indians were in the woods around the fort, Major Daniel Beasley, Fort Mims' commander, neglected to prepare the fort for the impending attack. His fatal error was failing to order sand cleared from the fort gate so that it would close quickly. Major Beasley was one of the first to pay for his mistake, as he was killed trying to shut the gate. Some 250-400 men, women, and children soon shared the same fate in a bloody massacre. As the dinner drums beat the call to eat at high noon August 30, 1813, more than a thousand Red Stick warriors under William Weatherford (Red Eagle), Peter McQueen, and High-head Jim poured through the open gate killing and scalping. One of the survivors, the slave woman Hester, paddled a canoe downstream to Fort Stoddert to tell of the horror and staggering loss of life.

The carnage of Fort Mims alarmed neighboring areas and expeditions against the warring Creeks were launched from Tennessee, Mississippi, and Georgia. General Andrew Jackson led his "Tennessee Volunteers" south and, aided by friendly Chickasaws, Cherokees, and some Creeks, won several battles. But the Red Sticks remained a viable fighting force. General F.J. Claiborne led his Mississippi militiamen north and, assisted by Choctaws under Pushmataha, defeated the Creeks under William Weatherford at Holy Ground near Powell's Ferry in present Lowndes County (just north of U.S. 80). Short enlistments kept Claiborne from exploiting his success. General John Floyd moved west from Fort Mitchell (south of present-day Phenix City), but was defeated at the Battle of Calabee Creek (near where Victoryland Racetrack is now). With the retirement of Claiborne and Floyd, the Creek War was left to Jackson.

In February 1814, Jackson learned of a Red Stick concentration in the bend of the Tallapoosa River — "Horseshoe Bend." Jackson and his 2,000 militiamen found about 900 Creeks under Menewa entrenched behind breastworks in the open end of the Horseshoe with the river on three sides. Jackson sent General John Coffee across the river to cut off the anticipated retreat and led his main column against the breastworks. Some of Coffee's command, including friendly Cherokees, swam the Tallapoosa River, destroyed canoes, and burned the village of Tohopeka in the rear of the Creeks at about the same time that Jackson's men launched their attack. Although Menewa (who was wounded five times) escaped and some women and children were captured, more than 800 of the 900 warriors were killed.

The Battle of the Horseshoe broke the back of the Creek rebellion and opened the entire Southeast to American settlers. The Creeks surrendered about one-half of the present state of Alabama in August, 1814, at Fort Jackson (Jackson generously lent his name to the former Fort Toulouse general location but, to the confusion of site preservationists, new walls were added, making it difficult to distinguish between the two specific sites). By 1819, at least three-fourths of the state had been taken from the Indians, including land owned by the friendly Choctaws, Chickasaws, and

Cherokees. In a series of treaties between 1828 and 1835, the remaining Indian land was taken. For those who prefer the term "ceded" to "taken," consider the fate of Creek Chief William McIntosh and Cherokee trader, Major Ridge. When McIntosh signed the Treaty of Indian Springs (1825) ceding Creek lands in Georgia, in negotiation with his first cousin, Georgia Governor George Troup, over a hundred Alabama Creeks, following a tribal mandate, marched to Georgia to burn McIntosh's home and kill him. A decade later when Major Ridge signed the Treaty of New Echota (1835) giving up the last of the Cherokee land, angry Cherokees, enforcing tribal law which forbade individuals ceding land without the consent of the tribe, killed Ridge, his son, and Elias Boudinot, editor of the Cherokee Phoenix, a Cherokee weekly newspaper which had begun publication in 1828.

After his Alabama exploits, Jackson and his battle-tested troops took a little trip, but not down the Mississippi as the song goes, but overland to beat the British in the Battle of New Orleans. Occurring after the treaty ending the war with the British, it had no effect on the peace terms but the national prominence it brought Jackson propelled "Old Hickory" into the White House. Ironically, Jackson, the Indian-fighter and President who later implemented moving the Indians west of the Mississippi, alienated a strong Alabama supporter, Governor John Gayle, by not being harsh enough on the Indians. The treaty specifying removal (Cusseta, 1832) was signed in Washington and allowed resettlement in due course. But some Alabamians jumped the gun and crowded onto Indian lands before the Creeks had the opportunity to move. Jackson sent federal marshals and troops from Fort Mitchell to hold off the premature claim jumpers. In the ensuing scuffle, Hardeman Owens, one of the "jumper" leaders from Russell County, was killed. Governor Gayle said the federal government was infringing on Alabama's state rights. Gayle was reelected without opposition but Jackson sent anthem-writer-turned-diplomat, Francis Scott Key, to Alabama to appease him. When the Creeks delayed their exit, General William Wellborn was sent with the mission of moving them. Some Creeks fought and lost at the Battle of Hobody's Bridge on Pea River (1837), and others fled to central Florida to live with the Seminoles. Most were rounded up and moved to the Indian Territory (Oklahoma). Several harsh evacuations preceded the infamous "Trail of Tears" trek of the Cherokees but none were as brutal. The southeastern tribe that had tried the hardest to adapt to the white man's ways suffered the most. Forced from their homes with nothing but the clothes on their backs and rounded up like cattle, they were herded west. Several thousand died on the way. By the end of removal, some 50,000 southeastern native Americans were uprooted and made to migrate west of the Mississippi.

Menewa, Horseshoe Bend, and Creek Removal

Celebrated for his wild and reckless youth, when his name had been Hothepoya (Crazy War Hunter), Menewa was a member of the anti-American faction called "Red Sticks" and led them at Horseshoe Bend. He also was an arch enemy of the leader of the lower Creeks, William MacIntosh, who was pro-American. MacIntosh and several hundred Creeks were with Jackson at Horseshoe Bend, as were Yuchis under Timpoochee Barnard, and 600 Cherokees accompanied by Sam Houston, a young white Tennessean who had been living with them.

Special Collections, AUM Library

Menewa, Creek leader at Horseshoe Bend

Of the 900 Red Stick warriors in the battle, only 70 survived. All but one were wounded, he having jumped into the river to swim to safety soon after the first shot. Forty-nine of Jackson's men were killed (including 23 Indian auxiliaries) and 154 were wounded (of which 47 were Indians). One of the casualties was Sam Houston, whose battle wounds plagued him the rest of his life.

Menewa fell after being hit several times by rifle fire. He regained consciousness after the battle was over and shot a passing soldier and was, in turn, shot through the head — the bullet going in one side of his face and out the other, carrying with it several teeth and disfiguring him for life. He revived again at night, crawled to the river and floated in a canoe downstream to a swamp where some of the Red Stick wives and children were hiding. By the time Menewa's wounds healed, the war was over and Red Stick land had been opened to white settlement. Menewa lost his store at Okfuskee (present day Wetumpka), 1,000 head of cattle, and hundreds of horses and hogs.

Although MacIntosh had been on the winning side at Horseshoe Bend, Menewa lived — and waited his turn. It was not long in coming. MacIntosh and 12 other Creek chiefs, collectively representing about 10 percent of the Creeks, ceded 15 million acres of Creek land by 1821-1823 treaties with Georgians. In the pay of the Georgia commissioners, MacIntosh and his party signed away the remaining 10 million acres of Creek land to the state of Georgia in 1825. The MacIntosh treaties were in violation of Creek custom and a specific law that decreed the death penalty for any Creek who sold land without the consent of the entire Creek nation in council. Formal sentence was passed on MacIntosh and the appointed executioner was Menewa. On May Day, 1825, a party of Creeks under Menewa carried out the sentence.

The illegal treaty of 1825 was annulled and the following year Menewa went to Washington, D.C., and signed a new treaty retaining the Creek lands. He promised his loyalty to the United States. After being pressured into signing a removal treaty in 1832 in return for federal protection from intruders, which they never received, the Creeks were finally forced to move. A resistance movement under the 84-year-old Eneah Emathla prompted Jackson to send an army to Alabama. True to his promise, Menewa and nearly 2,000 other Creek warriors joined the U.S. Army in rounding up the rebellious Creeks. Manacled and chained together, the captured hostiles began the trek west in a double-filed procession. As the departing Creeks went about touching leaves, trees, rocks, and streams in a farewell ritual to their ancestral homes, some watching whites were moved and others were amused. Washington Irving quoted Chief Emathla as commenting: "They cannot appreciate the feelings of a man that loves his country."

The Creek treaty permitted individual Creeks to stay under the jurisdiction of state laws. Many planned to do so, including Menewa. In the final days, the federal government abrogated these provisions, however, and even Menewa was forced to move. He spent the night before his exile alone in his home village at Okfuskee. The next morning he spoke to an old white friend. "Last evening I saw the sun set for the last time, and its light shine upon the tree tops, and the land, and the water, that I am never to look upon again." With tears in his eyes, he walked away.

Source: William Brandon, **Indians,** (Boston: Houghton Mifflin Company, 1987), 225-241.

Alabama Bureau of Tourism and Travel

The pioneer house, Hepsidam, between Grayson and Moulton, Alabama, in Bankhead National Forest

II
Frontier Alabama

Life and Travel

Chapter synthesized from **"Indian Trails to Interstates,"** *an unpublished manuscript in the Alabama Department of Transportation Library, Vol I, pp. 20-107.*

It is difficult for someone living in the contemporary world of automobiles, airplanes, missiles, space shuttles, and interplanetary exploration to conceive of the primitive nature of Alabama society two centuries ago. Only in this distant setting, however, can frontier and antebellum institutions be understood or appreciated.

In the society of our great-great grandfathers, a man's rifle and axe and a woman's spinning wheel, cards and loom, and iron pot were the ingredients of "easy" living. Every girl had a public record as to the number of "cuts" she could card and spin in a day, an important consideration for prospective grooms. Salt and coffee were luxuries, one almost indispensable and the other to be used only for special guests. The home was no more than a small cabin of one or two rooms, sparsely furnished with crude furniture. The family's clothing was homemade and "Sunday clothes" were dyed homespuns. Babies died from "croup," "infantile," "intemperance" and "teething" and had little more than an even chance of living until they had passed the critical second summer. Adults died of "remittent," "intermittent" and "puerperal" fever as well as from "dropsy" and "consumption." Grandmother's "yarbs" were the chief medicines, and doctors and lawyers were educated by training under older members of the profession. There were almost as many sheep as cattle, and oxen instead of mules were used to plow. Poles, brush, and logs were used to fence out wild and "domestic" animals. Mountain lions and bears stalked the settlers' livestock, and rattlesnakes were commonly six feet long. Community work activities and religious assemblies were the main social events. Corn liquor was the chief beverage and was served at most group functions. Gambling and fighting characterized most public meetings and taverns were operated by some of the most respectable citizens. A major road was "twelve feet wide and clear of stumps and roots" and a toll had to be paid by travelers unless they took a "stole" route around the toll-gate. The man-towed cart was a common vehicle of travel. There were no public schools or hospitals, few churches, doctors, lawyers, or ministers, and no dentists. Visualize these and hundreds of other unusual customs, conditions, and unique notions and one may begin to approximate the society and transportation problems of frontier Alabama.

Travel was hard. The modes of conveyance were primitive, stream crossings were major undertakings, stage travel was frightening, and the taverns used as meal stops or overnight lodging, crude.

Conestogas, Ferries, and Covered Bridges

Pack horses were commonly used over the early trails, but the most common conveyance was the wagon, the most picturesque being the Conestoga or "covered" wagon. The Conestoga was responsible for our current practice of driving on the right side of the road instead of following

The Montgomery Advertiser

The log cabin is one of several 19th century buildings preserved by Landmarks Foundation's "Old Alabama Town" in the Hull Street Historic District north of the State Capitol in downtown Montgomery

the English tradition of driving on the left. The sliding board by which the teamster could drive the horses and operate the brake was on the left side of the wagon. To get a clear view of the road ahead, the teamster, often smoking rolled tobacco called "stogas," drove the wagon on the right side of the road. Soon other vehicles adopted the right side driving as it was easier to follow the ruts of the heavy Conestogas than to cross them.

As the old Indian paths became more heavily traveled by traders, local Indians often ferried the traders across the streams. Traders would often hide a boat near the crossing for later use. In 1775 William Bartram, the famed botanist, and his Indian guide made their own raft to cross a swollen Alabama stream (identified by Peter Brannon as Pintlala Creek). After lashing logs and dry canes together with vines, they attached two strong vines to each end of the raft to tow the raft across the creek. Bartram continued:

The Indian took one of the grape vines in his mouth, plunged into the river and swam over with it, and the vine fixed to the other end was committed to my charge, to steady the raft and haul it back again after being unloaded .... The last load, with other articles, contained my property, with all clothes, which I stripped off, except my breeches, for they contained matters of more value and consequence than all the rest of my property put together; besides I did not choose to expose myself entirely naked to the alligators and serpents in crossing the flood. Now feeling all the goods safe over .... I plunged in and being a tolerable swimmer, soon reached the opposite shore. **"Indian Trails,"** p. 43

But streams could generally be forded at shallow points and, for narrow streams, a felled tree (called by Bartram a "raccoon bridge") sufficed. Bartram noted that in crossing such bridges "my Indian friend would trip as quick and light (as a raccoon), with one hundred weight of leather on his back, when I was scarcely able to shuffle myself over it astride." Conveniently for Bartram and other travelers not conditioned to frontier life, pathways soon widened into wagon roads and non-fordable streams began to be served by ferries.

Sam Mims, of "Fort Mims" fame, operated a ferry at the "Cut-off" (channel which connects the waters of the Alabama and the Tombigbee). He ferried passengers to Nannahubba Island and Adam Hollinger took them from there to the west bank of the Tombigbee. Lorenzo and Peggy Dow, a Methodist circuit rider and his wife, crossed on Mims' Ferry on an unsuccessful mission to convert the citizens of St. Stephens. They were to discover, as Alabama historian A.B. Moore stated, "The immigrants who settled ... in the localities of Fort Stoddert and Fort St. Stephens generally were not of the stuff that angels are made." (p. 129.)

Bridges gradually replaced ferries over the major streams and were the main methods of crossing the minor streams on the leading roads by the end of the antebellum era. The earliest bridges were normally covered bridges and, like turnpikes, they required each user to pay a toll — a direct road use "tax." The Alabama legislature first authorized a bridge in 1821, to connect the two sides of the town of Cahaba (Cahawba then) across the Cahaba River. Later they approved bridges for the falls of the Warrior River in Tuscaloosa and across the Tennessee at Florence and the Cahaba at Centreville (Bibb County).

Roads

In the territorial days and early statehood of Alabama, the two major roads, the Federal Road (1805) and the Natchez Trace (1801), linked Washington and New Orleans. Regular travelers were going through Alabama rather than to Alabama. Most other frontier roads were expansions of Indian paths to facilitate military movements: the Jackson Trace, Jackson's Military Road, Gaines' Trace (1810), and the Three Notch Road (1824). The exceptions were the Tuscaloosa-to-Huntsville, state-authorized toll roads by John Byler (1819) and Wyatt Cheatham (1824). The two roads also connected Huntsville with Mobile by linking with the Tombigbee River system through its northernmost terminus at Tuscaloosa on the Black Warrior River.

Only two days after the state of Alabama was admitted to the Union, the legislature authorized a road to be built from Muscle Shoals on the Tennessee River south to Tuscaloosa. William Wyatt Bibb, the first Governor of Alabama, approved the act in Huntsville on December 16, 1819. John Byler built the first state road, clearing all stumps and roots for a width of twelve feet. He collected the following toll: 75 cents for a four-wheeled

Alabama Bureau of Tourism and Travel

Corn crib at pioneer homestead in Noccalula Park, Gadsden. The corn crib's walls were made from "matched logs" and then hand hewn to desired thickness. The roof was made of weathered shingles.

carriage and team; 50 cents for a two-wheeled carriage; 12½ cents (one bit) for a man and his horse; 6¼ cents for each pack horse; one cent per head of cattle; and half a cent for each head of hogs or sheep. Anyone caught going through or around the turnpike (on a "stole road") without paying the toll was required to pay triple the amount due for the toll. Connecting the Tennessee River with the Warrior-Tombigbee Rivers, this road facilitated travel between Tuscaloosa and Nashville. When Tuscaloosa became the capital of Alabama in 1826, the Byler Road became the "Main Street of Northwest Alabama." Traffic was apparently heavy as Wyatt Cheatham, in 1824, built a competitive road, the Cheatham Road, on the Moulton-Tuscaloosa portion of the Tennessee-Tombigbee connecting road.

Also built in 1824, the Three Notch Road expedited communication and transportation between military posts at Pensacola and Fort Mitchell. Secretary of War John Eaton, in an 1831 memorandum to the House of Representatives, noted it was 233 miles long and constructed by the Army for military purposes at a cost of $1,138.78. The Three Notch Road, or "Three Chopped Way," was named for the triple gashes on trees left by the surveying party. Only short sections of the old road are still in use, a portion being Three Notch Street in the city of Troy. The name is also perpetuated by Three Notch village in Bullock County southeast of Union Springs.

Stagecoaches, the 'Horse Express,' and Taverns

The frontier and antebellum stagecoach driver was described by some as a cocky, cursing individual and by others as an accommodating, lighthearted, jovial type. This "grand figure, a hero to all the boys and girls," was the radio and newspaper of his time. Whether he was Tom Green on the Byler Road run between Moulton and Tuscaloosa or James J. Lovelace on the stageline from Columbus, Georgia, to Fort Gaines, he was a central figure of the Alabama frontier.

The folk hero's vehicle was the stagecoach — so named because a change of horses was required at periodic intervals, thus trips were made in stages. The distance traveled by one team of horses was a "stage," normally about 16 miles. Frontier stagecoaches were considerably different from the ones now observed in western movies. Early stages had four benches similar to country church benches and passengers loaded from the front as they would in a railway coach. Rear passengers had to crawl over the other three benches.

As the stages often carried the mail, the stops were normally post offices as well and a person looked for and met the stage in the same general manner as one awaits the mail man in rural and suburban areas today. The mail routes were called post roads.

Many distinguished visitors to Alabama passed over these roads. Some of the better-known travelers in the 1825-1850 era were the Marquis de LaFayette, Washington Irving, President Martin Van Buren, Henry Clay, P.T. Barnum, and President James K. Polk. An unusual local dignitary traveling to sessions of Congress was the 490-pound Alabama Congressman Dixon Hall Lewis. Lewis "booked" the entire stagecoach in advance for his trips and was the only passenger. He also occupied two seats in Congress (but got only one vote). The Georgia-born, South Carolina-educated Lewis had a keen mind and was an active man despite his bulk. An effective orator and politician, he represented the states rights view in Congress for eight terms.

Major stagecoach owners in early Alabama were Major James W. Johnston, Lewis Calfrey, Robert Jemison, and John R. Powell. In 1821, Johnston and Calfrey established the first stage route east from Montgomery to Milledgeville, Georgia. The stage left Montgomery on Monday, Wednesday, and Friday mornings at four o'clock and arrived in Milledgeville early on the following mornings. Robert Jemison of Tuscaloosa and John R. Powell of Wetumpka and Montgomery were vigorous competitors and almost broke one another until they combined their stage companies into a virtual monopoly of the stagecoach business in Alabama. Both Jemison and Powell were later involved in the development of the mineral district of Alabama and the early promotion of Birmingham.

Peter Brannon surveyed a stagecoach ledger for the 1842-1844 years and was amazed at the disparities in rates. He especially noted the record of a black passenger who paid three dollars for passage from Irwinton to Fort Gaines when, at the same time, a 100-pound box was transported all the way from Columbus to Irwinton for 45 cents. Apparently freight rate discrimination did not start with railroads.

Perhaps the rates reflected the hazards of travel — the degree of Indian and bandit danger or the condition of the roads, as well as distance and "what the traffic would bear." In the 1830s, a number of stage holdups in southeast Alabama were attributed to bands of roving Indians. The stage from Tuskegee, Alabama, to Columbus, Georgia, was held up several times and burned twice. Two stage travelers were killed near Marvin in 1836, and the stage south of Columbus to Eufaula quit after Major William Flornoy was ambushed and killed on Wiwalaste Creek, south of old Cilula, in Russell County. A more common hazard, however, was the wretched condition of many roads.

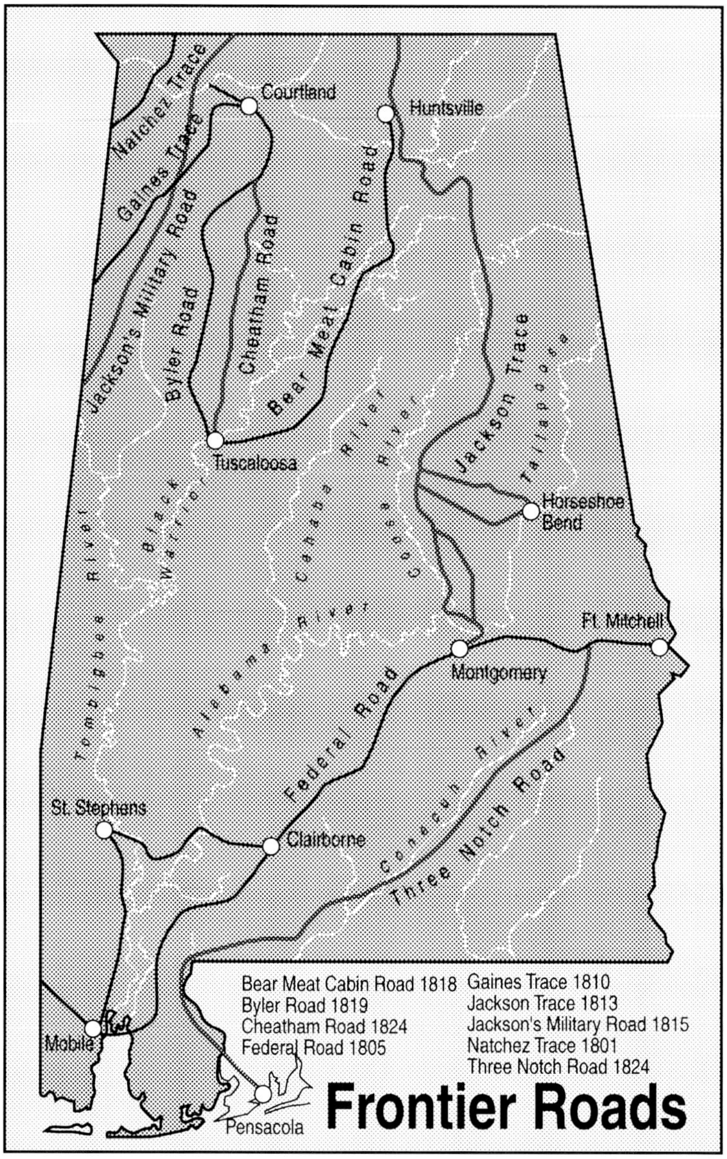

Graphic by Phil Coley

Road conditions in frontier Alabama were considered among the worst in the United States. The frequency with which stages got hung up on stumps in or near the road gave rise to the expression, "I'm stumped," meaning "I'm baffled." To avoid being "stumped" passengers were often asked to rock the stage by shifting their bodies one way or the other. On rough terrain and in wet weather they would often be asked to walk either to lighten the load or to avoid injury if the stage overturned. Preparing for a trip from Alabama to Virginia in 1836, James Davidson recorded in his diary:

> *But I am now to venture upon the perils of stage travelling — cracked skulls —broken bones — dislocated shoulders ... loss of sleep — hard jolts — rough fare — upset stages — mud — wind and cold are to be my portion of the next ten days.* Everett Dick, ***Dixie Frontier,*** (p. 207)

The 'Horse Express'

The 1860 Pony Express from Missouri to California is a historical phenomenon of legendary proportions but, unknown to most Alabamians, a pony express or "horse express" through Alabama preceded the well-known

The Montgomery Advertiser

The distance one team of horses would pull passengers was about 16 miles or a "stage," thus the term "stagecoach" for the conveyance vehicle. Stage stops often evolved into taverns, post offices and general merchandise stores.

mail riders by a quarter of a century. Neil Blue, a local Montgomery historian long associated with the Montgomery Post Office, recorded that the federal government's "Horse Express" through Montgomery was established November 15, 1836. There were three routes out of Montgomery: to Columbus, Georgia, to Huntsville, and to Mobile. A one-page letter from Mobile to Montgomery cost 56 cents, and 37 cents from Columbus to Montgomery. In contrast, a one-page letter from Montgomery to New York cost one dollar and, with three enclosures, weighing about an ounce, the charge was four dollars.

A private "Pony Express" operated between Montgomery and Mobile from 1844-1846. Owned by John C. Riddle and David H. Carter, it communicated financial intelligence (for example, fluctuating bank note values) 24 hours ahead of the regular mail. The fastest regular mail, by stage, was 36 hours. One of the horse express riders, Fred Tyler, on transmitting the news of the Mexican War battles of Palo Alto and Resaca de la Palma, made the Mobile-Montgomery run in 12 hours despite having to open the stables, and bridle and saddle his own horses (because he was ahead of time on the run). When a London newspaper doubted the feat, Riddle and Carter offered to bet $10,000 that Tyler could make the trip in 10 hours time. No one took the bet.

Alabama's "Pony Express" operated until shortly after the Mexican War when the telegraph line was completed from Montgomery to Mobile. Apparently the promoters of the St. Joseph, Missouri, to Sacramento, California, Pony Express of 1860 did not profit from the historical example of their Alabama predecessor, as they were superceded by the same technological innovation in 1861.

Taverns, Inns, or 'Stands'

Alabama taverns and inns fell far short of Hollywood images of a magnificent structure with a high-pillared veranda seductively beckoning the weary travelers to give up their carriage for waiting mint juleps. A realistic picture was much less enticing. A 1784 traveler said of southern inns and taverns: "three-fourths of them are in reality little better than mere shelters from the weather; yet the worst of them is by no means deficient in charging high." Another traveler advised companions to take the steamboat rather than travel by roads due to the "wretchedness of the roads, and still worse conditions of the inns."

Anyone who has stopped at contemporary commercial establishments along the Interstate for gas, food, or tourist trappings has seen amusing "Tavern Rules" posters or plaques. Actual guidelines for the proper running of a tavern are rare. A 1783 "guideline for running a tavern" was constructed by an experienced traveler for his daughter who was about to open an inn. Some of the more quaint rules were:

> *Have your cooking done free from coals and ashes.*
>
> *Avoid making smoky or greasy tea.*
>
> *Let your water bucket stand so high that your children shall not dabble in it.*
>
> *Keep a spit box in each room: this will teach vulgar persons that the floors were not made to spit on.*
>
> *Don't allow your children to examine the baggage of your guests; nor to belch up wind at the table.* ***"Indian Trails to Interstates,"*** pp. 59-60

Unfortunately, most inns did not subscribe to these "high standards." A Georgia lodger related the following incident regarding the clean bed sheets he was so fortunate to have acquired.

> *(He) was awakened at five o'clock in the morning by someone knocking violently at his door. Jumping up he ran to the door, calling out, 'What is the matter? What on earth do you want disturbing one at such an unreasonable hour in the morning?' 'Only want your sheets, sir.' 'My sheet! What do you want with my sheets?' ... To his astonishment the man replied, 'It is time to lay the table for breakfast, and I want your sheets to put on the tables, because they are the cleanest!' The gentleman thought if the sheets were to take the place of tablecloths, he would prefer his own to any other person's, and therefore allowed the man to come in and take them. When he made his appearance at breakfast, he was disgusted, but could not help being at the same time amused, to see so many persons innocently breakfasting off the supposed table-cloth.* **"Indian Trails to Interstates,"** p. 60

It may be possible that the most common traveler on Southern roads could not afford better accommodations and the extra cost of preparing most adequate lodging would have "priced" the inn-keeper out of business. Although inn prices were considered high, the bulk of the price was for food rather than lodging for the night. When one considers that the most criticism was of the lodging rather than the food the following prices of a hotel at Huntsville in 1820 (and the disparities between the price of food and lodging) gives food for thought.

Breakfast	37½¢
Dinner	50¢
Supper	37½¢
Horse for the night	50¢
Lodging	12½¢
Boarding without lodging, per week	$3.50
Boarding with lodging, per week	$4.50
Horse, per week	$3.00

"Indian Trails to Interstates," p. 70

A complaining lodger may have been accurate in his observations, but he may have been "getting what he paid for."

The veteran chronicler of Alabama travel, Peter Brannon, alleged that more than one writer had proclaimed an east Alabama tavern — Lewis' Tavern at Fort Bainbridge in the "Wilds of the Indian Country" (Russell County) — as being the "finest hotel in North America." Captain Lewis, the proprietor, a former Army officer, had a chef "lately from the best hotel in the City of Washington." The stage graced his establishment by arriving around four o'clock in the afternoon and remaining until the next day.

The majority of the rural taverns, often referred to as "stands," were a day's journey apart, as no one wished to travel after dark. For example, in 1820, there were nine taverns from Fort Mitchell to Mobile. Sometimes nightfall would catch a traveler on the road, however, and he would have to take what shelter he could find. Normally he would board in a private home. This also had its perils, as a group of travelers during the antebellum era was to discover. They stopped at a small cabin to seek lodging and later related the experience:

The woman who met them at the door refused for a time to take them in on the plea that her husband was absent and she was unwilling to take in strangers. But she was assured that they would be content to take the fare she was able to give them, without putting her to extra trouble, provided they could find shelter for themselves and horses. There was only one room to the house and the woman was compelled, therefore, to stretch a sheet across the corner of the room behind which she put down a pallet for the men. In the preparation of the supper she used but one cooking utensil, and that a frying-pan, for cooking the meat, then the bread and afterward the coffee. When they had eaten their supper and the gentlemen had smoked their pipes, the woman warmed some water in the frying-pan and asked the travellers if they wished to wash their feet before retiring; but they declining, she remarked that she could not rest well without bathing her feet, and began immediately to wash them in the pan to the great horror and disgust of the gentlemen. This revelation was quite unpleasant to them and the next morning they breakfasted only on roasted potatoes and water.

"Indian Trails to Interstates," p. 72

Photo courtesy of Alabama Bureau of Tourism and Travel

Sturdivant Hall, Selma, is one of the South's finest examples of Greek Revival architecture. Designed by the cousin of General Lee, the home was built in 1853-1855 for Edward T. Watts. Selma banker John McGee Parkman bought the mansion for $65,000 in 1864, but misused bank funds and wound up in Cahawba's "Castle Morgan" prison. He tried to escape and drowned in the Cahaba River. In 1870, Emile Gillman paid $12,000 for the house, which remained in the family until 1957, when the city of Selma purchased it. Bolstered by a sizable bequest of funds and antiques from Robert Daniel Sturdivant, the Sturdivant Museum Association was organized to preserve the house. Befitting such a mansion, a resident ghost in the form of Parkman is said to still roam the upstairs rooms of Sturdivant and his daughter's playful laughter is periodically heard in the parlor. Source: Lee Sentell, ***The Best of Alabama*** *(Birmingham: Seacoast Publishing, Inc., 1993) 258-259.*

III
Antebellum Alabama

From Statehood to Secession

By the terms of the Northwest Ordinance (1787), an area could become a territory when it had 5,000 adult males and a state when the territory had a population of 60,000 (the approximate population of Rhode Island in 1787). Satisfying these conditions, Alabama became a territory in 1817 and a state, after a constitution was duly submitted to Congress and approved, in 1819.

In July 1819 the Constitutional Convention met at Huntsville and John Williams Walker (see the sidebar on page 30) was elected president. A committee of 15 drafted the constitution — a distinguished group as four became governors of Alabama, three U.S. senators, one a U.S. Supreme Court justice (John A. Campbell), and one the vice president of the United States (William Rufus King). They produced a liberal constitution: all white males could vote, the governor was elected by the people, it included a bill of rights and a provision protecting slaves, and, as a concession to non-slaveholding areas, the white population was the basis for reapportionment. There was even an unsuccessful effort to allow the legislature to grant free blacks the right to vote.

Alabama's first Constitution of 1819 provided that the state legislature would meet at Huntsville and all subsequent sessions at Cahaba, at the confluence of the Cahaba and Alabama rivers near Selma. But the Cahaba site was on low ground and when the legislature met to discuss a permanent capital in 1825 they had to row to the temporary capital as an unprecedented high-water flood had inundated the area. The Tennessee, Tombigbee, and Warrior river valley representatives successfully supported Tuscaloosa's bid to be the capital but Autaugaville, Centerville, Greensboro, Selma, and Wilson's Hill (Montevallo) had their advocates. A joint session of the legislature chose Montgomery in 1846, although there were varying degrees of support for Tuscaloosa, Wetumpka, Marion, Mobile, Selma, and Statesville.

The moving of the capital from Tuscaloosa to Montgomery heralded the arrival of the Black Belt as the dominant section in the economic and political life of antebellum Alabama. Cotton was "King" and its barons were Black Belt planters. The story of one such baroness, Judith Anthony Greene Ware of Montgomery, and her kin is told by her descendant and namesake Judith Paterson. (See sidebar, pages 32-33.)

The plantation productivity of families such as the Wares and the Walkers had a national impact. Cotton alone provided an awesome 57 percent of the total exports of the United States in 1860 and one-fifth of that cotton came from Alabama. Mobile received raw cotton from the plantations near the Tombigbee and Alabama rivers and ranked second only to New Orleans as the largest cotton port in the South.

Steamboats were the major transportation vehicles for the antebellum cotton trade. They moved cotton bales from the nearest river landing to a cotton plantation to the Gulf Coast ports and international trade beyond. By the late antebellum era there were about 200 landings on the Alabama River and 300 on the Tombigbee-Warrior rivers. A steamboat, the Alabama, was built at St. Stephens in 1818 but its engines were too weak to go upstream.

The Montgomery Advertiser

Theodore R. Davis's "View of Montgomery, Alabama," made from pen and watercolor sketches by the artist when he and William Howard Russell of the London Times visited Montgomery in May 1861. Davis (1840-1894) was an artist-correspondent for Harper's Weekly during the Civil War and was wounded twice. ***Battles and Leaders,*** *I, 99.*

The Tensas, a sternwheeler (most antebellum paddle boats were sidewheelers, with paddles at the side), reached Cahaba in 1820 and the Harriett the next year — the latter going all the way to Montgomery, the first steamboat to do so. The Cotton Plant, built at Point Clear, was the first steamboat to go all the way up the Tombigbee to the head of navigation at Cotton Gin Port in Mississippi. The Native Georgia was built at Fort Gaines in 1834, the first steamboat on the Chattahoochee. Mississippi and Ohio River steamboats ascended the Tennessee River to Florence west of the Muscle Shoals. Boats working the Florence-New Orleans cotton trade included the Eastport, Cherokee, and Choctaw. The Coosa, operated on the river by the same name from Rome, Georgia, to Greensport, above the falls of the Coosa at Wetumpka.

The Black Belt was also the most densely populated part of the state, primarily because 45 percent of the state's black population was concentrated there as a part of the slave-cotton-plantation complex. Secondary areas of population density were the Tennessee, Coosa, Tombigbee, and Alabama river valleys.

A negative concomitant of "Cotton Kingdom" prosperity was the lack of educational opportunity for slaves. Alabama's illiteracy rate in 1870 was highest in the antebellum South. Although the Public School Acts of 1854 and 1856 had instituted a statewide public school system, the better public schools were in cities such as Mobile.

The urban areas in 1860 were not notably superior in culture, however, as they were principally central collection and distribution points for the agricultural economy. Although the Mobile area had almost 30,000 residents, Montgomery's population was less than 9,000, and Tuscaloosa's and Selma's population were both under 4,000. There was a theater at Mobile and portrait painters roamed the state, but the intellectual life of antebellum Alabama cities was primarily centered on the local newspaper, of which there were almost 100 by 1860.

As newspapers were the cultural focus, the editors were the intellectual leaders and their presses turned out the early literary efforts of the state. Leading the Alabama antebellum writers were a group of young idealistic University of Alabama students and faculty members now known as the "Tuscaloosa Bards." Destined to balance their literary pursuits with careers as lawyers, journalists, and politicians, the Bards in their youth symbolized the romanticism of the Old South. Three, William Russell Smith, Jeremiah Clemens, and Alexander Beaufort Meek, were in the first class at the University under the 23-year-old professor of literature, Henry Washington Hilliard. All four were lawyers, politicians, and published at least three books in their lifetimes. Smith, "The Father of Alabama Literature" published a book of poems, **College Musings,** while a student at Alabama, fathered the state's first literary periodical, "Bachelor's Button," the first play, "Aaron Burr," and had a distinguished public career capped by three terms in Congress.

Clemens, a cousin of Mark Twain, wrote four historical novels — the first two based on Clemens' service in the Texas revolution and Mexican War, the third favoring Burr over Hamilton in **The Rivals,** and the fourth on the Confederate mistreatment of Unionists during the Civil War. As a U.S. senator in 1850 he supported the California Compromise of that year and, with Smith and Hilliard, opposed secession in 1861. All three accepted Confederate commissions but performed only token service. Professor Hilliard left college teaching ranks to become the leader of the Whig Party in Alabama, a Unionist and, with Clemens, adversary of William L. Yancey in 1850 and 1861. Hilliard, like Smith, served three terms in Congress.

A.B. Meek opposed secession also but was more vigorous in pursuing southern rights within the Union than the other Bards. Like Smith, he was a Tuscaloosa newspaper editor and publisher of a short-lived literary journal, The Southron ("Southron" was a term of contempt Scots once used for Englishmen — from Sir Walter Scott). Meek's political career was marked by appointments rather than elections but by 1860 he was Speaker of the House and the leader of public education forces in the state. An orator and poet known for his elegies of nature, native Americans, women, and public figures, he was, despite his 6-foot-4, 240-pound frame, less energetic and confrontational than Hilliard or Clemens. But he was as versatile as Smith and devoted his life to promoting the arts, preservation of Alabama history, and the cause of public education. One of his final compositions was a tribute to the fallen heroes of the Confederacy, "Martyrs of the South," published in the Mobile Register in 1864, thus anticipating the post-war "Lost Cause Poets of Mobile."

Although beginning their careers in Tuscaloosa, the Bards spread all over the state — Smith a few miles north to Fayette, Clemens to Huntsville,

The Legacies of John Williams Walker

By LYNDA BROWN
Co-author of **Bibliography of Alabama History**

In his short life, John Williams Walker achieved what the aspiring young gentlemen of his generation considered the pinnacle of success: plantation ownership and high political office. Between 1810 when he arrived in Madison County and 1823 when he died of tuberculosis, Walker distinguished himself as one of the most able lawyer-planter-politicians who steered Alabama to statehood. In addition to his intelligence and a Princeton education, Walker had the further good fortune of marrying well. There is every reason to believe Walker married Matilda Pope for love, but marriage to the daughter of LeRoy Pope, a wealthy planter, banker, and land speculator, did nothing to hinder the young man's ambitions. Shortly after the wedding in Petersburg, Georgia — where both families had prospered and been members of the social elite — the Popes and Walkers migrated to Huntsville with every intention of transplanting their aristocratic way of life on the Alabama frontier.

Walker began his rise to political power as a member of the territorial legislature. An early advocate of statehood, he enlisted the aid of his old Georgia friends who held influential positions in Washington. When the time came for a constitutional convention, Walker was elected as a delegate and then unanimously elected as president of the convention. One of the delegates observed that Walker knew no more about parliamentary procedure than the average schoolboy and that he was "amazingly spoilt by the flattery which is lavished upon him," but another observer concluded that Walker was "decidedly the most talented member of the convention." With his credentials established, Walker was mentioned as a possible candidate for governor, but he was not interested, he said, in "the irksome routine of office." He aspired instead to be a United States senator "not only for its dignity" but for the opportunity to improve himself and to associate with "superior men." Walker got his wish and by November 1819 he was on his way to Washington. Exactly three years later, as his health deteriorated, Walker resigned from the Senate and died shortly afterward at the age of 39. Although his political career was brief, Walker made a substantial contribution in the formation of the state and is thus counted among Alabama's foremost founding fathers.

As a planter, Walker was only moderately successful. When his estate was settled — the debts and taxes paid — there was little wealth to distribute among his heirs. In his biography of Walker, Hugh C. Bailey concludes that Walker's greatest legacy to his six surviving children was an example of public service that "they would notably embellish by their own subsequent careers" (John Williams Walker, 1964). There is no question that the children and grandchildren of Matilda Pope and John Walker were high achievers. Among them were senators, judges, Confederate officials, and diplomats.

There is another Walker legacy. It is the legacy of a friendship preserved in family names. At Princeton in 1805-1806, Walker met Thomas Percy of Mississippi. After graduation, Walker — already suffering from tuberculosis — went on an extended journey to try to improve his health. He traveled south and west via New Orleans to the Percy plantation near Natchez. There, on the western edge of the Mississippi Territory, the young men solidified their friendship, and Walker decided that he, too, wanted to be a cotton planter in the new territory.

The Walker-Percy ties were drawn more tightly in 1814, when Percy joined Walker in Madison County where he promptly fell in love with and married Matilda Pope's sister Maria. When Walker went to Washington as a senator, it was Percy as brother-in-law and as friend who oversaw the Walker plantation and watched over the family. The two men honored their friendship by each naming a son for the other, and the Percy family continued the practice for four generations.

One Walker Percy (1864-1917) was a prominent Birmingham lawyer who married into the powerful DeBardeleben family, but the namesake whose life and career would most likely have interested Walker is the physician-philosopher-novelist who was born in Birmingham in 1916. Although not a publicly political man, this Walker Percy lived the kind of intellectually active, morally earnest, genteel life that John Walker would have respected — a late 20th-century version of the "superior men" he yearned to know. (In an eerie coincidence, Percy also suffered from tuberculosis.) Although Walker Percy is best known for his novels such as **The Moviegoer** (1961) and **The Last Gentleman** (1966), his name was a living legacy of the friendship founded in another era by two Southern boys a long way from home.

Hilliard to Montgomery, and Meek to Mobile. Tuscaloosa and the University remained a literary center. Yale graduate and professor of mathematics, F.A.P. Barnard, graced the Capstone for 16 years, until his prolific scientific writings and international reputation propelled him to the presidency of the University of Mississippi and later of Columbia College in New York. Caroline Lee Whiting Hentz, who, with her husband ran the Locust Dell Academy in Florence, 1834-1843, lived in Tuscaloosa three years. Hentz, who had written for Meek's Southron, also published 16 novels, including **The Planter's Northern Bride** (1854), a pro-Southern response to Harriet Beecher Stowe's **Uncle Tom's Cabin.**

Surpassing Tuscaloosa in the quantity and variety of literary activities was Alabama's cosmopolitan seaport city of Mobile. The first permanent repertory theater was established in Mobile in 1824 and Noah Ludlow and Solomon Smith became leading developers of the Mobile theater. William R. Smith's "Aaron Burr" played there in 1837.

Two Georgians moving to Mobile greatly facilitated the port city's literary progress — Octavia Walton Le Vert, internationally known hostess of the rich and famous and author of the two-volume **Souvenirs of Travel** (1857) chronicling two European tours from within the charmed circles; and John

Before Montgomery Was a Place

By JUDITH PATERSON

Excerpted from **Sweet Mystery,** a family memoir to be published by Farrar, Straus, and Giroux in September 1995.

"The Wares were here before there was a place," my maternal great-aunt Bessie Ware Walker liked to say. What she meant was that nobody in Montgomery had a longer local pedigree and more right to pride than we did. Be that as it may, her great- grandfather, Robert Alexander Ware, had left Colonial Virginia with his dissenting Baptist parents around 1770 and gone to the backwoods of North Georgia, where, though the living was precarious, the land was cheap and nobody cared how you worshipped. There, the young Robert fought the Revolution with his father and brothers and afterward prospered off military bounty grants and cotton made profitable by a newly patented cotton gin. But prosperity in post-Revolutionary Georgia had not been enough to stop him from buying 3,000 acres in the Alabama wilderness as soon as he could get his hands on it and eventually selling all he had in Georgia to go there.

When he arrived near Montgomery in 1822, he was 62 years old. His second wife, a widow named Judith Anthony Greene, was 50. What they had bought was a piece of an Indian plantation near the banks of a river along a line of the most cantankerous soil anybody ever tried to plow. Robert lived only five more years in Alabama. Long enough to weep on the aging neck of the Revolution's "boy-General" Lafayette during his triumphal 1825 tour of America, and to survive the malaria epidemic that took a fifth of the settlement's population that same year. Long enough to build a long log house and hack a working plantation out of the wilderness and see the eight children he and Judith had between them well married among the rising class of planters.

Judith, who survived her husband by 30 years, lived long enough to see their children grow enormously rich off cotton and slaves and see the 3,000 acres Robert had bought quadruple among their heirs and the number of slaves they had brought to Alabama go from 40 to over a thousand souls. Long enough to see their son, James Anthony Ware, marry a Georgia kinswoman named Jane Stokes and exchange the long plantation house for a finely styled Italian villa (now under restoration by the Landmarks Foundation of Montgomery) and eight years later swap it for the Greek Revival mansion that now houses the Alabama Chamber of Commerce on Perry Street.

Judith Anthony Ware, who had been raised among abolition-minded Quakers in Virginia, lived long enough to be disturbed by what the exponential growth of cotton had done to the institution of slavery — which she, like other lapsed Southern Quakers, had believed to be a temporary evil doomed to die a natural death. "The woman you are named for was an abolitionist," Aunt Bessie said to me once, lowering her voice as if to prevent the portrait of Judith's highly Confederate son (Bessie's grandfather), from hearing what she was saying about his mother. "The family was just mortified."

By national standards, almost no one would have called Judith Ware (who had owned slaves her whole life) an abolitionist. What she was, I believe, was a woman deeply troubled by what Alabama Fever and cotton had done to slavery and to her family in the 34 years between the coming of the Ware-Anthony-Greenes to Alabama in 1822 and her death in 1856. With the resurfacing memory of old age, she may have remembered traveling Quaker preachers predicting the fall of the South and "brother fighting brother" in the times of their children.

Be that as it may, ten years after Judith's death it had all come true. Her descendants and Robert's had backed the Confederacy with all they had and, in the process, lost incalculable amounts of wealth and pride and also — I believe — their moral moorings. James Anthony had turned his face to the wall and died (perhaps from drink) at 54 rather than endure the repercussions of it all, and when the conquering cavalry had taken over their house and read the proclamation of surrender from the steps of the Greek Revival mansion, Aunt Bessie's 42-year-old grandmother Jane had stood behind them and declared "This damned war though she had backed it as fiercely as he had has killed Mr. Ware, but it shan't kill me." And when the Congressional Reconstruction began in 1867, she moved her family upstairs and rented the downstairs and the stables to the officers of the occupying army for $125 a month and thereby saved the Wares Ferry Road plantation when all around them were losing theirs.

Aunt Bessie had other interesting and eminent forebears, but it was the Ware-Anthony-Greenes — as prototypes of the kind of people who created the mentality of the Alabama Black Belt — that fired Bessie's imagination and mentored mine.

Forsyth, longtime editor of the *Mobile Register*. Le Vert attracted national and international luminaries to Mobile. Forsyth brought in assistants with literary abilities such as Theodore O'Hara, Thomas Cooper DeLeon, Henry L. Flash, and A.J. Requier, as well as providing a publishing outlet for other young writers in Mobile. DeLeon, the most distinguished of Forsyth's recruits, managed Mobile's theater for a decade and the Mardi Gras for 25 years besides publishing 14 titles, the most significant being **Four Years in Rebel Capitals,** based on his wartime service as secretary for CSA President Jeff Davis. Charles L.S. Jones published two volumes of poems focusing on historical themes — Columbus's voyage, the Revolution, and the War of 1812 — and Flash, Requier, and Father Ryan glorified the Confederacy in poetry. Of course, A.B. Meek, who lived in Mobile 20 years, was the best-known Mobile poet.

Caroline Hentz was Alabama's first best-selling author with 93,000 sales by 1853, but she was eclipsed by Alabama's most successful 19th century novelist, Augusta Evans Wilson of Mobile, the master of domestic sentimentalism. Her second novel, **Beulah** (1859), sold 20,000 copies in nine months and her fourth, **St. Elmo** (1866), was said to have sold one million copies by 1949. She finished her ninth novel at age 72 and died two years later.

The antebellum industrial and transportation developments also focused on the cities. The manufacturing center of the state was the Montgomery-Prattville area. In Prattville, for example, Daniel Pratt had the largest cotton gin factory in the world. Alabama also ranked fourth among Southern states in textiles.

Photo courtesy of Alabama Bureau of Tourism and Travel

The Teague/Ware House, one of Montgomery's fine antebellum homes, was built in 1848 and was once the home of the James Anthony Ware family (see Page 32). Formerly housing the State Chamber of Commerce, the home now hosts the Alabama Historical Commission.

Stagecoach lines still served most Alabama cities, but railroads had begun to arrive by the 1850s. By 1854 the Memphis and Charleston Railroad had become an alternate means of transportation for residents of the Tennessee Valley, and Montgomery and Atlanta were connected by rail.

The Montgomery Advertiser

University of Alabama cadets before the Civil War

Montgomery had a rail link to Mobile by the end of the Civil War. Mobile, in turn, was the southernmost stop of the Mobile and Ohio Railroad, which ran north to Cairo, Illinois. The railroads, combined with the navigable rivers, made Alabama's transportation system one of the best in the South.

A major undeveloped area was the hill region of North Alabama, which cut the transportation and cultural link between the Tennessee Valley and South Alabama. The disparity between hill and plantation culture was reflected in an intrastate sectionalism that resulted in bloodshed during the Civil War. The cotton-producing areas supported the extension of slavery westward into the United States territories, opposed the election of Lincoln, and voted for secession delegates to the 1861 Secession Convention. In contrast, other areas were generally not as enthusiastic for slavery or secession.

The Sectional Crisis, 1832-1861

Two national issues crystallized Alabama political sentiment from the 1830s through the mid-1850s: the nullification crisis in the 1830s featuring South Carolina ruling null and void the national tariffs of 1828 and 1832; and the Compromise of 1850 by which California entered the Union as a free state. Henry Clay, the "Great Compromiser," and Stephen A. Douglas, the "Little Giant" of Illinois, engineered the 1850 Compromise aided by a

The Montgomery Advertiser

Wetumpka-Montgomery secessionist leader William L. Yancey's dog-trot summer home preserved in Old Alabama Town

sectionally conciliatory speech by Daniel Webster. John C. Calhoun of South Carolina, the sectional leader of the South, saw little for the South in the package and, on his deathbed, counseled the South to reject it and, if necessary, resort to arms. Secession seemed possible and delegates met at Nashville to consider joint Southern action. Webster's speech declared the Northeast logically wrong and politically motivated for using the slavery issue to divide the country as slavery had climatic limits confining the institution to the southeast. The followers of Calhoun, primarily South Alabamians, formed a states-rights or southern-rights faction and the more nationalistic and North Alabama followers of Jackson constituted the second party. A third party, the Whigs, opposed Jackson but found the states-righters too radical. Thus the Jackson Democrats and Whigs joined to curb the radicalism of the states-rights Democrats through the nullification and compromise of 1850 crises. In the 1850s, the Jacksonian Democrats and Whigs were for the most part unionists and the states-righters, secessionists.

The Montgomery Advertiser

William L. Yancey

After the death of Dixon Hall

The 19th Century Culture Shift In the South: Old South Romanticism To New South Utilitarianism

By AL HEAD,
Executive Director, Alabama State Council on the Arts, from his Masters of Liberal Arts (MLA) thesis at Auburn University at Montgomery.

In the three decades leading up to the Civil War a group of writers, now referred to as the "Tuscaloosa Bards," epitomized the classical eloquence and romanticism of the Old South. William R. Smith, Alexander B. Meek, Henry W. Hilliard and Frederick A. P. Barnard, the most prominent of the "Bards," led lives that sparkled with refinement and intellect in an otherwise crude Alabama environment.

In the ashes of the Civil War, the Bards' classical charm, scholarly orations, poetry, and prose seemed frivolous to a beaten, bitter, poverty-stricken population. Many Alabamians agreed with the ex-confederate general, D. H. "Harvey" Hill that "Men needed to learn that the effete, aristocratic educational values of the Old South were the cause and consequence of the economic failures the South had sustained..." and he asks, "What will a knowledge of the ancient classics of metaphysics and belles-letters do to relieve our poverty?" Henry Grady, the *Atlanta Constitution* editor who coined the term "New South", was also fond of saying "What the South needs now is fewer stumpspeakers and more stump pullers."

The Bards bemoaned the "horrors of utilitarianism." As early as 1841 Meek professed: "A people to become refined must have some motivation else than to grow rich." Frederich A.P. Barnard condemned "the narrow exclusiveness of that spirit (utilitarianism) which will not tolerate anything that fails to contribute directly to the supply of our animal necessities." But Barnard conceded "the undeniable truth that before the mind can be cultivated or improved, the body must be provided for." In the post-war world, being vivid examples of Alexander Meek's "apostles of an impractical creed," the Tuscaloosa Bards became icons of an extinct culture.

Lewis, William Lowndes Yancey became the leader of the states-righters in Alabama. Yancey was born in Georgia but educated in New York and Massachusetts. He studied law in South Carolina before moving to Alabama to practice law and edit newspapers. Ralph Draughon, Jr., who closely studied Yancey's childhood years in New York, described Yancey's stepfather, an abolitionist minister, as cold, sarcastic, and self-righteous. Yancey's mother was emotional, hot-tempered, and in her frequent uncontrollable rages would scream at her husband and slap her children. Sometimes she would hit them with the heel of her shoe. The stepfather required Yancey's mother to confess her sinful ways to his congregation. After his wife's inheritance was exhausted, he abandoned her. Draughon thought Yancey got his temper from his mother and his crusading zeal from his stepfather. Yancey also got an early start on hating abolitionists.

The 'Lost Cause' Poets of Mobile: Ryan, Requier, and Flash

Odes to the "Lost Cause," in the form of poetry in the *Mobile Register*, were so common to that city during the last one-third of the 19th century that the port city can be considered the capital of "Lost Cause" poetry. The most famous of the group was the poet-priest Abram Joseph Ryan (1836-1886), popularly known as Father Ryan. After his brother David, a Confederate Cavalry officer, was killed the summer of 1863, his heart and soul were with the Confederacy. "Conquered Banner," bemoaning the death of the Confederacy, was his response to Lee's surrender. His duties as a Catholic priest brought him to Mobile in 1870 and he was buried in the Catholic cemetery there 16 years later. His first volume of poems, **Father Ryan's Poems,** was published in the *Mobile Register* in 1879. Forty-seven editions had appeared by 1930.

Augustus Julian Requier (1825-1887) resided in Mobile 15 years. His offerings include "Ode to Victory" and "Our Faith in 61" but his best known was "Ashes of Glory." Requier sees triumph in defeat and no cause for loss of spirit.

....
No trumpet's note need harshly blare—
No drum-funeral roll—
Nor trailing sables drape the bier
That frees a dauntless soul!
....
Sleep! in thine own historic night—
And be thy blazoned scroll,
A warrior's Banner takes its flight,
To greet the warrior's soul!

Henry Lynden Flash (1835-1914) had Confederate service on the staffs of Lt. Gen. William J. Hardee and Lt. Gen. Joe Wheeler but was a war correspondent in the latter part of the war and known for his elegies of dcad Confederate heroes — Stonewall Jackson, Leonidas Polk, Felix Zollicoffer. The first and last stanzas of "Zollicoffer" were:

First in the fight and first in the arms
of the white-winged angels of glory;
With the hearts of the South at the feet of God,
And his wounds to tell the story.
....
But a handful of dust in the land of his choice,
A name in song and story,
And fame too short with her brazen voice,
"Died on the field of Glory!"

Source: Benjamin Buford Williams, **A Literary History of Alabama in the Nineteenth Century** (Cranbury, NJ: Associated University Presses, 1979), 124-130.

When Congress passed the 1850 Compromise package, Yancey and John J. Seibels, publisher of the *Montgomery Confederation*, opened their attack declaring that the only issue was one of "submission or secession." With the threat of secession imminent, Senators William Rufus King and Jeremiah Clemens, both of whom voted for the Compromise, returned to Alabama to conciliate the people. King had a distinguished career as a lawyer-politician in North Carolina before coming to Alabama and becoming the state's second U.S. senator, a post he held 1819-1844. After a stint as Minister to France, he was again a senator until selection as Franklin Pierce's vice president in 1853. He took the oath in Cuba where he was trying to conquer tuberculosis. He returned to Alabama to die at Cahawba in 1853 without ever functioning as vice president. Jeremiah Clemens, Alabama's other senator, had moved from Whig to Jacksonian Democrat to Unionist. He opposed secession but briefly served the Confederacy before becoming a Memphis newspaper editor and again pro-Union before his 1865 death in Huntsville. Clemens defended his support of the Compromise on the grounds that the South had gained more territory than she had under the Missouri Compromise. In any case, it was "the law of the land" and to oppose it would only promote a sectional feeling that would best be left buried. The *Alabama Journal* (August 17, 1851) attributed the efforts of Clemens and "the old Jackson democracy of North Alabama" as instrumental in crushing the "hopes of all the nullifying school of South Carolina editors and politicians."

The controversy of the 1850 Compromise carried over into the 1851 Alabama elections with the Unionists and secessionists furnishing candidates. In the Congressional races of 1851, the Unionists won five of the seven districts losing only in the Wetumpka and Mobile districts. In the winning districts, the Unionist position was to favor the Compromise but retain the right of revolution in the event the North did not respect it. The most spirited race was in the Montgomery district with the Unionist James Abercrombie opposed by the Southern Rights candidate John Cochran. This campaign was spiced by three debates between the Unionist Henry Washington Hilliard and William Yancey. Hilliard, a lawyer and prominent Whig congressman from Montgomery, like Clemens, opposed secession and briefly served the Confederacy. He practiced law in Georgia after the war and was appointed Minister to Brazil by President Rutherford B. Hayes. A contemporary politician, William R. Smith of Tuscaloosa, contrasted the oratorical styles of the unionist Hilliard and Yancey, the states righter:

> *In all that was soft and smooth and easy, graceful and persuasive, Mr. Hilliard was unquestionably the better; in all that was fiercely stormy, vituperative, denunciatory, impetuous, and scornful Mr. Yancey excelled. Mr. Hilliard had ... a more sweeping range of literary accomplishments ... while Yancey had a better knowledge of men, was a more perfect master of the passions....* Al Head's MLA thesis, AUM, pp. 22-23

Cochran, a devout secessionist, was publicized for having censured a friend for aid to the enemy by subscribing to a Northern newspaper. Cochran's campaign song revealed the sentiments of many Southern Rights disciples.

Africatown: An African-American Community in Mobile with an 1860 Slave Ship Heritage

By HENRY "HANK" WILLETT, Director,
Alabama Center for Traditional Culture

In front of the Union Baptist Church, in the Magazine/Plateau community about three miles north of Mobile, there is a bust of Cudjoe Kazoola Lewis, the last survivor of a voyage on the slave ship Clotilde from the west coast of Africa in 1860.

The monument is an enduring symbol of the community's pride in its African history and heritage, and is the focal point for annual celebrations of that heritage. Beneath the bust is a steel shaft sunk 100 feet into the earth, symbolizing the 100 years that this group of African-Americans had inhabited Mobile County soil when the monument was dedicated in 1959.

Cudjoe Kazoola Lewis was born around 1840, a member of the Tarkbar tribe, which inhabited the interior region of the Gulf of Guinea on the west coast of Africa. The Tarkbars were an agricultural people raising hogs, goats, sheep, chickens and cows. They planted beans and yams, and gathered bananas and pineapples. Their main trade item was the oil from palm trees, which was traded to other tribes, eventually reaching the coast for export abroad.

Alabama Bureau of Tourism and Travel

Cudjoe Lewis, the last survivor of the last U.S. slave ship, the schooner Clotilde, which arrived in August 1859

In the late 1850s, West Africa was at war with itself. Defeated tribes were often sold into slavery. In November of 1858, the *Mobile Register* noted, "The King of Dahomey was driving a brisk trade in slaves at from fifty to sixty dollars apiece." And as secessionist fever was spreading through Alabama in the 1850s, there was much talk of reopening the African slave trade, which had been outlawed since 1808.

It was in this setting that wealthy Mobile shipper Timothy Meaher and shipyard owner William Foster planned the trans-Atlantic voyage of the Clotilde for the purpose of bringing an illegal cargo of slaves back to Mobile. The Clotilde set sail from Mobile on March 4, 1860, arriving at the port of Whydah on the west coast of Africa on May 15. Five weeks earlier, Cudjoe Kazoola Lewis and dozens of fellow tribesmen had been captured by Dahomean warriors and marched to the port of Whydah where Lewis and 114 others were sold to Captain Foster for one hundred dollars apiece.

By the time they arrived in Mobile, federal authorities, having heard about the scheme, were on the lookout for the Clotilde. Captain Foster entered Mobile Harbor on the night of July 9, 1860. He transferred his slave cargo to a riverboat and sent them into the canebrake to hide them. He then burned and sank his schooner.

The Africans were distributed to those having an interest in the Clotilde expedition, with 32 settling on the Meaher property at Magazine Point, three miles north of Mobile. This formed the nucleus of what came to be known, and still is known, as Africatown. Lewis was among that group. After the Civil War, they were joined by a number of their fellow tribesmen. For decades they continued speaking their native tongue, had disputes arbitrated by their tribal chieftain, Charlie Poteete, and had their illnesses treated by the African doctor, Jabez. Up until World War II, Africatown remained a rather distinct community in Mobile County.

Africatown is unique in that it represents a group of Africans who were forcefully removed from their homeland, sold into slavery, and then formed their own, largely self-governing community, all the while maintaining a strong sense of African cultural heritage. This sense of heritage and sense of community continues to thrive today, more than 130 years after the landing of the Clotilde in Mobile Bay.

Oh, Carolina, That's the land for me
of all the lands in the Sunny South
Carolina still for me.
Dorman, **Party Politics,** p. 57

Abercrombie, on the other hand, was willing to wall South Carolina up with Federal authority and let her starve to death on rice. Abercrombie won by 1600 votes.

Although winning five of the seven districts, the Unionists had an overall majority of only 5,000 votes of a total of 75,000. The two North Alabama districts of Florence and Huntsville contributed a total majority of 4,566 votes on the efforts of the "Bald Eagle of the Mountains," George S. Houston of Florence, and the popular candidate of the hill folks, W.R.W. Cobb of Huntsville. That the people of Alabama were not willing to secede from the Union in 1850-51 was apparent in the election results but only in North Alabama was the majority decisive. Even in Yancey's home district, Alabamians in 1850 still thought their interests would be best served in the Union.

The sheriff of Pickens County, William A. Davis, spoke for many Alabamians in a letter to the editor of the *Pickens Republican* in 1851:

Are we now not free? Are we not now independent, and in the enjoyment of all the rights, privileges and immunities of freemen? Let us not experiment with so dangerous a remedy as secession, for fear we may soon be called to write the epitaph of liberty, like the man in health who took a dose of medicine and died under its influence. He wrote his own epitaph before he died in the following language: 'I was well; I wanted to be better; I am here.' "Unionism," MA Thesis, Auburn, 1966, p. 20

After the settlement of the Compromise of 1850, there was a feeling of conciliation that swept the State and a tendency to sidestep the slavery issue whenever possible. But the presidential election of 1856 brought Clemens and Yancey back into the limelight. Crowds flocked to their debates in North Alabama. When Yancey accused Clemens of overdrinking, the latter replied that he had to drink his intelligence down to a level with Yancey's.

Moderation was shortlived, and its collapse paralleled increased Northern agitation. When Boston abolitionists condemned the Compromise of 1850 and all future compromises with slavery, the *Jones Valley Times* denounced these "never-dying sentiments of a large number of clergy of New England, and the higher classes that move in that fanatical atmosphere." A DeBow's Review author attributed the "nervousness, fanaticism, and superstition" of Northerners to a disease "resulting from a sedentary life through long winters over hot stoves." Yancey rejected the saving nature of a national party. He suggested the organization of Committees of Safety — in order to "fire the Southern heart, instruct the Southern mind, give courage to each other, and, at the proper moment, by one organized concerted action ... precipitate the Cotton States into a revolution." In answer to the crusading zeal of the northern abolitionists, Yancey suggested reopening the African slave trade.

The consolidation of the political forces into one party in 1857-58 was accompanied by revitalized efforts for economic independence. Although Senator James Hammond's "King Cotton" philosophy was echoed by many, the *Moulton Democrat* advised: "Altho' Cotton is King and we hold the balance of power of the world's commerce" the South should do her own "fetching and carrying ... manufacturing ... books ... schools ... system of internal improvements, and, in short, that she be independent in everything."

The growth of southern nationalism had a negative side. It became increasingly dangerous to express pro-Union sentiments. Robert Seymour Tharin, a Wetumpka lawyer, was "tried by a jury of citizens" in Lowndes County "for expressing...sentiments that were dangerous to the peace of society." The evidence had shown that he had "conversed with several non-slaveholders." He was accused of planning to start a secret abolition society and establish a newspaper at Montgomery to be called the *Non-Slaveholder.* After conviction, he was publicly whipped and exiled. A Wetumpka jeweler, who was a Douglas Democrat, was jailed for "Lincolnism." In Uniontown, "individuals in disguise" waylaid one James G. Bagley on a public road and "whipped" him. Bagley's alleged crime was publicly declaring:

If the Union is dissolved and civil war ensues, I will be damned if I do not go North, shoulder my musket and fight against the South; There is no one here that I care about anyway, except my wife, and I can very conveniently carry her with me. My folks are all North and I will be damned to H-ll if I don't fight against the South as long as there is any necessity for it. "Unionism" MA thesis, Auburn, 1966, p. 23

More moderate speakers could command an audience, however, and many of the Unionists of the 1850s sided with either Douglas or John Bell in 1860. Jeremiah Clemens expressed the sentiment of the Tennessee Valley in regard to the talk of secession. They preferred to wait and see what Tennessee would do before acting, as "Alabama and Mississippi are in a large part the children of Tennessee." Clemens further stated that he knew the people of Tennessee better and "have been more familiar with them from infancy, than those of my own state." Clemens further clarified the position of the people of North Alabama in letters to John Crittenden of Kentucky. Agreeing that the people had wrongs of which to complain, he disagreed with the remedy for redressing the wrongs: "The difference between Mr. Yancey and myself is, that I believe that redress may be obtained in the Union, while separate State action will only aggravate the evil." He could see no evil that would come of consultation with the North, and if it should fail then the remedy of revolution but not secession was available.

The entry of Abraham Lincoln as the candidate of the Republicans prompted southern newspaper editors to predict resistance by the southern states in the event of his election. The Alabama legislature passed a resolution requiring Governor Andrew Barry Moore to call a state convention to consider secession if Lincoln, as a sectional candidate for northern interests, was elected President.

The worst fears of the South were realized — Lincoln was elected. In South Carolina, a man lamented, "the die is cast; no more vain regrets; ... the stake is life or death" and a neighbor, less dramatically, expressed the fear that the radical Republicans would "Brown us all" (in reference to the abolitionist John Brown).

A few days later, the *Palmetto State* seceded. In Washington, the "Secesh" of South Carolina was dismissed lightly. One gentleman remarked that they would "be whipped back by the army and navy within ninety days" and a couple of blocks away a lady gently purred, "and oh! Isn't that nasty of those people in South Carolina! Why don't they behave themselves." In Alabama, however, there were many people who thought highly of the land of Calhoun and petitioned Governor Moore to call the convention resolved by the legislature. Moore replied that the election of delegates would be Christmas Eve, 1860 and the elected delegates would meet in Montgomery two weeks later.

The Cradle of the Confederacy

The delegates who met in Montgomery January 7, 1861, to resolve the "crisis" voted 54 to 46 for immediate, separate-state secession from the Union. Seven anti-secessionists later switched sides to make the final vote 61 to 39. The majority reflected the stance of south Alabama states-rights Democrats who represented the top cotton-growing counties.

South Carolinians had already proposed a convention of seceding states to meet at Montgomery in February 1861. Montgomery was chosen because of its central location, railroad facilities, and because it was the home of the

The Montgomery Advertiser

The Exchange Hotel in Montgomery, 1843-1905

"silver-tongued" orator of secession, William L. Yancey, a towering figure soon to be relegated to lesser status as actual armed conflict drew near.

Although Alabama followed Yancey into secession, the closeness of the vote and the spirit of the opposition angered Yancey. His bitterness deepened as he and other ardent secessionists were passed over for more responsible leadership for the Confederacy. Yancey was not even a member of the Alabama delegation to form the Confederate government. As University of Georgia Civil War historian Emory Thomas pointed out, "The fire-eating radicals who had devoted much of their lives to Southern nationalism found themselves elevated to roles as irrelevant elder statesman in the Southern nation." Miffed by being offered a minor cabinet post, the Attorney-Generalship, Yancey took instead a diplomatic mission to Europe.

Jefferson Davis of Mississippi was chosen President. His composite profile was impressive. He was a West Point graduate and had military service in the Mexican War. His administrative ability was demonstrated as U.S. Secretary of War and by his senatorial service. He had a moderate stance on secession and, as one writer expressed it, "he carried himself like a President." Journalist John Beauchamp Jones, a CSA War Department clerk during the war, observed that Davis was nearly six feet tall and "when he throws back his shoulders he is straight as an Indian Chief ... and no one gazing at his profile would doubt for a moment that he beheld more than an ordinary man."

Varina Howell Davis, wife of the President, was singled out by the critical diarist May Boykin Chesnut as one of the greatest women she had ever known. Varina was the daughter of William B. Howell, who is buried at Oakwood Cemetery in Montgomery and, according to Mary Ann Neeley, director of Old Alabama Town, apparently was engaged in the mercantile business in Montgomery at the time of his death. Varina's grandfather, Richard Howell, served as governor of New Jersey for eight successive terms. She and her three children — Maggie, 6, Jeff, Jr., 3, and baby Joe — arrived in March to live in the two-story dwelling now called the White House of the Confederacy. She observed Miss Letitia Tyler, daughter of long-time *Montgomery Advertiser* editor Colonel Robert Tyler and granddaughter of the ex-President, hoisting the first Confederate flag. Mrs. Davis described it as having "a blue union containing the stars in white at equal distances ... one broad white and two red stripes the same width." Montgomery's four-month tenure as the "Cradle of the Confederacy" included some warm weather and Mrs. Davis did not like this aspect of Montgomery living: "This is a very pretty place and were not the climate as warm as is the enthusiasm of the people, it would be pleasant ...." Commenting that her patriotism sort of "oozes out" at the pores on hot days she added that she had "deliberately come to the conclusion that Roman matrons did up their chores, patriotism, and such public duties in the winter."

The Montgomery Advertiser

Jefferson Davis (Harper's)

A contemporary observer, Thomas Cooper DeLeon, using a like metaphor, noted "Montgomery, like Rome, sits on seven hills. The city is picturesque in perch upon bold, high bluffs ... Main street runs from the river bluffs to the Capitol ... on a high hill a full mile away. This street, wide and sandy, was in the cradle days badly paved ... streets, various in length, uncertain in direction and impractical as to pavement, ran into Main street at many points." The Capitol dominated the lesser structures "as it stared down the street with quite a Roman rigor." As to the political climate: "Montgomery was Washington over again; only on a smaller scale, and with the avidity and agility in pursuit of the spoils somewhat enhanced by the freshness of scent."

The *London Times* correspondent was less charitable. He stayed at the Exchange Hotel which he pronounced "in a frightful state — nothing but noise, dirt, drinking, wrangling" and came to the conclusion that he and his party were the only ones not armed with a bowie knife or pistol. "Had it not been for the flies, the fleas would have been intolerable but one nuisance

The Montgomery Advertiser

Montgomery True Blues on parade, 1848. They became a part of the 3rd Alabama Regiment in the Civil War

neutralized the other." On Montgomery, "I have rarely seen a more dull, lifeless place; it looks like a small Russian town in the interior." The Capitol building was described as "one of the true Athenian Yankeeized structures ... erected on a site worthy of a better fate and edifice." The English observer suggested the Exchange would be better run by Yankees (actually it was Northern owned at the time). In any case, it was the center of political discussions on the secession of other states, Cabinet personnel, the latest appointments, and Cabinet deliberation ... all, to DeLeon, "canvassed with heat equaled only by ignorance."

The most pressing issue to the Cabinet was the instructions the Secretary of War was to give to the Louisianian General Pierre Gustave Toutant Beauregard as he sought a bloodless surrender of Fort Sumter in Charleston harbor. The Secretary of War, recommended by U.S. Senator from Alabama C.C. Clay and Yancey, was Leroy Pope Walker of Huntsville, son of Alabama's first U.S. Senator John W. Walker. Like many Southerners, he underestimated the Northerners' and particularly Lincoln's resolve. In fact, a basic misunderstanding between North and South was that neither side realized, until it was too late, that the other side was serious to the point of fighting and dying. After Lincoln's election, Walker told an audience "that he would wipe up with his pocket handkerchief all of the blood shed as a result of the South's withdrawal from the Union." In any case, the Secretary sent a telegram to Beauregard from the Winter building (which still stands near the fountain at the opposite end of Dexter Avenue from the Capitol) for the General to give the Fort Sumter defenders the opportunity to state a specific time to evacuate the fort and if they did not to "reduce the fort as your judgment decides to be most practical." At 4:30 a.m., April 12, 1861, a Confederate mortar fired the first shot. Major Robert Anderson surrendered at 2:30 p.m. the next day.

Both sides were now galvanized into action. Lincoln called for 75,000 volunteers and four border states, Virginia, North Carolina, Tennessee, and Arkansas, joined the Confederacy. Rump conventions voted Missouri and Kentucky out of the Union and, although the Confederacy added their two stars to its flag, both states were occupied by the Union throughout the war.

As Virginia's secession was subject to a referendum in May, the Confederate emissary, Vice President Alexander Stephens, proposed a temporary alliance with Virginia suggesting if that came about, the CSA government could well be moved there. On April 27, the Virginia convention issued a formal invitation for the Confederate government to move to Richmond. On May 11, Congress voted 5 to 3 (Alabama, Florida, and South Carolina opposed) to have their next session in Virginia. Ensuring Virginia was solidly in the Confederacy was thus a major reason for the move. Contributing factors were the poor hotel accommodations and particularly hot summer in Montgomery, the lack of office space for the expanding Confederate government, and the aggressive mosquitos. In Richmond's favor were the Tredegar Iron Works, flour mills and tobacco factories, the prestige and power of Virginia and good transportation facilities. The move also placed Davis, as military commander-in-chief, close to the buildup of troops facing Washington.

By June, 1,000 government employees had moved from Montgomery, where they had barely settled in, to Richmond. By the end of July, the Confederates had routed the Union Army in the first major battle of the Civil War — Manassas Junction (Bull Run).

Courtesy of Alabama Bureau of Tourism and Travel

Battle of Selma Reenactment, third weekend in April, the largest Civil War commemoration in Alabama, with 2,000 reenactors. The weekend is highlighted by a ball in authentic period dress at Sturdivant Hall on Saturday night.

IV

The 'Civil' War

The War Between the Union and the Confederacy

The Confederacy called the Civil War the "War Between the States." The official records of the war compiled by the United States government was titled War of the Rebellion (130 volumes). The Civil War has emerged as the accepted compromise between the two, although there was nothing "civil" about it.

The Confederacy and the United States means the government and men in uniform supporting the respective governments — not a geographic area. In view of 32,068 Virginians and 31,092 Tennesseans fighting in the Union Army and Missouri, Kentucky, Maryland, and Delaware being slave states in 1860, the terms "North" and "South" are somewhat misleading. The "North" did not defeat the "South" in the Civil War. The United States won a military victory over the Confederacy — aided by thousands of Southerners, including most of the 186,000 blacks who fought for the Union, and perhaps a equal number of white Southerners, predominantly from the mountain South. Thus the best term was provided in 1905 by the one-armed ex-Confederate and ex-governor from Henry County, William C. Oates, who titled his reminiscences The War Between the Union and the Confederacy.

The Confederacy referred to Civil War battles by the nearest town, community or church (Manassas, Virginia; Sharpsburg, Maryland) and the United States by terrain features (Bull Run Creek, Antietam Creek). The Confederate method is more precise so it will be used first and with the U.S. terms following in parenthesis, for example, 1st Manassas (1st Bull Run), Sharpsburg (Antietam).

Alabama Invades the North

Alabamians fought on all fronts in the Civil War and their sacrifices were many. One of the most romantic figures was John H. Pelham, one of six sons contributed to the Confederacy by Dr. Atkinson Pelham, a planter and country doctor near Jacksonville. Resigning from West Point in 1861, Pelham became an artillerist in Jeb Stuart's cavalry. Dubbed "gallant" by Lee, he became the "boy major" at 24. When the blond, blue-eyed, handsome youth was killed at Kelley's Ford in March 1863, three Southern girls allegedly "put on mourning."

Other Alabamians made significant contributions to both major Confederate offensives: Sharpsburg (Antietam) the fall of 1862 ending Lee's first invasion of the Union and Gettysburg (July 1863) stopping Lee's second and last invasion north.

Sharpsburg, Maryland (Antietam Creek)

More Americans died in battle September 17, 1862, than any day in American history. It was the bloodiest day of the Civil War — 22,719 casualties — 12,401 Union or 25 percent of those in action; and 10,318 Confederate, 32 percent of those engaged.

For days armed with knowledge of the disposition of Lee's forces (via a lost CSA order found concealed in three cigars) and with twice as many troops and shorter supply lines, George McClellan had the potential to

Antietam Today

The battlefield at Antietam is picturesque. Civil War battlefields normally have rail fences, cannon galore, visitor centers with a film, colorful maps, a souvenir shop, and tons of statues. Most have a church, some sort of depression, like a sunken road, someone's farm forever immortalized, and a bridge. Antietam has it all, without the commercialization/urbanization of other sites.

decisively defeat Lee and perhaps end the war in 1862, But "Tardy George," afflicted with the "slows," turned the lost orders into one more lost opportunity.

On Sunday, the 14th of September, 1862, Robert Rodes' 1,200 Alabamians moved into position north of Turner's Gap, South Mountain, a couple miles east of Sharpsburg, Maryland. Rodes' brigade was part of Gen. D.H. "Harvey" Hill's command trying to buy time for Lee to reassemble his scattered forces. Rodes ordered the 12th Alabama to form a skirmish line of sharpshooters in the woods to his front to slow the Union advance. Dodging tree to tree Indian fashion, they made life miserable for the oncoming federals. General George Meade's Pennsylvanians spearheaded the assault on the left flank of Hill's forces defended by Rodes. Before reinforcements arrived from Longstreet's Corps, accompanied by "Old Pete" himself (a South Carolinian who got his West Point appointment through Alabama), the Alabamians experienced four hours of the hardest fighting they had in the war. The 6th Alabama under Colonel John B. Gordon, who may have been the best regimental commander in the Army of Northern Virginia, repeatedly repulsed Meade's attacks until the Pennsylvanians broke them off at nightfall on the 14th. Lee gained precious time. One third of Rodes' Alabamians were killed, wounded, or captured.

At dawn on the 17th the battle of Antietam Creek began, with Joe Hooker's 1st Corps attacking Jackson on the Confederate left flank. The most savage fighting occurred in David Miller's 30-acre cornfield across the turnpike from Dunker Church. When it appeared the federals were carrying the day, John Bell Hood's division, including the 4th Alabama, counterattacked. Hood's seven regiments at the cornfield had 60 percent killed or wounded. Hooker's 1st Corps had nearly one third casualties.

Alabamians were also heavily involved a few hundred yards away at the "sunken road," a depression between two slopes caused by years of road use. The 6th Alabama, heroes of South Mountain, saw their commander, Colonel Gordon, receive five wounds this day. Gordon, in his **Reminiscences of the Civil War,** recalls the sunken road defense vividly and was a personal testament as to why it was called Bloody Lane. General Lee, realizing the position of Gordon and adjacent regiments to be the center of the CSA line soon to be assaulted en force, rode along the line to encourage the men. As they came by the 6th Alabama, Gordon called out: "These men are going to stay here, General, till the sun goes down or victory is won." The first Union volley included one minie ball that went through the calf of Gordon's right leg; higher up the same leg he was shot again; a third ball pierced his left arm; and a fourth ripped through his shoulder. He

The Montgomery Advertiser

Stuart (C.S.A.) and Averill (U.S.) cavalry clash at Kelly's Ford on the Rappahannock, where "The Gallant" Pelham was killed, March 17, 1863.

Alabama Department of Archives and History

John Pelham (1838-1863), Major, C.S.A. Pelham fought under Jeb Stuart at 1st Manassas, Sharpsburg (Antietam) and Fredericksburg. Promoted before Antietam, the "Boy Major" led Stuart's Horse Artillery effectively and courageously, his coolness under fire reminiscent of Thomas Jackson's artillery heroics in the Mexican War. Lee, after Fredricksburg, noted: "It is glorious to see such courage in one so young." Pelham was killed shortly thereafter at Kelly's Ford, Jackson two months later at Chancellorsville, and Stuart one year hence at Yellow Tavern.

recalled his pledge to General Lee. "I looked at the sun. It moved very slowly; in fact, it seemed to stand still." Gordon attempted to go to his men to remind them of his pledge when "I was shot down by a fifth ball, which struck me squarely in the face, and passed out ... I fell forward and lay unconscious with my face in my cap." Gordon would have drowned in his own blood except for a bullet hole in the cap which allowed the blood to drain. Gordon woke up in a field hospital and lived to fight another day. His replacement, misinterpreting an order from General Rodes, ordered them to abandon their fence-rail breastworks to scamper up a slope to their rear. Primarily as a result of this miscommunication, the regiment had 52 killed and 104 wounded. Elsewhere on the battlefield the Union rifled artillery was outranging its Confederate counterparts — dramatized to the 9th Alabama when one of its members was beheaded by a solid shot.

Antietam ended in a stalemate. But Lee's invasion of Maryland was stopped, and after the battle his beaten-up army recrossed the Potomac to Virginia. McClellan was satisfied with his "victory." Lincoln was not. After a post-battle tour, he relieved McClellan.

Gettysburg

From the Confederate perspective, Gettysburg featured a flanking attack on the left the first day by Richard Ewell, a flanking attack on the right the second day by James Longstreet, and a straight-ahead assault on the Union center the third day, the so-called "Pickett's Charge." The egg-bald Ewell was said to have lost his leg at Manassas and his nerve at Gettysburg. His troops, including Robert Rodes' Alabamians, drove the Union troops from the small town of Gettysburg but did not take the more significant high ground beyond the town — Cemetery Hill. On the second day Longstreet's men made a determined and costly assault through the wheat field, the peach orchard, "Devil's Den" and almost to victory at Little Round Top. On the third day 15,000 Confederates charged the Union center across an open field and 7,000 went down. Longstreet's second-day attack on the Union left received a leadership setback when Hood was wounded. A regimental commander from Alabama almost saved the day.

Oates and the 15th Alabama at Little Round Top

William Calvin Oates (1835-1910) was born in a part of Pike County now in Bullock County, taught school in Henry County, studied law in Eufaula (Barbour County), and practiced law in Abbeville before joining the 15th Alabama Infantry, CSA. He lost his right arm in August 1864 at Fussell's Mill (near Petersburg). After the war Oates served the 3rd District as congressman for seven terms (1880-1894) until elected governor in the famous Kolb-Oates campaign of 1894.

But the high point of his life was far from Alabama. On the second day of the greatest battle of the Civil War, Oates was in control of the highest point of the battlefield, the top of Big Round Top on the extreme left flank of Meade's Union Army. He noted, "within a half an hour I could convert it into

The Montgomery Advertiser

Antietam. The Sunken Road (Walton Taber's Battles and Leaders sketch).

Alabama Department of Archives and History

John Brown Gordon, commanding officer of 6th Alabama at South Mountain and the Sunken Road (Antietam).

a Gibraltar." But his orders from his brigade commander and fellow Alabamian, General E. McIver Law of Tuskegee, were to take Little Round Top.

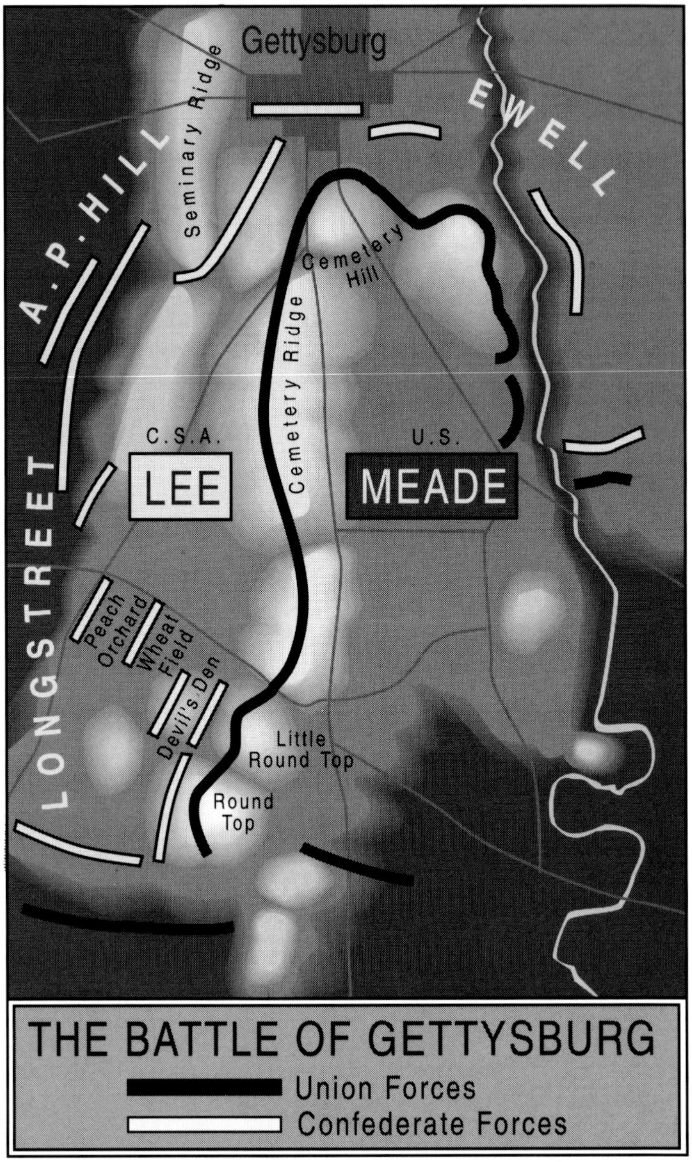

Graphic by Phil Coley

Little Round Top was defended by a Maine infantry regiment under Colonel Joshua Chamberlain, a pre-war Bowdoin College professor. Oates, a rough-and-tumble sort and one of the toughest soldiers in perhaps the hardest fighting Confederate division (Hood's) left the field with nothing but respect for the professor and his regiment: "There never were harder fighters than the Twentieth Maine men and their gallant colonel. His skill and persistency and the great bravery of his men saved Little Round Top and the Army of the Potomac from defeat." Oates' 15th Alabama drove the Federals from their strong defensive positions but "five times they rallied and charged us" — twice with bayonets. Colonel Oates lost his brother John, and the commander of his supporting regiment, Michael J. Bulger, (47th Alabama) was wounded and captured with over 300 men. Bulger, an anti-secessionist from Tallapoosa County, was left for dead on the field. He carried the minie ball under his shoulder blade to his death, at age 94.

Despite his losses, Oates made what he thought would be a final victorious charge — "It was our time now to deal death and destruction to a gallant foe ...." His charge carried the 15th to a large boulder less than 100 yards from the top of Little Round Top. Looking around, Oates suddenly became aware that he had Union infantry to the front, right, and left. "When one man was shot in the face, his right-hand or left-hand man was shot in the side or back. Some were struck simultaneously with two or three balls from different directions .... The ground was soaked with the blood of as brave men as ever fell on the red field of battle." Oates passed on the order that, on signal, everyone would run "in the direction from whence we came"

Alabama Department of Archives and History

William Calvin Oates (1835-1910). Commander of the regiment "on the other side" from Chamberlain's 20th Maine at Little Round Top. Oates subsequently lost his right arm near Petersburg, Virginia, in August 1864. After the war he served seven terms in Congress, 1880-1894, before winning a disputed election for governor in 1894 as a "Bourbon" against the farmers' candidate, Reuben F. Kolb. Like Joe Wheeler, he was appointed a general in the Spanish-American War and, ironically, was stationed at Fort Meade, Pennsylvania.

and regroup on the top of Big Round Top. The Union account (by the 20th Maine's regimental historian, a chaplain, and according to Oates, "Doubtless ... at prayer a safe distance in the rear.") claimed a federal charge and a rebel rout. Oates argues that he waited until the Union charge was repulsed "as it would give my men a better chance to get out unhurt," and then signaled the retreat, upon which the 15th "ran like a herd of wild cattle, right through" the federals.

Chamberlain was awarded the Medal of Honor for his Gettysburg heroics, became a general, and commanded the Union troops for the surrender ceremony at Appomattox. Oates was not at Appomattox but a post-war fellow Bourbon Governor of Alabama and then Major Thomas Goode Jones was. Jones, a VMI student of Stonewall Jackson and wounded four times in the war, carried a flag of truce to Appomattox with General Lee. Goode served two, two-year terms as Governor of Alabama, 1890-1894, being succeeded by Oates. Chamberlain likewise became governor in his native state and immortalized by Michael Shaara's Gettysburg novel, **The Killer Angels** (1974) — must reading for people who think they have no interest in the war between the Union and the Confederacy.

The Third Day and the 'Charge'

Alabama had 16 regiments at Gettysburg — several concentrated in the brigades of Cadmus M. Wilcox of North Carolina and James J. Archer of Maryland — both in the 15,000 under Longstreet who charged the center of Meade's line on the third day. George Pickett of Virginia led less than one-half the number but formed the brigades before the attack so his name is forever linked with the charge. Wilcox's "Alabama Brigade," noted for capturing 1,500 prisoners at Salem Church (outskirts of Fredericksburg), consisted of the 8th, 9th, 10th, 11th, and 14th Alabama regiments. One of the most colorful Alabamians in "Pickett's" charge was Colonel Birkett Davenport Fry, commander of the 13th Alabama, who led Archer's Brigade because the Marylander had been wounded and captured the day before. Bounced out of West Point for failing math, Fry fought in the Mexican War, was a filibuster general under Walker in Nicaragua, an antebellum cotton mill manager in Tallassee, and had been wounded at Seven Pines, Antietam, and Chancellorsville before being wounded and captured at Gettysburg. Brigadier General James Henry Lane of North Carolina was also in the "charge." Lane was a colorful professor of civil engineering at Alabama Polytechnic Institute (API, now Auburn University), from 1882 to his death in 1907.

Lee lost one-third of his army at Gettysburg. He accepted responsibility for the loss and offered his resignation, which Davis refused. After the war both he and Ewell were credited with the statement: "It took a great many mistakes to lose that battle. And I myself made most of them." Ewell seems to have had the better claim.

From an Infantry Regimental Perspective, War Is Hell

The impact of the war on individual regiments was drastic. In some cases a series of small engagements took a greater toll than the major battles. The

The Montgomery Advertiser

Stevenson, near Bridgeport: (Harper's) 1863 Union occupation as a part of the Chattanooga campaign

The Montgomery Advertiser

Huntsville during federal occupation, 1862. (Harper's sketch.)

The Montgomery Advertiser

Tuscumbia (Leslie's sketch, circa 1862.)

experiences of three Confederate infantry regiments from Franklin County in northwest Alabama illustrates the point.

Franklin Countians fought both for the blue and the gray cavalry — in the 1st Alabama Cavalry, USA; Roddy's 4th Alabama Cavalry, CSA; and the 11th Alabama Cavalry, CSA — but their heaviest losses were from service in the Confederate infantry regiments, particularly the 16th, 27th, and 35th. All three units served together during the 100-day battles, Dalton to Atlanta, Georgia, the summer of 1864. After Jeff Davis replaced Joe Johnston with John Bell Hood, the "fighting Texan" promptly ordered a series of assaults legendary for their ferocity and futility.

Atlanta fell and the Texan led his crippled army into Tennessee for more carnage at Franklin and Nashville. Inadvertently or not, Atlanta burned, and in "Hot Lanta" today a popular button reads "Gen. William T. Sherman: The Father of Urban Renewal."

Meanwhile the three Franklin County-laden Confederate Infantry Regiments followed Hood north. Unlike the other two, the 16th was with the Army of the Tennessee before the Atlanta engagements: Fishing Creek (64 lost), Shiloh (162 lost), Murfreesboro (168 killed or wounded), Chickamauga (244 killed and wounded), and in the Atlanta campaign (200 lost — 150 at Jonesboro); so half its force and all commissioned officers were gone before Hood's move north. At war's end, 50 survived to surrender.

The 27th Alabama had a similar fate. Captured at Fort Donelson, they spent most of 1862 in the Union prison at Camp Douglas, Illinois (Chicago). After being exchanged, their regimental commander, Colonel Adolphus A. Hughes, died of disease at Port Hudson. His replacement, Colonel James Jackson, lost an arm at Kennesaw. Retreating south after Nashville, their ranking officer was a captain and he commanded 16 men — of the 1,000 in the regiment three years earlier.

The 35th Alabama Infantry fought at Corinth, Baton Rouge, Baker's Creek, the Atlanta campaign, Franklin (150 killed), and Nashville. Although faring better than the 16th or the 27th, half of their force had been killed by the time Hood was relieved by his own request in January 1865.

Approximately 618,000 Americans died in the Civil War and a large number of counties North and South had losses as great as those of Franklin, but the county's three infantry regiments did experience especially hard service. Few 1865 survivors would disagree with the post-war quote of the opposition general most responsible for their tragic losses:

> *I am tired and sick of war. It is only those who have neither fired a shot nor heard the shrieks and groans of the wounded who cry aloud for more blood, more vengeance, more desolation. War is hell.* (Sherman, 1879)

Not All Alabamians Wore Gray

The official number of Alabama white unionists in federal service is 2,576, most serving in the 1st Alabama Cavalry. The total number is well over 3,000 because, for example, approximately 400 were known to have joined the 51st Indiana in July 1862 and 20 the 4th Indiana in August 1863. In surveying cemeteries in the vicinity of one county of North Alabama,

Winston, it was discovered that of the 93 Union soldiers buried with federally funded markers, 69 were in the 1st Alabama Cavalry. Union units the other 24 served included the 12th Tn Cav, 7th Ill Cav, 1st Middle Tn Cav, 10th Mo Cav, 5th Tn Cav, 14th Mi Inf, 2nd Tn Inf, 41st NY Inf, 56th Ill Inf, and the 11th Wisc Inf. Sixteen members of the 1st Alabama Cavalry were buried in the infamous Confederate prison at Andersonville Station, Georgia. All died May-October 1864, seven in August, when the dead totaled 2,993 (of approximately 32,899 prisoners in the 26½-acre enclosure). It is obvious Alabamians served in a number of units besides the 1st Alabama Cavalry — especially in the Tennessee regiments and Union regiments operating in North Alabama during the war.

The first companies of the 1st Alabama Cavalry were formed in late 1862 and engaged in scouting duty until their first major raid soon after Colonel George E. Spencer took charge in the fall of 1863. Lincoln's South Carolina-born friend and Spencer's corps commander, Stephen A. Hurlbert, ordered the 1st Alabama to proceed through Jasper, Alabama to Montgomery to destroy the Montgomery-West Point railroad. The 650 raiders encountered a force of 2,000 Confederates under General Samuel W. Ferguson soon after arriving in Alabama and were turned back. April-September 1864 the 1st Alabama acted as scouts in Sherman's Atlanta campaign and from September to December participated in the march to the sea. As Spencer's brigade approached Williston, South Carolina, with the 1st Alabama in the front, they struck a force of Confederates and drove them seven miles before the rebels dispersed into the woods and swamps. The Confederates were an Alabama brigade formed of the remnants of the 1st, 3rd, 5th, 9th, 12th, and 51st Alabama regiments. At Monroe's Crossroads in North Carolina Spencer's brigade was attacked in the early hours by cavalry under Wade Hampton and Joe Wheeler, which they repelled after a 2½-hour fight. Spencer's brigade also guarded the Union left flank at Bentonville, in the concluding battle of Sherman's campaign. In a recent book on **Lincoln's Loyalists,** Richard Nelson Current noted that "In proportion to their numbers, the Union troops from Alabama contributed as much to the war's outcome as did those from any other Southern state" (p. 173). The story of Alabama's Unionism is immortalized by an outdoor pageant, "The Incident at Looney's Tavern," Lakeshore, Alabama, performed Thursday-Saturday nights May through September.

Current further estimated the total number of white Southerners in the federal army at 100,000 — in contrast to 850,000-900,000 Confederates. Fully one in 10 white Southerners wore the blue rather than the gray. When one adds 178,000-186,000 blacks fighting in the Union Army, the majority Southern, (including 10,000 black soldiers from Alabama), it is apparent that the Civil War was a war, not between the North and the South, but, as Colonel Oates called it, "The War Between the Union and the Confederacy."

The Home Front In Collapse

The major cause of the war's sudden end in the state was the collapse of the home front. Specific problems that weakened and finally caused this failure, according to the late Malcolm McMillan of Auburn University, included opposition to conscription, wanton desertion, and the impressment of property without just compensation. General problems were sectional discord between north and south Alabama, a breakdown of the democratic election process, and improper use of the militia. Transportation problems also prevented the distribution of food and other essentials, and contributed to the inability of the government to feed and clothe the destitute. Inflation, extortion, the tax-in-kind, and the Union blockade all made life rougher on the home front and reduced the population's will to fight.

Wholesale desertions followed the fall of Gettysburg and Vicksburg the summer of 1863 and Atlanta's surrender in September 1864. A major cause was a soldier's conscientious effort to relieve the suffering of his family at home, a reason condoned by public opinion on the home front in Alabama. When steady reports from home of hunger, near starvation, and mistreatment by marauders was accompanied by Confederate reversals in the field, desertions became commonplace. Particularly disheartening was the news that their families were being abused by agents of their own government such as the conscript cavalry, "foraging" regular cavalry, or overzealous enforcers of impressment and tax-in-kind laws. The communities recognized the validity of the family's hardships and that the duty of taking care of one's family transcended that of fighting for the Confederacy.

The Confederate government had a "Catch 22" situation — damned if they do and damned if they don't. Trying to raise manpower for the war effort by enforcing conscription and rounding up deserters was forcing an unwilling population to fight. It also accented the injustices of the system which permitted larger slaveholders to be exempt from conscription. Politically influential men could also avoid military duty in the field by becoming members of the local militia. For example, 30,000 were in a classification which could not be deployed outside the county. In the same way, attempting to consolidate resources for the war through confiscation, under the impressment laws, of horses, mules, wagons, and other needed supplies, or the tax-in-kind which confiscated foodstuffs, increased the suffering of the civilian population. Such wartime shortages, compounded by the Union blockade, encouraged unreasonably high prices. The Confederate government tried to meet its needs by printing more money, thus inflating the currency. A CSA dollar in 1864 was worth about 5 cents in gold. Some items became critically short such as cotton cards for making cloth at home and salt for curing and preserving meat.

Probably the safest haven in Civil War Alabama was Governor John Gill Shorter's hometown of Eufaula, where subsequent Governor Thomas Hill Watts moved the state capitol when Montgomery fell to Wilson's raiders in April 1865. A fortunate aspect of this sanctuary is the preservation of gorgeous antebellum mansions showcased in annual pilgrimages. But this Barbour County village was also touched by inflation and shortages, as recorded by Parthenia Antoinette Hague, a plantation school teacher residing near Eufaula during the war. Coffee rose to $30 per pound, then to $60 and $70. Good workmen received $30 per day so it took, "two days hard labor to buy one pound of coffee." Improvisation was in order. Matured okra seed and parched yams substituted for coffee, and raspberry, blackberry, or huckleberry leaves for tea. Corn cob ashes, especially red cobs, produced

Mobile and the C.S.S. Hunley

From **Alabama: Its History and Geography,** p. 197

The most famous submarine of the Civil War was the C.S.S. Hunley. About 25 feet long, it was named for one of its builders, Horace L. Hunley, who also financed the submarine.

The Hunley's chief designer was William Alexander of Mobile. He was the only person closely tied to the Hunley who did not die either testing or on a mission in the submarine. The first crew of seven went down in the rough waters of Mobile Bay. The Hunley was then moved by rail to the calmer waters of Charleston Harbor in South Carolina. After another crew drowned, Mr. Hunley went to Charleston to train the next crew himself. And in October of 1863, he went down with the third crew, making more than 30 men drowned testing the submarine.

Despite the Hunley's reputation as an "iron coffin," Lieutenant George Dixon and six of his men from the 21st Alabama Infantry Regiment volunteered to take the Hunley into combat. The mission was to attack the U.S.S. Housatonic anchored in the shallow water of an inlet into the harbor. The Hunley was armed with explosives fastened to the end of a long pole attached to the submarine.

On February 17, 1864, Lieutenant Dixon and his fellow Alabamians rammed the Housatonic near the magazine (munitions storage). There was a loud explosion. The Housatonic sank ... but so did the Hunley. Because the Housatonic went down in shallow water all but five men survived. Not so fortunate were those in the submarine. The crew of the Hunley, the first submarine to sink a ship, all perished.

alkali to raise dough (as bicarbonate of soda did "before the war"). A blue dye was extracted from fermented indigo weeds. Hats, fans, baskets, and mats were braided and plaited from palmetto and straw. Shoes were made from cloth or knit. Miss Hague also noted that the woods were their drug stores. Dogwood-tree berries were taken for quinine. Blackberry roots or ripe persimmon made cordials to treat dysentery. Extracts from the barks of wild cherry, dogwood, poplar, and wahoo trees were used for chills and agues. Wild castorbean plants yielded castor oil. Everyone had a garden, which often included "a few rows of poppies ... to make opium, from which our laudanum was created" (a popular sedative at the time). The heads of poppies, plucked when ripe, would be penetrated by a large sewing needle, and placed in a cup for the opium gum to "exude and to become inspissated by evaporation. The soporific influence of this drug was not excelled by that of the imported articles." The blockade was endured. (There were attempts to break it. One scheme was submarine warfare. See the special feature on "Mobile and the C.S.S. Hunley.")

Raphael Semmes of Mobile was the Confederacy's premier naval hero and made life a bit more difficult on the Union homefront. He commanded the CSS Sumter, which captured 18 ships in six months, but his greatest triumphs were as commander of the CSS Alabama. In two years the Alabama captured 69 vessels worth more than $5 million. In June 1864 the

The Montgomery Advertiser

The C.S.S. Alabama and its commander, Raphael Semmes

Alabama was outgunned and sunk off Cherbourg, France, by the Kearsarge, effectively protected by a chain cable making it a partial ironclad.

The Governors

The three Civil War Governors of Alabama were Andrew Barry Moore of Marion, John Gill Shorter of Eufaula, and Thomas Hill Watts of Greenville and Montgomery. All three were slaveholders and plantation owners from the cotton-growing Black Belt of central and south Alabama.

Moore was a National Democrat in the 1850s and a strong voice for moderation until John Brown's raid on the federal arsenal at Harper's Ferry, Virginia in 1859. The Northern support for Brown convinced Moore there was no hope for sectional compromise so he led the state into secession. Moore also had a ringside seat at the forming of the Confederacy during the "cradle days" when Mary Chesnut painted him a graceful host but somewhat of a bore. He was an aide to both of his Civil War governor successors, Shorter and Watts.

John Gill Shorter of the pro-secession "Eufaula Regency," was a States Rights Democrat in the 1850s and, as governor, cooperated fully with the Confederate government. He supported conscription, which was regularly met by force in the mountains and the wiregrass, especially in the Pea River swamps. Shorter, as a long-time secessionist, was well-known in north Alabama and not politically effective there in supporting CSA acts. But Shorter finally alienated even his south Alabama supporters by the impressment of slaves for war labor. In the 1863 elections, he was defeated by the former Whig Thomas Hill Watts by almost a 3 to 1 majority. He lost his home county of Barbour by 400 votes.

Alabama's third war-time governor, Thomas Hill Watts, with 179 slaves,

The Montgomery Advertiser

Governor John Gill Shorter, Civil War governor, 1861-1863.

The Montgomery Advertiser

Governor Thomas Hill Watts, Civil War governor, 1863-1865

had been the largest slaveholder in the 1861 secession convention. When he joined the Yancey forces, the outcome was inevitable. Although, like Yancey, he accommodated the cooperationists' request that secessionist leaders not be a part of Alabama's delegation to form the Confederacy, he lived in Montgomery and was active socially. As a wealthy man, the affable and genial "Big Tom" lavishly entertained the Confederate officials and his judicial expertise came to the attention of Jeff Davis who appointed him Attorney-General under the permanent constitution in 1862. Helped by his able Assistant Attorney General, Wade Keyes, also an Alabamian, Watts served well for 18 months, writing more than one hundred opinions, compared to 20 for his two predecessors.

The conscript cavalry and Confederate cavalry carrying out impressments and "foraging" continued to be major sources of citizen complaints to Governor Watts. E.C. Betts of North Alabama, later Alabama's commissioner of agriculture, wrote in February 1864, that "The approach of a body of Confederate cavalry fills every neighborhood with dread and any man upon whose premises they camp regards himself as already ruined." Betts thought the CSA cavalry in the Tennessee Valley was as destructive as the enemy.

The tax-in-kind was particularly odious. Under it, one-tenth of all corn crops (the "tithe" corn) had to be given to the government. Abundant corn in central and south Alabama but a lack of transportation to get it distributed to the north fostered the practice of some north Alabama women walking south (the "corn women") to obtain corn and carrying it back north in sacks. In December 1864, Watts asked the CSA General Richard Taylor (son of ex-

President Zachary Taylor) to withdraw 5-6 companies of cavalry from Walker County as they were "doing no good there" and their "eating of the tithe corn is simply depriving a great many people of bread." Watts suggested to Taylor if their purpose there was to fatten the horses then they should be moved to the rich prairie country of south Alabama "as the cries of starving people are coming up to me almost every day" from north Alabama.

Unfortunately for state wartime morale, the section which opposed secession the most — north Alabama — suffered the most during the war. The Tennessee Valley was occupied with federal gunboats coming to Florence in April 1862 and remained occupied except when two Confederate Armies were in the vicinity — Bragg in middle and east Tennessee in late 1862, early 1863 and Hood in his retreat from Atlanta and advance on Nashville in late 1864. It was the consistent Alabama battleground of the war.

In contrast, far to the south in Montgomery, as late as April, 1865, on the eve of the one threat to the area during the war — Wilson's Raid — life went on as usual in Governor Watt's house:

> *On April 4, the day after Richmond and Selma fell, the governor gave his daughter Kate in marriage to Robert M. Collins of West Point, Mississippi, a lawyer and Confederate soldier and the son of a Mississippian who owned seven plantations. Kate's bridal gown of ivory satin was brought to Montgomery through the blockade by Meyer Lehman, a blockade-runner and a friend of the family, at a cost of $700. Since railroads were unavailable, the couple made their way to West Point in a magnificent carriage drawn by matching bay horses in silver-mounted harness.* McMillan, **The Disintegration of a Confederate State**, (p. 119)

The Intrastate War

Most of the conflicts between the Union and Confederate forces in Alabama in the years 1861-1864 occurred in the Tennessee Valley. There were, however, two major Union raids into south Alabama in 1864-65 — Rousseau's Raid (1864) and Wilson-Croxton's Raid (1865). Gen. Lovell H. Rousseau accomplished his prime purpose of cutting the railroad link between Montgomery and Atlanta before joining Sherman at Atlanta, and James Harrison Wilson destroyed the Confederate ordnance and manufacturing center at Selma. Croxton's raiders, a detachment from Wilson's main column, burned the University of Alabama. The University was a military school during the war and its students, as cadet drill instructors, trained 12,000 of the first 18,000 recruits raised during Governor Shorter's administration. After the war, Congress gave the University public lands to compensate for this wartime loss. But the major raid was the two-month springtime sojourn of Wilson through Alabama in 1865.

Wilson's Raid

In the spring of 1865, 13,480 Union cavalrymen armed with seven-shot Spencer repeating carbines crossed the bend of the Tennessee River near Waterloo to strike deep into the heart of Dixie in one of the most awesome cavalry raids of the entire war. Led by the 27-year-old West Point graduate

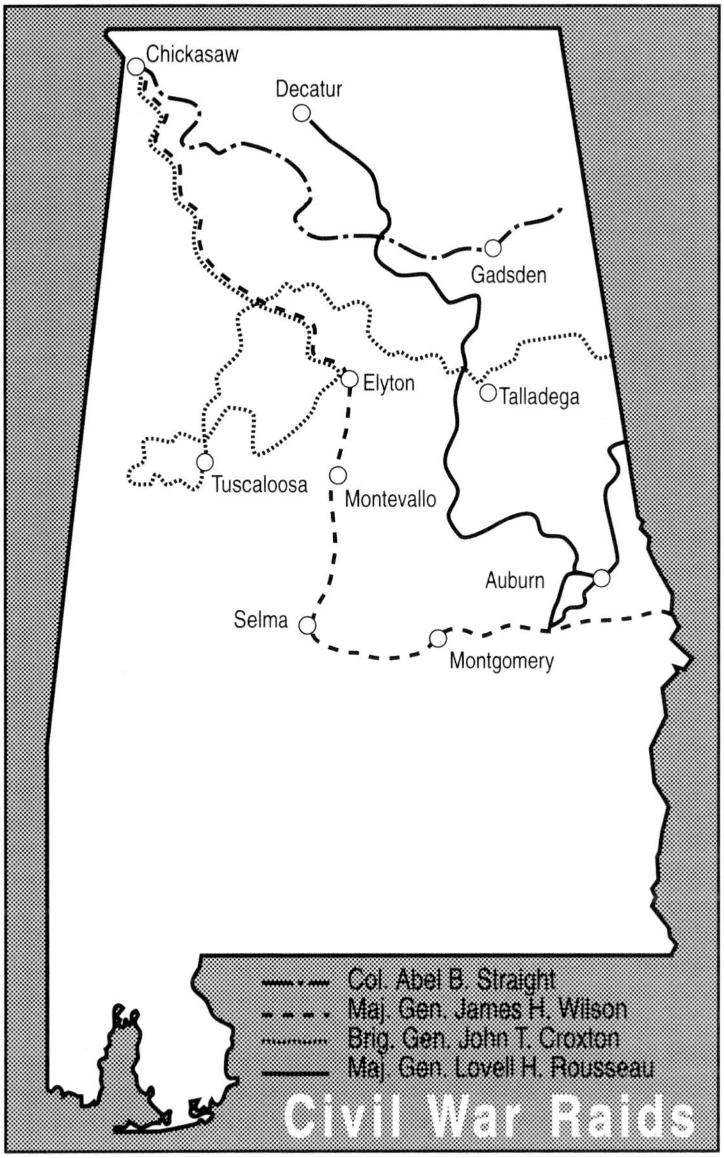

Graphic by Phil Coley

Based on Bill Letford and Allen Jones's Federal Raids in Alabama 1861-1865, Alabama Highway Map, 1961

James H. Wilson, the raiders were Grant-directed to tie up Confederate forces who otherwise would defend Mobile, and to destroy CSA forces in the field, lines of communication, and military resources. Wilson, a veteran of Antietam, Vicksburg, and the Wilderness, had fought under Phil Sheridan and William T. Sherman. Like his adversary, Nathan Bedford Forrest, he tried to get there first with the most, strike weak spots in the flank or rear, and break the enemy's means of communications and supply. He used the horse for speed and maneuverability but, once engaged, his men dismounted to make better use of their repeating carbines. His cavalry was, in fact, mounted infantry.

Forrest, on the Confederate side, was a well-to-do Memphis businessman dealing in cotton, real estate, and slaves before the war. A couple of inches over six feet tall, he was a lithe and powerful man with steady eyes, a man of striking and commanding presence. He joined the Confederacy as a private and rose to the rank of lieutenant general. Yet he was an unlettered man who had contempt for the well-educated. In his own words, "I ain't no graduate of West Point; never rubbed my back agin any college ...." He projected soldierly simplicity and engaging frankness in normal conversation but, once aroused, he had a terrible wrath. After being seriously wounded by a pistol shot by one of his own lieutenants, Forrest killed him with a penknife. Forrest was a tough man, and perhaps the best cavalryman in the war.

The Union cavalry had crossed the river and were in the hills before Forrest had intelligence of their movements. As three cavalry divisions would fill up a level valley two miles long and one-half mile wide, the four days it took to report the river crossing to Forrest seems incomprehensible.

The raiders divided into three columns to pass through the "barren and Godforsaken land" of the northwest Alabama hill country as quick as possible. They converged at Jasper — "a cluster of houses, a courthouse, and a jail." South of Jasper, the formidable Black Warrior River forced Wilson to leave his wagon train on the northern bank. After a laborious but unchallenged river crossing, the raiders continued to Elyton, the fledgling iron production center which would become Birmingham. At the time it was a village of 3,000 described by Wilson as "poor" and "insignificant ..." in contrast to the "pretty little town" of Montevallo and the "beautiful town with broad streets" (Selma) farther south.

On the way to Selma, a foraging party under Indiana Captain Ross Hill was taking advantage of the fertile area's wares when he was shocked by a woman shouting: "You Ross Hill! How dare you rob my plantation! If you don't call your men ... I'll go up to Indiana and make your mother whip you within an inch of your life." It turned out that the young woman had once lived in Hill's hometown. The plantation was spared.

The destruction of Selma was a prime objective of the Union expedition. An estimated 10,000 workers labored in the city's factories. In the last two years of the war they produced two-thirds of the fixed ammunition used by the Confederacy and one-half the cannon. They also built the Selma, the Morgan, and the Tennessee iron-clad gunboats.

Estimates of the size and quality of the Selma defenders varies but James Pickett Jones's **Yankee Blitzkrieg: Wilson's Raid Through Georgia and Alabama** cites 3,000-4,000 rebels and 6,000-8,000 Yankees. It was not an equal contest. Wilson had more and better trained men, who were better equipped, and, from top to bottom, better led than the defenders of Selma.

On the eve of battle, Wilson received an accurate diagram of the Selma defenses from an Englishman who helped build the works. As the United States troops massed for an assault on the afternoon of April 2, a Confederate force attacked their rear. Rather than fight on two fronts, the bluecoats charged the CSA works, and, as the militia abandoned their posts, the whole defense collapsed. Forrest escaped, but otherwise it was a total Union victory.

Wilson occupied Hotel Gee and the week-long wrecking of Selma's war-waging capacity got under way. So much cannon and machinery were dumped into the Alabama River that it formed heaps above the water line. Approximately 1,000 horses and mules were killed. The military destruction of Selma was total.

En route to Montgomery, a brief engagement was fought at Benton, a trooper (not deterred by a smallpox rumor) was flogged for stealing at Lowndesboro, and a group of "good-looking ladies" brought the raiders food at Hayneville. As elements of the force encamped on Catoma Creek outside Montgomery, Mayor W.L. Coleman surrendered the city.

Wilson headquartered at the Exchange Hotel and an impressive parade up Dexter Avenue followed. One trooper asked of a group of observing females something to the effect: "Where are all the Confederate soldiers who were supposed to defend this place?" After some hesitation, one replied: "I guess they took a lesson from y'all at Bull Run."

The Montgomery Advertiser

Battle of Mobile Bay and capture of the C.S.S. Tennessee, August 5, 1864. (Harper's sketch)

The Montgomery Advertiser

Fort Morgan after its surrender on August 23, 1864. (Harper's sketch)

After Montgomery, Wilson's raiders had quick victories near current West Point and Phenix City, Alabama, before capturing Columbus and Macon, Georgia. They also captured Jeff Davis and his cabinet-member party of Richmond refugees at Irwinton. The capture of Davis, combined with the destruction of Selma's war-sustaining facilities, effectively ended all hope of Confederate resistance east of the Mississippi.

The Battle for Mobile, 5 August 1864-9 April 1865

On August 5, 1864, Union Admiral David Farragut, a Tennessean by birth, moved his attacking naval force past the three forts guarding the entrance of Mobile Bay to engage the Confederate Navy in the Bay under Admiral Franklin "Buck" Buchanan. The strength of Farragut's 30-ship fleet was the four iron monitors: the Tecumseh, Manhattan, Winnebago, and Chickasaw. The Confederate Navy was spearheaded by the iron-clad ram Tennessee built up river in Selma ... and well-built it was. It withstood six to eight rammings and numerous broadsides from nine- and eleven-inch guns.

The Tecumseh led the way into the bay and almost immediately hit a torpedo and sank. The Winnebago quickly forced Fort Powell's evacuation, Fort Gaines, on Dauphin Island surrendered shortly, and only Fort Morgan remained. The outgunned and outnumbered Confederate Navy was disposed of with dispatch, except for the Tennessee. Its formidable armor-plating took the rammings and a point-blank 15-inch shot but the remainder of the deck, a mere 18 inches higher than the waterline did not. The steering apparatus was completely destroyed and the smokestack had fallen so the Tennessee was dead in the water with the Union monitors firing broadsides at will. As Admiral Buchanan had received a broken leg from an iron splinter, Commodore James D. Johnson hoisted the white flag. The Confederate Navy was defeated and the siege of Fort Morgan commenced.

The Federals landed troops and guns at Navy Cove above the fort. High sand spits and rolling hills shielded their advance. Scouts found an abandoned trenchworks 1,400 yards from the fort and the Union artillery was put in place. While the monitor barrages sought to reduce the walls and Union sharpshooters picked off Confederate gunners, a dozen heavy mortars were brought up. Capable of lobbing large explosive balls into the fort, the mortars soon ignited the wooden barracks and endangered the powder magazines. Besieged on all sides and the land forces within 200 yards, Fort Morgan's Brigadier General Richard L. Page surrendered August 23, 1864. The battle of Mobile Bay was over.

Major General Dabney H. Maury defended Mobile with less than 10,000 troops. Union General E.R.S. Canby had a combined force of 45,000. Spanish Fort on the eastern shore of the bay was captured after a two-week siege in March-April, 1865. On April 9, 1865, the day after Spanish Fort fell, 16,000 Union troops under General Frederick Steele successfully assaulted the fortfications of Blakely and captured more than 3,000 prisoners. On the news of General Joseph Johnston's capitulation, General Richard Taylor surrendered the remaining CSA forces east of the Mississippi on May 4, 1865, at Citronelle. General Kirby Smith did the same for the Trans-Mississippi CSA forces on the 26th. The war was over!

The Aftermath

Alabamians participated on all fronts during the Civil War and in both armies. Various estimates allege 67,000 to 100,000 Alabamians served in the Confederate Army, and an estimated 13,000 in the Union Army (about 3,000 white and 10,000 black).

The war resulted in an impoverished Alabama. The sacrifices made to support the Confederate war effort and the ravages of both armies left much of the state destitute. Manufacturing made some advances during the war and the transportation system was improved through railroads, but the Union raids late in the war canceled these modest gains.

The emotional fires of sectionalism of the 1850s flamed into secession in 1861 but the reality of war and its impact on the home front had cooled and sobered the state's citizenry even before the fall of Vicksburg and the defeat at Gettysburg. After the 1863 summer, more and more Alabamians wanted to wind the war down and return to a more stable and peaceful life. As the war dragged on, the people progressively lost the will to fight. Alabamians saw no reason to continue the war except to maintain slavery and most were not slaveholders. By the spring of 1865, the people were defeated. Wilson's task was reduced to subduing scattered remnants of the once-proud but now battle-worn Confederate regulars under Forrest. Farragut and Canby had similar "mop up" operations in Mobile Bay. The war was over and the people were ready for peace and recovery.

Alabama Bureau of Tourism and Travel

Fort Gaines on Dauphin Island, Mobile Bay: On August 3, 1864, Union General Gordon Granger landed about 1,500 men on the western end of Dauphin Island two days before the Battle of Mobile Bay. With Farragut's naval victory on the 5th, Fort Powell on the sand bar at Grant's Pass fell. On August 8, 1864, CSA Colonel C.D. Anderson, after a token defense, surrendered his garrison of 800 at Fort Gaines — much to the dismay of Fort Morgan's commander, CSA General Richard L. Page (Robert E. Lee's nephew) and the citizens of Mobile. General Page surrendered Fort Morgan on the 23rd, after a more determined defense. With the fall of Atlanta a week and half later, Lincoln's 1864 reelection was assured. Source: McMillan, ***The Alabama Confederate Reader****, 310-311.*

V
Post-War Alabama
Reconstruction

A popular grade school textbook, used for years in the public schools of Alabama, followed the "happy slave" thesis for the antebellum years and glorified the role of the KKK during reconstruction. "The Klan did not ride often, only when it had to." And the questions at the end of the chapter didn't let up:

What did President Lincoln say about the Southern states after the war?

How did the Southern states feel about President Lincoln's plan to get them back into the Union?

What happened to President Lincoln?

Actually Lincoln's plan for reconstruction required Alabamians to do only three things: abolish slavery, nullify secession, and have 10 percent of the number of voters in the 1860 election take an oath of allegiance. If Lincoln had lived and his reconstruction plan could have prevailed over alternative ones by Congress, the reconstruction era would have been much milder. In any event, Lincoln's successor, Andrew Johnson, an East Tennessee Unionist but no Lincoln, was not able to effect a similar plan of presidential reconstruction. The 1866 congressional elections gave the congressional reconstruction forces a two-thirds majority and, in effect, the ability to dictate the terms by which the southern states reentered the Union. In the 1868-1877 years the Confederate States were readmitted as their new constitutions incorporated the 13th, 14th, and 15th amendments which required the South to free the slave and grant the freedman citizenship rights, including voting. The 14th amendment contained the "equal privileges and immunities" and "equal protection of the law" clauses, basic to the civil rights gains in the post-1950s era. From a legal and constitutional perspective, the clauses were also central to the process of gradually converting the antebellum state-based power of the federal union to a post-war American nation ruled from above.

Immediate post-war, presidential reconstruction was doomed from the start because it was too lenient from the viewpoint of even the most moderate of Northern Congressman. Under it, former Confederates dominated the Southern congressional delegations and they were not in favor of political rights for the recently freed slaves. Most importantly, by the freedom of the slave, the old constitutional provision for only 3/5th of the slave population counting for representative purposes in the House of Representatives was now, in effect, changed to 5/5th which meant that the South picked up 12 more congressional seats than the region had in 1860. In essence, the same type antebellum Southern leadership was back, with the same views, and there were more of them than there were in 1860! Northerners wondered aloud who won the war. Thus Congressional reconstruction gave Northerners the opportunity to consolidate their gains resulting from winning the war.

White conservative Southern Democrats were pragmatic too. They recognized the post-reconstruction political value of discrediting the

Northern-backed Republican regimes in the South. The South militarily lost the Civil War but won the battle of the pen, historians said about the reconstruction era. Early designation of the Republicans as "radicals," the Northern politicians in the South as "carpetbaggers," and native-born reconstruction leaders as despised "scalawags" has stuck to the present. Accommodating the national desire for sectional reconciliation at the turn of the century, a Northern educator — William A. Dunning of Columbia University in New York — encouraged his Southern history students to complete dissertations on Civil War and Reconstruction in their home states. The general philosophy by Dunning and his students was — "radical" republican reconstruction regimes were corrupt and inefficient; illiterate blacks dominated the era assisted by corrupted northern "carpetbaggers," and native-born "scalawags;" the South was occupied by the Union Army and literally ruled at the point of the bayonet; "radical" republican reconstruction lasted 12 long years; no good came from the era; conservative whites, led by the KKK, finally tired of this oppression and overthrew the "radicals;" the corrupt and inefficient "radicals" were replaced by honest white conservative "Bourbons" restored to their rightful place in the manner of the House of Bourbon in France.

Alabama Department of Archives and History

Robert Burns Lindsey, Democrat governor in Reconstruction Alabama

As noted by subsequent historians, the Dunning school overstated their case on all accounts. The state governments were not uniformly corrupt or inefficient, and in Alabama, not even all Republicans, as the 1870-1872 administration of the Democrat Robert Burns Lindsay attests. Blacks did not dominate a single state, although two South Carolina legislatures were majority black. The Palmetto State also had the only black Supreme Court Justice. But there were no black governors, only two black United States Senators (Mississippi) and 10 U.S. Congressmen. Of the 108 major black officeholders in Alabama listed by Richard Bailey in **Neither Carpetbaggers Nor Scalawags,** 97 were members of the state House and five in the state Senate (two of the senators were in the House also).

Three of the ten black Congressmen were from Alabama — Benjamin Sterling Turner, Selma businessman and city councilman who also served as the Dallas County tax collector before his 1871-1873 Congressional term; Jeremiah Haralson, a Selma minister who was in both houses of the state legislature and president of the Labor Union of Alabama before elected to Congress in 1874; and James Thomas Rapier, born in Lauderdale County in 1837 of free parents, educated in Canada, a lawyer and a successful Tennessee Valley farmer before his election to Congress in 1872. The moderation of Turner and Haralson appeased many white constituents in their largely Black Belt First District but Rapier was more activist. In the Constitutional Convention of 1867, his rhetoric was seen as "violent and

Courtesy of Alabama Bureau of Tourism and Travel

Benjamin Sterling Turner (1825-1894) of Selma, Reconstruction Congressman

highly inflammatory" by whites who Virginia Hamilton, in **Alabama: A History,** observed were "unaccustomed to being challenged by blacks." Rapier was particularly incensed when, after being royally regaled abroad as a part of the Congressional delegation representing the United States at the Vienna Exposition of 1873, he was refused service at inns from Montgomery to Washington and relegated to second-class status on public conveyances. In supporting a civil rights act to prevent such abuse, he noted to his colleagues: "Here I am the peer of the proudest but on a steamboat or railroad car, I am not equal to the most degraded. Is this not anomalous and ridiculous?"

Even when successfully allied with each other and the "carpetbagger" and "scalawag" factions, the coalition of "radicals" had very limited tenure. There were never enough Union forces in Alabama to coerce Alabamians to the national will, and military rule under General Wager Swayne ended in 1868. As lenient Presidential reconstruction preceded Swayne's 1867-1868 tenure, and Democratic governors served from 1870-1872 and after 1874, the Radical Republican or Congressional-dominated Republican rule in Alabama was only for a total of five years and these not cohesive or continuous. It was certainly not 12 years of military or radical dominance. Nor have the Dunning school arguments on the heroic role of the KKK in deposing the despised "radical" or the honesty of the "Bourbons" who replaced them gone without challenge. Klan activity no doubt helped elect the Democrat Lindsey in 1870, but a coalition of scalawags and white conservatives aided by division in the ranks of blacks and carpetbaggers yielded a victory by the Unionist George Smith Houston in 1874, not Klan leadership. And "Honest Ike" Vincent's fleecing the state of $230,000 in 1883 and similar Bourbon activity in five other Southern states detracts from the credibility of persistent claims of strict honesty on the part of the Bourbons. In the **Origins of the New South,** Comer Vann Woodward documents Bourbon corruption and doubts their public morality exceeds that of the "radicals."

The Dunning School's assessment of the era as all bad is likewise in error. Alabama constitutional authority Malcolm McMillan, late head of the History Department at Auburn, gave the Constitution of 1868 high marks. Of the 100 delegates who wrote it, there were 51 native Alabamians ("scalawags"), 30 "carpetbaggers" or Freedmen Bureau officials, 18 blacks, and 1 conservative. Patterned after Midwestern constitutions, McMillan dubbed it more democratic and more liberal than Alabama constitutions before and after. It provided for the popular election of all executive and judicial officials by the people. More emphasis was put on public education, women's rights, industrial resources, and property tax exemptions for the less affluent. One fifth of all public revenues was earmarked for education, whereas the total annual antebellum appropriation had been $100,000. The constitution also created a state superintendent of education and a strong Board of Education. While the white conservative antebellum southern leadership was out of the Union, the United States Congress passed the Morrill Act of 1861, allotting 30,000 acres of land for each congressman and senator for support of an agricultural and mechanical college. Thus Auburn University was created during the reconstruction era in 1872 by the same "radical" legislature that elected Confederate Alabama's adjutant general George Goldthwaite to the U.S. Senate. And in the 1872 elections, although the anti-secessionist David P. Lewis was elected governor as a Republican, both houses of the legislature were Democratic. The most notable radical abuse was leaving the state with a $30 million debt, mostly due to state endorsement of railroad bonds. Even this is misleading because the Bourbons only paid the $13 million that they considered to be valid. Unfortunately for Alabama's education forces, the Bourbons returned to the antebellum system of poorly financed public education via their Constitution of 1875. Clearly the Dunning School interpretation of reconstruction still popular with much of the public is largely mythical. Sarah Woolfolk Wiggins, an authority on Alabama Reconstruction, captures the essence of the popular misconception of the era:

> *The Alabama public then and now has been preoccupied with vilifying the Republican party for disasters that were basically the readjustments of a people defeated in a war, adjustments that represented unwanted, unpleasant, wrenching social, economic, and political changes.*

Wiggins also questions the stereotypical picture of scalawags and carpetbaggers. In an analysis of five major scalawags (Samuel F. Rice, Alexander H. White, Lewis Parsons, David P. Lewis, Alexander McKinstry), she notes that none fit the popular image of a small farmer with little education or political experience and rabid Unionist sympathies. In contrast, they were men of property who were lawyers and had active public careers as Democrats before becoming Republicans. Four served the Confederacy — two in politics and two in the army. Only Lewis was a Unionist. They exemplified "clear-sighted political realism in assessing the political situation for what it was in Alabama, not as they might have wished it to be." Like the Congressional Republicans, they were political pragmatists.

In regard the carpetbaggers, Wiggins' basic point was that their control over Alabama Reconstruction has been vastly overestimated. None were gubernatorial candidates or justices of the Supreme Court and, of the 38 Congressmen of the era, only 9 were northerners. Wiggins classifies the carpetbaggers into two contrasting groups: idealistic men of moderation who sought to better the lot of the freedmen and remake the South into the northern image; and corrupt plunderers securing political offices for the spoils. The enlightened group included General Wager Swayne, head of the

Freedmen's Bureau before becoming military governor, and U.S. Senator Willard Warner. The latter group of spoilsmen were represented by District Judge Richard Busteed, Lieutenant Governor Andrew J. Applegate, and former Union General George E. Spencer. Spencer was a friend of President Grant and the major dispenser of federal patronage in Alabama. Busteed and Spencer supported the Democrat Lindsay for one purpose or another during reconstruction as both used their politics "as a gambler shuffles his cards — to suit the occasion."

But the scalawags were the real leaders of the era. And on close examination, they were not much different in socio-economic status or education from the Alabama political leaders before or after reconstruction.

The Ku Klux Klan (KKK)

The alleged origin of the reconstruction era KKK in Pulaski, Tennessee, with former Confederate General Nathan Bedford Forrest as its head, is an oft-told and perhaps accurate tale. But its strength in the era, its central control and regional cohesiveness, and its significance in effectively fighting or ending political reconstruction is overstated.

For sure there was some sort of white conservative night-riding terrorist group, often made up of young rowdies, in most parts of the South. They were especially active when there were blacks trying to vote, become office holders, secure a square deal economically, or get an education. Most were local and temporary. In Alabama, they included the Pickens County Night Owls, the Tuskegee Knights of the White Carnation, the Black Cavalry of Tallapoosa County, and the Tuscaloosa County Sipsey Swampers. As a regional organization, the Klan had strong rivals in the Knights of the White Camelia. Forrest himself was more explicit in public statements about membership in the Order of Pale Faces than the Klan. The glorification of the reconstruction Klan by the early 20th century "Birth of a Nation" motion picture, its subsequent resurrection in the 1920s and national growth to a membership of 5 million or so, and its continued skeletal existence to date accounts, in large part, for its strong historical image in the immediate post-Civil War era. And the Klan is a convenient umbrella designation for the multitude of white conservative night-riders of Southern reconstruction.

The chronological and geographical focus of Klan and Klan-like violence in Alabama, as documented by Allen W. Trelease's **White Terror: The Ku Klux Klan Conspiracy and Southern Reconstruction,** was the years 1868-1871 in four western Alabama counties bordering Mississippi — Fayette, Tuscaloosa, Greene, and Sumter. They encompassed the towns of Tuscaloosa, Eutaw, and Sumter. The spiritual leader was Ryland Randolph, editor of the *Tuscaloosa Independent Monitor* whose masthead motto was "White man — right or wrong — still the White Man." The targets of the violence were Republican and Union League political leaders, northern teachers in black schools, and any black man who resisted political intimidation. Night-riders murdered five men in Sumter County in 1869, including black legislator and minister Richard Burke of Gainesville, and seven men in three months of 1870 in Greene County, including black legislator Jim Martin of Union and the white county solicitor Alexander Boyd of Eutaw.

Governor William H. Smith and the University of Alabama were singled

Why Not Be a Teacher?

By JUDITH PATERSON

Excerpted from **Sweet Mystery,** a family memoir to be published by Farrar, Straus, and Giroux in September, 1995.

My paternal great-grandfather, William Burns Paterson, was hardly more than a boy when he came to Alabama and started teaching black people to read and write in freedmen's shacks and wagon beds — in dusty Black Belt heat so hot you could hardly breathe in it — at a time when the Ku Klux Klan was still driving such people out of the state and burning down their houses. Wanting to go as a missionary to Africa but not having the money to get there, he had left a close family of poor farmers, weavers and brewery workers in a rural Scottish village called Tullibody and gone one day in 1867, near the time of his 18th birthday, to the docks at Glasgow and hired himself out as a deck hand on a freighter headed for New York.

For three years, he roamed America, often walking long distances "with just a dog, a gun and a fishing line," working at anything that paid and falling in love with a country vast and free beyond anything he could have imagined in Scotland. In the spring of 1870, he followed Reconstruction railroad work north from New Orleans to West Alabama and found himself standing at the heart of the band of dark soil that had made cotton king and now bled like a wound across the belly of the state, where black bodies and black dirt had made a few white people very, very rich, where impoverished freedmen now made up over half the population and blacks and whites alike now labored night and day just to feed their children.

Proud of the learning he had come by the hard way and confident of his own intelligence, affability and good sense, at first Will saw only the chance to make money and rise socially in the place he had come to. In a letter to his brother John, he said that he might bring a colony of skilled Scottish workers to Hale County. He thought about a career in politics. and so it went for a while, until a national economic crisis and local politics squeezed railroad contracts, and the scales began to fall from the hazel eyes of the ruddy-cheeked Scotsman. "There is nothing but politics (meaning conflict over race) here," he wrote his brother in 1871, his high spirits dampened by the turmoil and political violence that erupted between the Reconstruction Republicans (whose party he joined) and Bourbon Democrats (who had befriended him and introduced him to their daughters) at the end of Reconstruction in Hale County.

It must have been during that dark time that black railroad workers began begging him to teach them to read and write and do figures. And he must have begun at that moment to dance the fine line between his belief in education and human betterment and the traditions of a place built on class and caste, where learning was often ridiculed, where public education was still inadequate for whites and nearly nonexistent for blacks.

For 15 years he had piled learning on top of learning — poring over school texts in a steamy kitchen in Scotland, borrowing books from strangers across America and mailing them back from wherever he

Alabama Department of Archives and History

William Burns Paterson (1849-1915) founded a school for blacks, Tullibody Academy (named for his place of birth in Scotland) in Greensboro in 1871, and served as its principal until 1878, when be became president of the Normal School at Marion. A fight between one of his Normal students and white cadets of Howard College, also in Marion, escalated into a racial dispute that caused both colleges to leave Marion — Howard College to Birmingham, where it eventually became Samford University, and the Normal School to Montgomery, where it evolved into Alabama State University. Paterson served as president until his death in 1915.

happened to be when he was done with them, carrying a German dictionary and a grammar for thousands of miles in order to read the Bible in that language — pursuing a peculiar urge far beyond any practical purpose, or so he thought. Now this, to start at the bottom among a people who for generations had been forbidden by law to pick up a pencil, who know nothing, some of them already too old to learn easily and some of the children too hungry some days to think at all.

But something in the sight of grown, strapping men, wet with their own sweat, begging for the few years of schooling that even the poorest farm child in Scotland could take for a birthright touched something in the heart of a young immigrant a long way from home. And so, one day, standing in unthinkable heat — seeing the longings of his own childhood written on faces so different from his own — he nodded his head and turned toward them.

At first, he taught the men (and soon a few women and many children) sitting in wagons over lunch under the trees and then on the weekends in an abandoned slave cabin using hymnals and newspapers sent from Scotland. Finally, in the fall of 1872 — with the help of an odd consortium that included many ex-slaves, the Freedmen's Bureau, two Baptist churches (one black and one white) and several planters (one hoping to stem the flood of farm laborers leaving the county, another wanting to educate four golden-skinned children sired by him in slavery) — he built himself a long one-room schoolhouse in the county seat at Greensboro. And there in a school called Tullibody Academy, modeled after the little one-teacher, each-one-teach-one schools of rural Scotland, the 23-year-old, largely self-taught Scotsman began educating Alabama's first generation of black scholars and teachers.

out for personal abuse by editor Ryland A. Randolph, who spurred the "Sipsey Swampers" into action and ran off most of the students and faculty in the 1868-1871 years, including Smith's son. The governor's nephew, also a University of Alabama student, proved a more difficult victim as he, before fleeing to Illinois, had a street brawl with Randolph resulting in the editor's loss of a leg. Randolph, clearly out of control, finally became inconsequential after public statements attacking Confederate and white conservative heroes Nathan Bedford Forrest of Tennessee and John C. Breckinridge of Kentucky.

Outside of west-central Alabama, the major Klan-like violence in reconstruction occurred at Cross Plains in Calhoun County, in July, 1870. A major racial conflict erupted from a white youth picking a fight with a black youth. Shots were exchanged and four blacks and a white Canadian, William C. Luke, were arrested. Luke, a school teacher of a black school at Patona, was not involved but unpopular with the white community as a race mixer. Fifty to 60 fully disguised Klansmen overpowered the guard and lynched the five prisoners. Governor Smith sent a special investigator, prosecutor, and federal troops. Nine men were arrested but the local grand jury wouldn't indict them.

In the November 1870 election, Smith, despite his lack of success against the nightriders, was renominated by the Republicans. The Democrats nominated Robert B. Lindsay, a Tuscumbia lawyer and moderate. Prior to the election Klanlike activity peaked. Republican congressman Charles Hays was dragged from the platform October 25 at a Eutaw Republican gathering. Despite the presence of Smith, former governor Lewis Parsons, and U.S. Senator Willard Warner, white conservatives fired into the mostly black crowd, killing four and wounding 54. In Tuskegee, the foremost black Republican, James H. Alston, was run out of town by a Klanlike organization headed by his former master and former CSA General Cullen A. Battle. Trelease noted that "Nearly every Negro church and school in the county was burned prior to the election." In Greene County, black Republican leader Guilford Coleman was taken from his home, murdered and mutilated. The violence in Sumter, Macon, and Greene counties was effective. Lindsay, the Democrat, won by 1,400 votes statewide out of a total of 150,000. Greene County went Democratic by 35 votes compared with a majority of 2,000 for the Republican Grant in 1868. Sumter County Democrats won by 600 votes in 1870 whereas they had lost by 1,000 votes in 1868. The Republican Smith carried Macon County but by less than Grant had in 1868. Trelease concluded that the "Klan became in effect a terrorist arm of the Democratic Party, whether the party leaders as a whole liked it or not."

As time passed, white public opinion very gradually turned against the terrorist tactics of the Klan. Unfortunately, during its heyday, local authorities could not effectively counter systematic terrorism although there were unsuccessful efforts to do so by Sheriff F.M. Treadway and his "Mossyback" supporters in Fayette County, by Judge Charlton of Morgan County (murdered in March 1870), and by state agent and ultimate U.S. Attorney John A. Minis. But the state refused to act decisively. The federal government was the only hope for protection and, by 1871, there were only three Union companies in the state — one at Huntsville and two in Mobile.

(Ironically, a century later, a descendant of Sheriff Treadway and a namesake of attorney Minis, Judge Frank Minis Johnson, Jr., of Montgomery, was more successful in seeing the law enforced in Alabama.)

Again, ironically, or perhaps logically, the center of nightriding violence against blacks in the Alabama-Mississippi vicinity of Sumter County during Reconstruction was the same area and time which produced a large volume of black folk music, especially the blues. (See the sidebar by Lynda Brown.)

Bourbons, Farmers, and Birmingham

The last quarter of 19th century Alabama history is generally referred to as the Bourbon era, which featured "the rule of the brigadier generals." The pro-Confederate forces were restored to power and a Confederate war record was practically essential for political success.

George Smith Houston, the first Democratic Governor of the era, served two consecutive two-year terms (1874-1878) as Governor and was U.S. Senator from 1879 to 1883. He had opposed secession in 1861 and was therefore not typical of the Bourbon era.

Houston was succeeded by seven consecutive governors who had served in the Confederate Army. The senatorial seats were likewise dominated by ex-Confederates James Pugh, Edmund Pettus, and John Tyler Morgan. Pettus and Morgan (both were from Selma and died in 1907) were Confederate brigadier generals as was Governor Edward O'Neal.

Besides Confederate service, the Alabama Bourbons shared an appeal to white supremacy and a dedication to laissez-faire governments with low taxes and few services, including minimum aid to education. The economy-in-government position resulted in the reduction of the state debt from 30 to 13 million dollars, but the Bourbon claim to honesty in government received a severe blow in 1883, when it was learned that three-time state treasurer "Honest Ike" Vincent had fleeced the state of $230,000. After his capture in Texas, he worked as a convict leasee in Birmingham coal mines before being pardoned by Governor and fellow Bourbon Thomas Goode Jones in 1893.

The indifference of the Bourbons to the social ills of the day fostered opposition from the forces of reform, particularly for the economically depressed farmers of the state. The farmers were opposed to trusts, high protective tariffs, and convict leases, and favored a more equitable tax structure (tax on something besides land), more money in circulation, better schools, and direct election of U.S. Senators.

The farmer opposition was expressed through various "independent movements," the Grange or Patrons of Husbandry, the Greenback Party, the Agricultural Wheel, and the Farmer's Alliance.

The Grange: The National Grange or the Patrons of Husbandry

Oliver H. Kelley, a statistical gatherer for the Department of Agriculture, organized the Grange in Washington, D.C., in December 1867. Kelley envisioned a social and educational organization to overcome the general demoralization after the Civil War and achieve sectional reconciliation. It grew rapidly in the Middle West and expanded into the South in the 1870s.

Courtesy of Alabama Bureau of Tourism and Travel

William Christopher Handy, popularly acclaimed as "Father of the Blues," was born in a log cabin in Florence, Alabama, on November 16, 1873, and died in New York City on March 29, 1958. Handy gained fame and finally fortune as the composer of St. Louis Blues, Memphis Blues, and Beale Street Blues. The Handy family's donations of the composer's personal piano, his famous trumpet, his library, and a wealth of other memorabilia, make it one of the most complete museums of its kind in the world.

The Devil's Music in Sumter County

By LYNDA BROWN

Co-author of **Bibliography of Alabama History** in progress

To some religious people, secular songs are the music of the devil. The blues, in particular, have been associated with all manner of wickedness. When W.C. Handy was growing up in Florence in the 1880s, his Methodist minister father would not let him have a guitar because he thought the instrument was "one of the devil's playthings." In order to please his father, Handy gave up the idea of playing the guitar and learned instead to play sacred music on the organ. Later this son of the straitlaced preacher would write one of the most famous of all blues songs — "St. Louis Blues" — and become known as the Father of the Blues.

Handy did not invent the blues; he just helped to make them popular. His blues are a citified version of the authentic African-American folk music that arose out of fields, cabins, and kitchens somewhere in the South — probably in Mississippi and Alabama — sometime after the end of slavery. Sumter County might not have been the birthplace of the blues, but in the early 20th century it was the home of an exceptionally rich store of black folk music.

Ruby Pickens Tartt was the first white person to give serious attention to the black musicians of Sumter County. As an amateur folklorist, Tartt started writing down the stories and songs she heard as she traveled the back roads and visited the black churches near her home in Livingston. When the federal government started collecting folk songs for the national archives in the 1930s, the folklorists in Washington soon heard about Tartt and the music she had discovered in Alabama. In the spring of 1937, John Lomax, one of the foremost collectors of folk songs, arrived in Livingston with his new wife and his recording machine. Tartt took them in, introduced them to the singers, and arranged for interviews and recording sessions.

Lomax was not disappointed in what he heard, and he eventually recorded more than 600 songs in Sumter County for the Archive of American Folk Song in the Library of Congress. Lomax became friends with several of the singers, and Vera Hall was one of his favorites. She was a cook and washerwoman who often sang spirituals with her cousin Dock Reed. Reed was too religious to sing the "devil songs," but Hall liked secular songs as well as the hymns and spirituals she sang in the Baptist choir. One evening Lomax coaxed Hall into singing a blues song that became one of his treasures.

The lyrics of the blues are about "natural facts" as one bluesman put it — hardship, suffering, loss, separation, work, love, and lust. Often they are about escape, and Hall's song, "Another Man Done Gone," is about a black man who had escaped from jail and was running through the night. "You see his face," Lomax wrote, "you know him, but at the same time you put him out of your mind, so that when the white man asks after him, you can say:

I didn't know his name,
I didn't know his name.
I don' know where he's gone,
I don' know where he's gone."

Vera Hall sang these words in her fine contralto voice, and Lomax's recording of the song became a classic.

In singing about almost intolerable truths, blues singers bare their souls to the world, and singers and listeners alike often feel comforted and strangely uplifted. Ironically, the devil's music — like spirituals — emancipates the spirit. It was entirely fitting, then, that in observing the 75th anniversary of the Emancipation Proclamation, folklorists at the Library of Congress selected and played Vera Hall's recording of "Another Man Done Gone."

Sources: Virginia Pounds Brown and Laurella Owens. **Toting the Lead Row: Ruby Pickens Tartt, Alabama Folklorist.** University of Alabama Press, 1981.

W.C. Handy. **Father of the Blues: An Autobiography.** Macmillan, 1941.

John A. Lomax and Alan Lomax. **Best Loved American Folk Songs.** Grosset and Dunlap, 1947.

Olivia Solomon and Jack Solomon, eds. **"Honey in the Rock": The Ruby Pickens Tartt Collection of Religious Folk Songs from Sumter County, Alabama.** Mercer University Press, 1991.

In 1872, a Mississippi agent organized eight granges in Pickens and Sanford (now Lamar) counties of northwest Alabama. But Alabama's Grange really took off under the leadership of ex-Confederate Major General Evander McIver Law of Tuskegee. Law, who was William C. Oates' and Michael Bulger's brigade commander at Little Round Top, ran the Tuskegee Military High School before the war. A South Carolinian by birth, he returned there after the war, but again moved to Tuskegee in 1872. The next year he received a commission from the National Grange as a deputy for Alabama and organized Tuskegee Grange No. 9. By the time of the state convention in Montgomery in November 1873, there were 320 granges in Alabama in 50 of the state's 65 counties. Law served as secretary of the state organization, 1873-1876. Its well-educated head (or master), William H. Chambers of Oswichee in Russell County, was Emory University's top student in 1847 prior to earning a law degree from Harvard. He became a law partner of later Civil War Governor John Gill Shorter in 1854 and editor of the *Southern Cultivator.* He served in the state legislature before and after the war and in the CSA Army during the war.

Although the Alabama Grange had a temporary resurgence in 1887, its heyday was the 1870s. After 1880 it was not a powerful force, giving way to the more aggressive Farmers' Alliance and the Agricultural Wheel. Its major failure was not relieving farmer distress through its pet scheme of cooperative buying and selling nor was it able to replace sharecropping with cash wages. In addition, many granges were carelessly formed, had ill-informed members, placed non-farmers in policy-making positions, and held anti-democratic secret meetings.

Though short-lived and hampered by being thematically non-political, the Grange introduced Alabamians to large-scale agricultural organization, provided educational and social activities for farmers, instituted cooperative economic action, and educated farmers on better methods such as crop diversification and soil improvement. The Alabama "Grange Legislature" of 1875-1876 and subsequent legislatures yielded Grange-supported acts regulating cotton weighing and sampling, forbidding trading in agricultural products at night, and providing for a geological survey, an immigration commissioner, and finally, in 1883, a Commissioner of Agriculture. Perhaps more than anything else, the Grange encouraged the development of a high degree of farmer self respect and a pride in agricultural pursuits. A Grange Hall and other architectural preservations of Alabama in the 19th century can be seen at Old Alabama Town in the Hull Street Historic District, Montgomery. (See the sidebar by Mary Ann Neeley. Philosophical support for the diversity of old Alabama and encouragement for even broader architectural preservation efforts is in an accompanying sketch by architectural historian Bob Gamble.)

William Manning Lowe of Madison County and The Greenback Party

With the virtual disappearance of the Republican Party after 1876 and the non-political stance of the Grange, the only opposition to the Bourbon Democrats in Alabama by 1878 were independents and the Greenback

Old Alabama Town

By MARY ANN NEELEY
Executive Director, Old Alabama Town

Old Alabama Town captures the spirit of the architecture, history and life-style of 19th century Alabama. Located within sight of the state capitol, Old Alabama Town's three blocks recreates a lively streetscape of buildings ranging from the high-style 1850s Thompson House to the vernacular 1898 one-room school.

Architecturally, the area includes examples of Federal, Greek Revival, Italianate, Queen Anne, and Steamboat Gothic. A Log Cabin, Shotgun House, Dogtrot houses, Italianate townhouse, Greek Revival cottages and mansion depict the places people lived. The school represents educational values of rural Alabamians sacrificing to see that their children learned the three "R's" while the Corner Grocery portrays daily consumerism in an urban neighborhood. The Country Doctor's Office and the Drugstore Museum show the contrasts and similarities of rural/urban health care. The small 1890s church denotes the religious nature of Southerners, black and white. The Cotton Gin indicates the power of cotton in the economy, and the Grange Hall tells the story of the struggle post-war Southern farmers had to new systems of land management and labor while trying to break the hold cotton had on their existence.

Working craftspeople add lively drama to our interpretation of life in 19th century Central Alabama.

The Montgomery Advertiser

Cotton gin at Mitylene, near Montgomery, 1907

Alabama's Architectural Heritage: Columns and Cabins, Mansions and Mills

By BOB GAMBLE,
Alabama Historical Commission

Early Alabama architecture tends to be viewed largely in terms of a few long-favored images: Civil War-era forts, pioneer cabins, columned plantation houses, and perhaps more recently the gingerbread-festooned dwellings of the Victorian era. To be sure, from the prehistoric period — the several thousand years of native American habitation — nothing remains in terms of "architecture" except the romance-enshrouded earthen mounds still found occasionally along Alabama rivers and streams. Even a century of European colonization, beginning with the French on the Gulf coast around 1700, has left not a single vestige, architecturally speaking. But if Alabama's architecture as we think of it today begins less than two centuries ago, it has spawned a diversity that enriches our built environment.

Unproven claims would place a handful of log houses close to 1800 or even earlier. But the oldest documented structure in the state is Huntsville's Leroy Pope house of 1814, a dignified brick dwelling quite worthy of the town's leading citizen.

With the opening of newly surveyed Federal lands a few years later, settlers flooded into Alabama from the older states to the east and north. And depending on his economic circumstance, the pioneer's first shelter might be anything from a rude temporary "pole" structure or a sturdy one-room cabin with loft to that badge of frontier gentility, a commodious two-story log "dogtrot" house.

Perfect for long hot summers, the "dogtrot" dwelling took its name from the wide, breezy central hall that bisected the house from front to back and lay open to one and all, man and man's best friend alike. In fact, it would be the dogtrot house, in both humble single-story versions and grander varieties, that would become the typical rural Alabama homestead through most of the last century and into the beginnings of this one — in hill country, fertile cotton regions and coastal pinelands alike. Along with the crossroads store, the grist mill, the cotton gin, the lodge hall and the inevitable church or two, it was for generations a standard fixture of the Alabama landscape.

But in the most favored agricultural areas as well as early trade centers like Montgomery, Tuscaloosa, Demopolis, Florence and the port city of Mobile, King Cotton and its attendant prosperity quickly produced an appetite for a more ambitious architecture. It was an architecture that borrowed from established traditions in the Carolinas, Virginia and farther afield, while tailoring these to fit local conditions of climate, available materials and available skills. Thus porches were apt to be a little more generous against the Alabama sun, and ceilings a little higher, while decorative details often might be a little less skillfully executed than in eastern drawing rooms and public meeting halls.

Needless to say, the plantation house — not just the columned classical variety, but also less-known versions built in the Italian villa and Gothic styles — has assumed mythic proportions in Alabama history, along with its antebellum townhouse counterpart. This is not without reason, since such structures probably represent 19th-century Alabama's architectural high point. But this emphasis has hindered recognition of other types of architecture which are as valid in their own way, and as expressive of the state's development.

Early industrial complexes like Daniel Pratt's water-powered mills at Prattville or the great stone mill buildings at Tallassee (tragically gutted in the early 1990s) rank among the most important manufacturing establishments of the pre-Civil War South. Later in the century, the opening of the north Alabama mineral regions around Birmingham and Anniston produced a flurry of Victorian-era homes, churches and commercial structures that have only recently been appreciated — when it is almost too late. And post-1900 Birmingham itself would eventually boast a fine assemblage of early skyscrapers, along with streetscapes of spreading Prairie-style houses and wide-eaved bungalows more akin to Chicago and Pasadena than to cherished southern architectural preferences.

So from mill to mansion, cabin to skyscraper, each architectural imprint from the past has a story to tell if we know how to read it. The structures themselves link us to distant times out of which the present grew, and form a sort of vivid visual gauge by which both the achievements and limitations of our ancestors may be measured.

Party. The leading Greenbacker was William Manning Lowe of Madison County, a former Confederate lieutenant colonel on General James H. Clanton's staff. Lowe, brother-in-law of independent Nicholas Davis, Jr., of 1861 anti-secessionist fame, favored more money in circulation to help mortgage-ridden farmers pay their debts. He supported the unlimited coinage of silver or "free silver," (the later major issue of William Jennings Bryan) and other farmer movement goals such as $50 in circulation per capita. But his main thrust was paper money or greenbacks, as issued by the national government during the Civil War. Backed by the *Huntsville Advocate* and having heavy voting strength in Madison, Lawrence, Limestone, and Franklin Counties, Lowe won the 1878 Congressional election against incumbent Congressman William Willis Garth, a member of Longstreet's staff in the war who had a law degree from the University of Virginia. In 1880, Lowe was initially counted out in a congressional challenge from popular ex-Confederate General Joe Wheeler but eventually seated after a congressional investigation. During the 1882 campaign Lowe died after a prolonged attack of bronchitis and pneumonia. Had he lived, he would probably have carried his single-issue politics and the Greenbackers into the emerging farmers' movement coalition, the Farmers' Alliance.

The Farmers' Alliance

As the historian of the farmers' movement in Alabama, William Warren Rogers, notes, the Farmers' Alliance was the most important agricultural organization in Alabama between the Civil War and 1900. The first Alabama Alliance was formed by a Texas organizer in the heart of Greenback country — Madison County — in 1887. Various farm clubs entered the Alliance as a group and former Grange leaders embraced the Alliance with enthusiasm. Both small and large farmers made up its membership and ministers, especially rural Baptist, took an early interest. The red-haired and fiery-tempered Baptist minister of Bibb County, Samuel M. Adams, was elected president at the August 1887 state meeting of 3,000 held at Cave Spring, Madison County. Barbecues and picnics were held with Alliance meetings and the Alliance expanded the social and educational activities of the Grange by well-attended local and county meetings and annual conventions. In 1889, the Alabama Alliance met at Auburn, site of the Agricultural and Mechanical College, a meeting attended by national agricultural leaders and Alabama Commissioner of Agriculture, Reuben F. Kolb. At the Auburn meeting, the Alliance was merged with the Agricultural Wheel, a more politically active farm group strong in the Tennessee Valley. By late 1889, the Alliance had an estimated 120,000 or so members and 3,000 lodges.

Like the Grange, the Alliance engaged in business ventures, especially cooperatives. It also operated cotton warehouses at Opelika, Ozark, and in St. Clair County. Whenever possible, it cooperated with local merchants to get better prices for Alliance members. Their largest single endeavor, the Alabama State Exchange in Montgomery, purchased almost exclusively from local merchants. But the Alliance attempted too much too soon and earlier successes were soon followed by failures. One economic success was a boycott against the jute bag trust which brought the price down from 13 cents to 5 cents by 1890.

From 1887 to 1892, the Alliance was primarily non-political. When it was apparent its economic activities were failing, the order became political. Even after becoming an integral part of the populist movement, however, it maintained its separate existence to 1897. It survived by going political and, like the Grange earlier, it gave farmers a genuine sense of brotherhood and made them proud of their historic role in feeding and clothing America.

In the political arena, the Farmer's Alliance was led by Reuben F. Kolb of Barbour County. Kolb was defeated for the Democratic nomination for Governor in 1890 and 1892 by Thomas G. Jones of Montgomery. Kolb carried eight more counties than Jones but the large Black Belt vote (much of which was fraudulent, according to some Alabama historians) yielded an 11,435 majority, in a vote of almost a quarter of a million, for the Bourbon Jones.

The 1894 Kolb-Oates election was almost an "instant replay" as Oates, the one-armed Confederate hero of Henry County, defeated Kolb by 27,000 votes. Again, fraud was charged. The conservative Bourbons, manipulating the black voters of the Black Belt, had withstood the challenge of the reform-minded farmers for the last time.

The Montgomery Advertiser; inset of Jones from the Alabama Department of Archives and History

Governor Thomas Goode Jones' home, 353 Adams Avenue, built in 1855 and bought by Jones in 1879, had a major addition while Jones was governor in 1892. The house was said to have expanded with the Jones' family of 13. Judge Walter B. Jones (1889-1963), son of Governor Jones and a rigid segregationist, inherited the house and lived it in during his 43-year tenure as a state circuit judge, from 1920 until his death in 1963. Source: Advertiser files and J. Mills Thornton, ***Touched by History*** *(Montgomery, Alabama: printed by Black Belt Communication Group, early 1990s.)*

Two conditions paralleled the heavy black population in the Black Belt — high cotton production and a high percentage of illiteracy for the total population. In 1870, the Black Belt led the state in both categories as it did in 1900. But by 1900, there was an increase in cotton production statewide and a decrease in illiteracy. After 1910, the Tennessee Valley showed a marked increase in cotton production which continued to 1930 when the Valley, in consequence of the tremendous impact of the boll weevil on South Alabama cotton production, emerged as the leading cotton-producing area of the state. Although there was a significant decrease in the illiteracy rate statewide from 1900 to 1930, the Black Belt continued to have the highest rate. A private effort to improve black education in the Black Belt was the Snow Hill Institute in Wilcox County. (See the sidebar by Amelia Bartlett-Dodd.)

Under the "Bourbon" rule in the post-Reconstruction era, taxation was

Black Education in the Early 20th Century Black Belt: William J. Edwards and the Snow Hill Institute

By DR. AMELIA BARTLETT-DODD

In 1893, William Edwards graduated second in a class of 20 from Tuskegee Institute — no small feat as his early life had been spent in poverty and illness. Born in 1869 in the Snow Hill community of Wilcox County, Edwards' mother died before his first birthday. His father left him to be raised by a grandmother on three rented acres where cotton and corn were grown. In his childhood, his only shirt was often a "crocus sack" or corn sack his aunt had cut holes in for arms and head. Edwards remembered putting on a sack shirt for the first time: "It seemed as if a thousand pins were sticking me all at once, but after a few days ... I could wear it comfortably. For several summers this was my only garment."

Limited to two or three months of school each winter and ridiculed by the other children for having only bread to eat, Edwards still learned to read well enough to accomplish his one desire — to read the Bible for his very religious grandmother. In 1880 his beloved grandmother died and Edwards' father, who had been absent for a number of years, returned to take him and his sister to Selma. There for only a short time, he became very ill. Having no medical attention and in need of food and clothing, Edwards got progressively sicker. His aunt heard of his ordeal and came for him. Begging for nickels and dimes for medical care, "Aunt Rina" took him to Dr. George Keyser, who operated many times to remove dead bone from Edwards' arm and heel. The recovery was painfully slow. Unable to walk, Edwards often crawled outside to spend the day watching ants. The following year he could do a little work on his aunt's farm. Living in a one-room log cabin with three other people, seldom having enough to eat and too poor to buy oil, Edwards studied his books by the light of pine "light-wood." Always in his mind was the desire to attend school. In 1887 Edwards heard of Tuskegee, a school where boys and girls without money could work for their education. He immediately wrote "Mr. Washington" for a catalogue. Edwards reached Tuskegee the first day of 1889. Working, learning, realizing a dream, he graduated four years later. His class chose a motto which became the cornerstone of Edwards' life — "Deeds Not Words."

Greatly influenced by Booker T. Washington, Edwards desired to do whatever possible to help the Black Belt's unfortunate. Traveling on foot through Wilcox, Monroe, Butler, Dallas, and Lowndes counties, he observed living and farming practices. He found a black population of more than 200,000 uneducated and superstitious people and a school population of 84,500. He did not discover any accessible libraries or public schools and found only one private school. Edwards identified his life's work. He resolved to establish a school modeled after Tuskegee Institute, emphasizing practical and industrial arts. He sought to teach the beauty and dignity of all labor and instill a love for the soil and agricultural life.

Snow Hill Normal and Industrial Institute began in an old one-room log cabin with one teacher, three students, and 50 cents in capital. Mr. R.O. Simpson, the white man on whose plantation Edwards was reared, donated seven acres for the school. Deeply interested in the welfare of the black people of the area, Simpson later contributed 93 more acres and finally sold one-half of his plantation to the school, making Snow Hill's total holdings close to 2,000 acres.

There was no state appropriation nor any group responsible for funding. Edwards wanted a school for all blacks, thoroughly religious but not bound to any denomination. With encouragement from Dr. Washington, Edwards learned to solicit aid in the Northeast. Through Miss Susan Messinger's appeals to people of Boston and New England, money was raised for Snow Hill. Andrew Carnegie heard an Edwards' speech and gave $10,000. Miss Anna T. Jeanes of Philadelphia donated $5,000 and later established the Jeanes Fund.

Edwards encouraged blacks to build better school houses, lengthen the terms, own their land, and build dwelling houses having more than two rooms. At the time, less than 10 acres of land within 10 miles of the school was owned by blacks. Virtually everyone lived in one- or two-room log cabins. Not one home had a glass window. Edwards recalled that shortly after the founding of the school a black man built a house with glass windows and people came from miles around to see it.

Twenty-five years and 1,000 graduates later, the impact of Snow Hill could be felt. Over 50 percent of the students bought their own homes — many with five or six rooms. It was known that wherever a Snow Hill student taught, the school term lengthened and more people bought land and built better homes, schools and churches. The school had more than 400 students, 22 teachers and officers, 24 buildings, and 14 industries in constant operation.

Ill of health, Edwards resigned from Snow Hill in 1924. The Institute became a public school in 1936 but was closed in 1973 with the desegregation of the Wilcox County schools. But in Edwards' heyday, Snow Hill Institute was an impressive educational establishment. Its alumni, like its founder, William J. Edwards, and its godfather, Booker T. Washington, had cast their buckets down. In the process, they uplifted the quality of everyday life for generations of Black Belt blacks.

Source: **Twenty-Five Years in the Black Belt.** William J. Edwards (The University of Alabama Press, 1993). The book was brought to my attention by an AUM English teacher, Ann Depas-Orange.

light and appropriations to education slim. In 1900, the average amount of education money spent on each child in Alabama was 50 cents, compared with the national average of $2.84. In 1880, 25 percent of whites and 80 percent of blacks age 10 years and older could not read or write. Short school terms and underpaid and underprepared teachers accounted for the slightness of the change in illiteracy by 1900. Periodic public education movements gradually lengthened the school year — to five months by 1901, seven months by 1935, eight by 1943, and to the nine months term by

Photo courtesy of Dan Brothers, Alabama Bureau of Tourism and Travel

"Salute to the Peanut Industry" mural, depicting the contributions of Dr. George Washington Carver, the Wiregrass Festival of Murals in Dothan.

1947. In the meantime, Alabama ranked near the bottom of most education statistics nationally and illiteracy remained a major problem.

Higher education made some gains in the late 19th century with the establishment of Auburn University in 1872, the first normal school (teacher college) at Florence in 1872, and three black colleges — a state normal and industrial school at Huntsville (1873), Tuskegee (1881), and Alabama State (1884). Like the public schools, however, the state colleges were plagued by inadequate funding in the late 19th and early 20th centuries. In 1884 the University of Alabama's entire appropriation was $24,000, and in 1900 Harvard University received more revenue than all Southern colleges combined. Educational appropriations and academic excellence could have been worthy legacies for the South to adopt from the East but the Ivy League had a far different Deep South impact in the 1890s. (See "Auburn Goes Ivy League" by Andy Doyle.)

The Bourbons also had a particular dislike for the manipulations of the railroad lobby during the Reconstruction period, and in their Constitution of 1875 forbade state, county, and municipal governments from lending their credit to railroads, as was done with disastrous results during Reconstruction. Nevertheless, the railroads were able to make progress. In 1865, Alabama had only 962 miles of railroad. By 1873, there were 1,793 miles of track, and by 1900 this increased to 4,226 miles. Water transportation also survived without state aid. In 1880, there were 43 steamboats in the state and nearly a half million dollars had been invested in water transportation. The state was also assisted, as in other days, by the federal government. Alabama Congressman, F.G. Bromberg, a "Radical Republican," got the channel in Mobile Bay deepened in 1876 and, with a second dredging in 1888, an ocean-going vessel came to the Mobile docks for the first time. The federal government continued its dredging efforts in the Alabama River, and by 1892 had progressed to Montgomery. A greater federal effort on the Tombigbee, which included the building of 17 locks and dams, made this stream and the Warrior River navigable to Birmingham Port where iron, coal, and steel from Birmingham could be loaded for shipment to Mobile — some 350 miles away.

Auburn Goes Ivy League: 'The Gentlemanly Sport' on the Plains, 1892

By ANDY DOYLE, Ph.D. student, Emory University and adjunct faculty, Auburn University at Montgomery

Dr. George Petrie, professor of history and Latin and volunteer football coach at the Alabama Agricultural and Mechanical College (later Auburn University), met his 14-member team at the Auburn train station early in the morning of February 20, 1892. Along with several dozen tense and excited Auburn students wearing their neatly pressed gray cadet uniforms, they awaited an 8:10 a.m. train for Atlanta, where they would meet the University of Georgia in their first intercollegiate football game. The sport that would in later generations become as authentically Southern as a road sign full of bullet holes had yet to penetrate the Deep South despite its great popularity in the Northeast. Petrie had come to Auburn the previous summer determined to introduce to his native state this modern Ivy League sport that he had encountered while in graduate school at Johns Hopkins. Over the fall semester he had recruited athletically inclined students and, standing on the parade ground, rulebook in hand, had taught them this complex new game. He even purchased smart new white canvas uniforms from a Boston sporting goods dealer out of his own meager paycheck. Petrie came to Auburn with his freshly minted Hopkins Ph.D. determined to impart the progressive vigor of the modern age to southern higher education. Teaching his students to play "scientific football," as the sport was often called to distinguish it from the old-fashioned game of soccer, was an outgrowth of his ambitious New South vision.

Petrie, the Auburn cadets, faculty, and team joined a group of Auburn supporters from Montgomery on the special train, and the exuberant group practiced their newly composed college cheer during the four-hour trip to Atlanta. The two-hundred-member Auburn party stepped off the train platform into a city gone mad over a game that virtually no one had ever played or even seen. The Georgia team train had arrived from Athens 30 minutes earlier, and the city streets were filled with roving bands of Georgia students filling the air with ear-splitting cheers. The two teams and their supporters walked through streets filled with newsboys hawking special editions containing stories exhorting one and all to come witness the spectacle. They walked past downtown storefronts decorated with ribbons in both the red and black of Georgia and the orange, blue, and white of Auburn. Even the staid and genteel Kimball House Hotel, to which both teams retired for two hours of rest and last-minute instructions, rocked noisily with the sound of college cheers.

Remsen Crawford, the editor of *Atlanta Constitution*, had obviously made good on his promise to promote popular interest in the game. A fortnight earlier, Crawford had assured Petrie that he would "boom" the game, "whoop'er up in all the papers," and "really make things hum." Like Petrie, Crawford believed that football would serve the cause of

Southern progress. As the unofficial house organ of the New South modernizers, the *Constitution* unabashedly and persistently called for a transformation in Southern cultural and economic norms that would bring the South more in line with Gilded Age America. With the notable exception of racial issues, the New South advocates began comparisons of Northern and Southern culture with an unstated assumption of Yankee superiority and the presumption that Southern progress would hinge on the region becoming more like the North. Bringing to the South a modern, mass-market sport already hugely popular in the rest of the nation was an expression of the social vision of the New South ideologues. Henry Grady, Crawford's predecessor both as editor of the *Constitution* and as a leading cheerleader for the New South ideology, had been instrumental in bringing professional baseball to the Deep South in 1884. Grady helped organize the Southern League and had served as the league's first president. While Southern urban boosters considered professional baseball teams to be an asset for a modern, progressive region, college football suited their purposes even better. Football was a "gentlemanly sport" invented by Ivy Leaguers, was played only by the scions of the elite, and was heralded as the perfect sport for the machine age; whereas baseball was strongly identified with a working class constituency of players and fans and possessed a more pastoral image because of its folk origins.

In the ten days prior to the game, the *Constitution* and its arch-rival the *Atlanta Journal,* fairly bubbled over with breathless articles announcing the Deep South debut of this thrilling and fashionable Yankee sport. Southern progressives followed the interpretive lead of Walter Camp and other northeastern proponents of American football by describing the game as an allegory for a modern, rationalized industrial society. Football was a model of precision, orderliness, teamwork, and strategy that contracted sharply with the chaos and freebooting individualism of soccer. Football, claimed the *Journal,* was "a scientific as well as a physical" sport and was thus superior to the old-fashioned game of soccer. The *Constitution* declared, "Whether we be reconstructed or not, we cannot shut our eyes to the phenomenal growth of the sport in its new form." Old timers who witness the new sport will realize that "science has invaded" the sporting world and produced a modern and progressive successor to soccer. In a 1935 retrospective on that first game, Petrie interpreted football as a symbol of progress. "In the fall of 1891," he declared, "we undertook to bring order out of the confusion of mass football (soccer) at Auburn."

The interpretation of the new game was refracted through the lens of the New South belief that virtually any social, cultural or economic institution associated with the North was modern, progressive, and worthy of emulation. Southern college football began as a self-conscious imitation of the northeastern culture that Southern progressives so desperately wanted to emulate. Petrie declared that this game would be "the first in a series of annual contests after the manner of the Yale-Harvard games." The *Atlanta Journal* compared Georgia coach Charles Herty with the "coach of Yale's famous boat crew," and declared, "The game promises to be equally as interesting as the great foot-ball contests of the north have proved." The *Constitution* echoed this sentiment, declaring, "The excitement in Atlanta over the approaching game ... amounts to nothing short of the interest felt in the famous Yale and Princeton games in the north." Crawford had heard that the winner of the annual Thanksgiving Day college football championship game in New York City received a trophy, so he recruited a local jeweler to offer a silver cup to the winner of the Auburn-Georgia game. The *Constitution* praised the jeweler for making this game "as swell in every respect as the Yale or Princeton games." The *Constitution* even managed to invoke the talismanic power of the Ivy Leaguers in a gameday exhortation to fans to ignore the foul weather. "Yale and Princeton men," it declared, "want nothing better than cloudy, misty weather such as this for one of their great games."

If this assertion were true, then the Yale and Princeton men would have been thrilled with the weather in Atlanta that day. A steady rain fell uninterrupted all morning, stopped briefly in early afternoon, and began again a half hour prior to the 3:30 p.m. start of the game. The saturation newspaper coverage had generated plenty of interest, however, and a crowd of nearly two thousand braved the weather and filled the grandstand at Piedmont Park in the uptown section of Atlanta. Elite Atlantans awaited the start of the game from the comfort of their elegant horse-drawn carriages, nearly one hundred of which were arrayed opposite the grandstand along the backstretch of the horse track that surrounded the field. Just before 3 o'clock, an immense roar greeted the arrival of the Georgia team, which rode in aboard an immense horse-drawn carriage known as a tally-ho. Both the tally-ho and its team of four horses were extravagantly festooned with ribbons, streamers, and bunting in the school colors of red and black. The magnificant carriage dramatically rode up the backstretch of the horse track and deposited the team at midfield to the ecstatic cheers of the partisan crowd. The Auburn team made a far more prosaic entrance a few minutes later. Unsure whether his team's share of the gate receipts would cover travel expenses, Petrie and his team each paid the nickel fare and rode to the game on the electric streetcar along with the fans. The Auburn team walked into the exposition grounds through the main gate along with the ordinary paying customers.

The game was a sloppy affair in every sense of the word. The field was a virtual sea of mud, and Petrie cringed a bit at how quickly his players' pristine new uniforms, which he had forbidden them to wear in practice in order to keep clean, became covered with mud. Players who had only a hazy conception of both the rules and the plays that they were supposed to execute slipped and slid into one another all afternoon. The teams repeatedly fumbled, as the fat, oval ball, difficult for even experienced players to handle under perfect conditions, was rendered wet and slippery by the rain. An occasional punt or end run brought the crowd to its feet, but both teams followed the conventional strategy of the day and repeatedly sent ballcarriers "bucking" into the center of the line. The teams stumbled and slipped through a scoreless 45-minute first half, mistakenly called an inning in a muddled and confusing game account personally written by Remsen Crawford, who obviously knew even less about the game than the novice players he was describing.

The Auburn line, led by its 210-pound "centre rush," Floyd McKissick, had kept Georgia pinned in its own territory throughout most of the first half. McKissick, a young professor of electrical engineering who outweighed most of the other players by 40 or 50 pounds, used that bulk to help Auburn score its first-ever touchdown. The "closed game" of the 1890s encouraged an inside running attack in which backs plunged into the line behind a tightly massed wall of blockers who were allowed to push, pull, or even carry a ballcarrier through the massive pile of bodies in the center of the line. McKissick capped an early second half Auburn drive by grabbing Richard Dorsey, a 137-pound halfback, and shoving him through a wall of Georgia defenders for a touchdown. An Auburn cadet with a campus reputation for unruliness was so overcome with joy over the first-ever Auburn touchdown he ran out onto the field and kissed the diminutive halfback.

Touchdowns then counted four points and conversions two, so Auburn's touchdown and successful conversion gave them a 6-0 lead. Five minutes later, an Auburn guard scooped up a Georgia fumble and ran 40 yards through the misty rain for another touchdown, although he did not receive a kiss for his effort. The conversion was unsuccessful, and Auburn now led 10-0. The players slogged back and forth in the winter twilight for another 20 minutes, and Auburn held on for its first football victory. A boisterous crowd of Auburn cadets rushed onto the muddy field and cheered as a Georgia state legislator presented the highly touted silver cup to the Auburn team captain.

Football's boosters declared the game's Deep South debut to be a grand triumph. The game had drawn a good crowd despite terrible weather, inexperienced players, and near total ignorance of the game on the part of the general public. The *Journal* declared the game to be "a brilliant success" given that "the people in this part of the country know comparatively so little about this exciting game." The *Journal* maintained its infatuation with things Northern by noting that "the Auburn men played more like a Yale or Princeton team than the Georgia men," and found the 10-0 score significant because it "was the same as that made in the last great game between Yale and Princeton."

Both Petrie and Remsen Crawford were eager to gain Northern recognition of this Southern achievement, as if they believed their game was not quite real until it received legitimation from the Yankees they were imitating. Crawford gleefully informed Petrie that the game "did a heap of good" because several Northern newspapers had picked up the Constitution's account of the game off the wire. This publicity would inform the rest of the nation "how Southern collegiate athletes were booming up." Petrie sought unsuccessfully to get Caspar Whitney, the influential sports columnist for Harper's Weekly, to send a photographer to Atlanta to cover the game. Petrie persisted, sending newspaper accounts and photographs of the game to Whitney, and was rewarded with a brief mention of the game in Harper's. This eager desire for Northern recognition of Southern football would persist for two generations, vividly highlighting the almost pathetic compulsion of southern progressives to seek Northern approval.

Sources: George Petrie Papers; L.S. Boyd, "Reminiscences"; Scrapbook of Mrs. P.H. Mell; W.K. Askew, Class of 1917: World War I Class, privately published, 1981; all of above at Auburn University Archives; Michael Levy, "The Rise of Sports in the New South," unpublished thesis, Amherst College, 1993; *Atlanta Constitution; Atlanta Journal; Montgomery Advertiser.*

Changing population densities affected what growth there was in the transportation system of the state. As late as 1870, the Black Belt was the most populated area of Alabama, but within three decades the Birmingham area was first. Birmingham, already at the junction of two railroads, added water transportation advantages with the Birmingham Port development. With large deposits of coal, iron ore, and limestone in close proximity, the city enlarged rapidly from its modest beginnings in 1871. Daniel Pratt was an early promoter and his son-in-law, Henry DeBardeleben, carried on the work after Pratt's death in 1873. Truman Aldrich consolidated a large part of the coal reserves in the area through his Cahaba Coal Mining Company. Enoch Ensley, James Sloss, and others promoted steel-making in the early days. Birmingham's population increased in proportion to the growth of the steel industry, reaching 38,000 in 1900.

In 1887, the Tennessee Coal, Iron, and Railroad Company (TCI) of Birmingham was the largest single holder of ore lands and furnace plants in the United States. Five years later, TCI owned 17 large furnaces and 400,000 acres of coal and iron land. Birmingham became the largest shipping point for pig iron in the U. S. by 1898 and the third largest in the world. When the pig iron market fell, TCI built a modern open-hearth plant at Ensley and by the early 20th Century it was producing the majority of open-hearth rails in the country. In 1907, the Harriman lines ordered 150,000 tons of open-hearth rails. Shortly thereafter, J.P. Morgan's U. S. Steel bought TCI for $35 million. U.S. Steel, now USX, is still one of the largest landowners in the Birmingham area.

President Theodore Roosevelt sanctioned the acquisition, but a Senate committee later concluded it violated the Sherman Anti-Trust Act. By one purchase, U.S. Steel dominated the open-hearth output of steel rails, secured control of most of the U.S. iron-ore supply, monopolized the Southern iron and steel trade, and eliminated Birmingham as a competitor of Pittsburgh.

U.S. Steel mechanisms for subjugating Birmingham to Pittsburgh were "Pittsburgh Plus" and "Birmingham Differential." "Pittsburgh Plus" meant that a customer buying Birmingham steel paid the price of Pittsburgh steel plus the freight rate from Pittsburgh to the delivery site. Birmingham's growth was stifled. Some expansion was permitted by the "Birmingham Differential," that is, the Pittsburgh price plus a surcharge of $3 a ton (1909) ... increased to $5 a ton after 1920. Yale historian Comer Vann Woodward, in a chapter in his classic **Origins of the New South** titled "The Colonial Economy," concluded the metropolitan North retained for its tradesman the lucrative tasks of transporting, processing, and distributing goods by ingenious devices more effective than any employed by the British Board of Trade in the pre-Revolutionary era. The Alabama economy was but a colonial appendage of the northeast in the early 20th century and its residents with a per capita income of $321 in 1919 made Alabamians the poorest of the poor. One-time cotton farmer and novelist Andrew Nelson Lytle captured this plight in **I'll Take My Stand:**

He has been turned into the runt pig in the sow's litter. Squeezed and tricked out of the best places at the side, he is forced to take the little hind tit for nourishment; and here, struggling between the sow's back legs, he has to work with every bit of his strength to keep it from being a dry hind one, and all because the suck of the others is so unreservedly gluttonous.

Photo courtesy of Phil Coley

VI
The First Half of the 20th Century
The Good Roads Movement and the Automobile Revolution

The Good Roads Movement came out of the late 19th century farmers' need for adequate farm-to-market wagon roads, so it preceded the "Automobile Revolution" of the early 20th century. Railroad development dominated the last half of the 19th century. Transportation improvements in the 20th century focused on good roads.

By 1900 the main outline of the railway network of Alabama had been completed. The Tennessee Valley and the Gulf of Mexico had at last been linked by rail. All sections of the state were interlocked and tied into the transportation system of the nation, but the center was Birmingham where all the leading rail lines were connected. The focal points of the railroads in South Alabama were Montgomery and Mobile.

Railroad domination of the transportation picture in Alabama was echoed at the national level, but the seeds of technological change which were to make the internal combustion engine supreme on land, in the water, and in the air were being sown. While local citizens were ignoring the wretched state of disrepair and neglect on the public roads they were required by law to maintain, the inventors were making quality road and bridge construction easier, "paving the way" for the success of the Good Roads movement in the early 20th century.

The railroad lobby initially supported the farm-to-market or local roads part of the Good Road Movement because it enlarged the trade areas of the towns served by the railroad thus increasing railroad traffic. In contrast, interstate roads stimulated the Automobile Revolution and adversely affected the railroads' passenger-carrying business. Increased automobile registrations and the motor transport development during World War I moreover presented potential freight-carrying competition which cooled railroaders' enthusiasm for the Good Roads Movement.

> *Farmers had their own ways of combating rival interstate road improvements pushed by agents of the noise-producing horseless carriages:*
>
> *One Sunday motorist, forced to detour from a well-traveled route, unexpectedly plunged into a deep, muddy hole. A farm boy rounded the bend with a team of horses, set his price — a stiff one — and with speed and dispatch extracted the motorist.*
>
> *"Do you farm on Sundays around here?" inquired the motorist as the boy prepared to leave.*
>
> *"Nope, we just pull cars outta the hole."*
>
> *"What do you do Saturday nights. Go out?"*
>
> *"Nope," replied the youth. "... haul water to the hole."*
>
> **"Indian Trails to Interstates,"** Vol. I, p. 141.

The roads were bad enough without any additional help. An 18-year-old teacher recalled her days driving a Model T to a one-room school in rural Marengo County in 1926. In winter the "deep bogginess" made the roads impassable but "under the summer suns, they became hard like concrete, and when the first big rain came to soften the top layer of soil, they could be slick as glass." To avoid sliding into a ditch, the smart motorist would put chains on the rear tires, keep the car in high gear as much as possible, go at a moderate rate of speed, and never use brakes or low gear unless absolutely necessary. These were the Black Belt rules of the road.

Senator John Hollis Bankhead and the Federal Highway Act of 1916

As chairman of the Senate committee on Post Offices and Post Roads, Alabama's Senator Bankhead had periodically introduced bills appropriating money for the construction of post roads. A $500,000 appropriation in 1912 requiring local areas to pay two-thirds of the cost yielded 425 miles of improved roads in 17 states. More importantly, it brought the Federal government into road building and the Bankhead-Shackleford Federal Highway Act of 1916 resulted. Bankhead, President of the United States Good Roads Association, summarized his arguments in a 1908 speech in the Senate:

The country has the poorest roads ... in all else, we are progressive and stand first ... Good roads are avenues to progress, the best proof of intelligence; aids social and religious advancement, increases value of products, saves time, labor and money...The highways are the common property of the country; benefits are shared by all; needed by all ... and all should contribute to them. What fair-minded man will say that the people who live on public roads should be required to build and keep them in repair for use of the general public? The burden is more than they could bear. No government has ever enjoyed good roads where compulsory labor is relied on to build and maintain them. Are savings affected by good roads? There would be a reduction by half of annual cost of transportation ... Aid should be extended for a liberal appropriation for improving our roads ... Give farmers good roads and with the telephone, rural delivery bringing easy contact with the outside world ... he will prove the most prosperous and contented, patriotic citizen on the American continent.

"Indian Trails to Interstates," Vol. I, pp. 131-133

The Federal Highway Act of 1916 established the 50-50 ratio of cost sharing between the state and federal governments. One of the initial projects was the Bankhead National Highway, named in honor of the Alabama senator. It began with an improved highway between Atlanta, Georgia and Memphis, Tennessee, (through Birmingham and Jasper with a branch line to Sulligent) but the highway became transcontinental, with the Atlanta side extending to Washington, D.C., and the Memphis side continuing to San Diego, California, on the Pacific coast.

Kellers, Klaxons, and Jitneys

Nothing revolutionized Alabama life like the snorting, bucking "horseless carriage" which burst upon the American scene in the last five years of the 19th century and became a family necessity within 25 years.

The two stalwarts of early gasoline automobile manufacturing were Ransom E. Olds and Henry Ford. Olds' 1897 vehicle carried four passengers and its 10 mph speed was the fastest gasoline-driven auto around. Olds was the first auto manufacturer to demonstrate the possibility of a mass market for a low-priced car. Ford produced a homemade car in 1896 for the Detroit Electric Company before launching the Ford Motor Company in 1903 with $28,000 solicited from 13 investors. Ford is chiefly known for his willingness

'Henry Ford and the Muscle Shoals Proposition'

In the early 1920s Henry Ford offered $5 million to Secretary of War John Weeks for two abandoned World War I nitrate plants near Sheffield, the Waco Quarry southeast of Russellville, and the Warrior Steam Plant at Gorgas. Although he promised to use the facilities for wartime munitions should the need arise, his immediate plans were to produce commercial fertilizer and to separate Utah alunite into potash ... and aluminum to use in auto manufacturing.

The fertilizer would be sold to area farmers at no more than 8 percent above cost. If the government would complete the three dams necessary to overflow the rapids of Muscle Shoals, Ford also would distribute the 600,000 horsepower generated in return for paying the government 4 percent of the cost of building the dams each year. As for the 70-mile lake formed by the three dams, Ford envisioned land being subdivided into five- to eight-acre farms to be sold to factory workers for $50 per acre. As their farms would be self-supporting, their salaries from factory work would be supplementary income. His "Seventy-Five Mile City" was to make New York City "look like a prairie village." Although supported by the Farm Bureau and Alabama U. S. Senators Oscar Underwood and "Cotton" Tom Heflin, Ford's hydroelectric involvement prompted opposition from Alabama Power Company and other regional utilities. As taxpayers paid some $84 million for the properties Ford was to buy for $5 million, and 4 percent was deemed by many to be inadequate returns on the taxpayers predicted cost of another $50 million to complete the three dams, opposition became widespread. The press compared Coolidge's alleged favoritism to Ford to the Teapot Dome oil reserves scandal of the Harding administration. When Ford, Coolidge's main potential rival for the Presidency in 1924, was invited to the White House and subsequently endorsed "Silent Cal," the press speculated Ford got Muscle Shoals for his non-candidacy.

Finally, in October 1924 a politically weary Ford told the dour Coolidge (T.R.'s daughter, Alice Roosevelt, said he looked like he had been weaned on a pickle) that he was officially withdrawing his January 1922 bid. Muscle Shoals development was to await the creation of TVA by FDR's New Deal in 1933.

Source: Leslie Wright, "Henry Ford and Muscle Shoals," The Alabama Review, XIV (July 1961) reprinted in Sarah Woolfolk Wiggins, **From Civil War to Civil Rights: Alabama, 1860-1960** (University of Alabama Press, 1987), 297-308.

Photo by Chip Cooper, courtesy Alabama Heritage

Almost 5 million civilian autos were produced in 1941 and only 139 in 1943. Post-war America was car-starved. Hubert Mitchell of Hartselle saw the market for a low-cost car. By January 1949, after buying a defunct auto company and using off-the-shelf parts, Mitchell turned out 12 hand-assembled mini-station wagons from a makeshift factory at Redstone Arsenal, Huntsville. Naming his car after the well-liked "Big George" Keller, his chief executive and a 28-year Studebaker veteran, and centering promotional ads on Keller, Mitchell accumulated 1,500 dealers and half the stock sales necessary for mass production. Suddenly Big George died of a heart attack. And the Keller died with him. Without him, as engineer John Liefeld concluded, "We had no sparkplug left ... We paid everyone off and that was that." Source: G. Ward Hubbs and A.R. Gibbons, "Keller," Alabama Heritage, Summer 1991, 30-42.

to do the unorthodox and assume the risks necessary to make a mass-produced low-cost car a reality.

His most successful product was the Model T introduced in 1908. It was cheap ($800 initially, but less than $300 by 1920-1921), simply designed so almost anyone could repair it, and specifically built to meet the farmers' needs — high enough off the ground to travel over deep ruts and fair-sized rocks and stumps, and light enough to run through swamp, sand, and mud. Ford loved it. He sold more than 15 million "tin lizzies" before reluctantly replacing it with the Model A in 1927 to meet the competition of the General Motors' Chevrolet which, unlike the Model T, did not have the "buggy" look.

Photo by Dan Brothers, Alabama Bureau of Tourism and Travel

Blount County's Horton Mill Covered Bridge stands 70 feet above the Calvert Prong of the Warrior River, making it the highest covered bridge over water in the United States.

Roads and automobiles advanced side by side. State highway systems totaled about 200,000 miles nationwide in 1920. In Alabama, there were slightly less than 4,000 miles on the state system. By 1940, Alabama had over 6,500 miles of state roads and the total of all state systems was 329,000 miles. The marking of highways was very common by the 1920s. Federal numbers were placed on shield-shaped signs and state highway numbers were on round signs. These markings, in turn, made road maps easier to use.

An Alabamian who contributed to automobile-related inventions was Miller Reese Hutchinson (1876-1944), a Baldwin County native. Hutchinson attended military schools in Marion and Mobile, college at Spring Hill and Auburn, and the Medical College of Alabama. He patented the "Klaxon," an automobile horn, a hearing device for the deaf called the acousticon, and the dictograph. He became Thomas Edison's chief engineer of the Edison Laboratories, where he did pioneer work on storage batteries.

One temporary innovation in the 1920s was the "jitney," a sort of half-bus, half-car, which functioned as a taxi for the people of the era. The jitney was used in Alabama and in 1923, was the focal point of an urban transportation conflict in Birmingham. The "notorious jitney," according to competitive transportation sources, terrorized the streets of Birmingham in the roaring twenties. As explained by UAB urban historian, Blaine A.

'Where Illiteracy Lies Heaviest and the Needs of Childhood Are the Most Marked': Marietta Johnson and the Organic School at Fairhope

By DR. AMELIA BARTLETT-DODD

Progressive and revolutionary educational doctrines were spawned in a time and place where, according to John Dewey, "illiteracy lies heaviest and the needs of childhood are most marked ..." — the deep South in the early 1900s. Marietta Louise Pierce Johnson, founder of the School of Organic Education in Fairhope, Alabama, had experienced much success in traditional teaching methods but was profoundly affected by reading Nathaniel Oppenheim's **Development of the Child** and C. Hanford Henderson's **Education and the Larger Life.** Distancing herself from teaching for a period of time in order to study and define the best environment for the growth of children, Mrs. Johnson began practicing her theories with her own two young sons.

Marietta Johnson gave her methods of education the name of "organic" because they followed the natural growth of the pupil. She defined education as "growth" and emphasized the concept that schooling should nurture the immediate needs of the whole organism; spiritual, mental, and physical needs must always be kept in balance; and one part of a child's development could not be isolated from another without damaging the whole child. Mrs. Johnson found a receptive environment for the practice of her theories when she and her husband, Frank, moved to the Single Tax Colony of Fairhope, Alabama. In this model community were progressive-thinking followers of Henry George who believed all persons were equally entitled to the use of the earth.

The School of Organic Education opened in 1907 with six pupils and quickly grew so that by 1913 there were 150 students in kindergarten through high school. It was a free school to children from Fairhope, charging tuition only to those recruited from the North. It was a school distinctive in a number of ways. There were no fixed desks. Students were free to move around and sit wherever they were most comfortable. Classes were often held out of doors, arithmetic taking place in a sandstone gully, the "gym" a field nearby. There were no assigned tasks. Children worked according to their individual capacity and interests. Teachers were leaders (rather than instructors) who adapted the work according to the strength and weaknesses of the individual students. Mrs. Johnson recognized that true growth comes from the student's desire to study or need for information and not external demands. Children were grouped according to age, not academic ability, into "life classes." Mrs. Johnson prohibited all rewards for success or punishments for failure. She postponed the teaching of reading until students were eight or nine.

In 1913, John Dewey — an unrivaled authority on progressive education — visited the School of Organic Education and reported very favorably on the "Fairhope Experiment." His 14-year-old son accompanied him and begged to remain at the school. Dewey included a chapter in his book, **Schools of Tomorrow,** describing Mrs. Johnson's model. His favorable report was a great help to Mrs. Johnson as she traveled widely to secure funds for the Organic School, a progressive model for America, flourishing in the Deep South.

Marietta Johnson lectured widely in the United States and Europe. George Allen Brown, in his **Memoir,** wrote, "It had been said the Organic School was better known in Europe than in the United States, and better known in other states than in Alabama." Mrs. Johnson was one of the founders of the Progressive Education Association in 1920 and helped many schools follow her principles of organic education by writing, lecturing, conducting classes, and training teachers. Her association with the Edgewood School at Greenwich, Connecticut, spanned 13 years and produced many teachers prominent in progressive education.

Among the teachers recruited for her school were graduates of Cambridge, Oxford, Harvard and Yale. One of her teachers wrote of the Indian tepees built by the 8-, 9-, and 10-year olds. The group slept in the tepees and lived as Indians for a week on the beach at Mobile Bay. Mothers helped the students prepare meals over an open fire. Willard Edwards, a history teacher during the mid-twenties, directed some students in building a 34-foot schooner. It sailed the bay for many years after, transporting students to Biloxi, Mobile, and local outings. Grace Rotzel, who taught in Fairhope for five years, later founded her own successful progressive school in Pennsylvania. Wharton Esherick became America's preeminent furniture maker after acquiring his first set of carving tools while teaching at the Organic School.

The graduates of the Organic School were prized for their "freshness of intellectual attack" by the presidents of Antioch and Rollins. But at the 25th anniversary, Marietta Johnson was most pleased that no students or teachers had ever had a nervous breakdown.

There was an "intellectual alliance" between the colony of Fairhope and the Organic School. In 1921, Mrs. Johnson began what would become an integral part of the Fairhope winters — a six-weeks course uniting parents, teachers, and social workers from around the country to study the school and the organic education philosophy. By 1930, the highly successful winter course brought students from 31 states, Canada, and South Africa. It was a major cultural event that drew such notables as Clarence Darrow, who recommended the single tax and organic education as a means of reducing crime.

For 32 years, Marietta Johnson served her school without pay, donating to it the funds raised from her lecture tours and giving unselfishly of her own income. In the twenties, almost all of the school's revenue came from outside Fairhope. As the national depression deepened, there was a great decline in the number of boarding students. By the mid-1930s, the Organic School was in serious financial trouble and barely struggled through each year. Mrs. Johnson's health declined at the same time and in 1938, she suffered a fatal heart attack.

Marietta Johnson made a profound difference in the lives of her students. Margaret Mead told of her sister Elizabeth's experience with organic education: "At Fairhope," she wrote, Elizabeth "learned practically nothing at all — except how to teach, how to waken children to enthusiasm, and how to treat each individual as a person. This she has carried all through her life." (p 115, **Women of Fairhope**)

Sources: John Dewey, "Professor Dewey's Report on the Fairhope Experiment in Organic Education, The Survey, (May 16, 1914), 199.

Paul M. Gaston, **Women of Fairhope** (Athens, GA: University of Georgia Press, 1984 reprinted by Black Belt Press, Montgomery, AL, 1993).

Marietta Johnson, **The Fairhope Idea in Education** (New York, NY: The Fairhope Educational Foundation, circa 1927). Includes the chapter on Fairhope from John Dewey's Schools of Tomorrow.

————, **Thirty Years with an Idea** (University, AL: University of Alabama Press, published for the Organic School, Fairhope, AL, 1974).

Brownell, the jitney was an unusually large touring car which could accommodate five to seven paying passengers. It held fewer passengers than the more widely used street railway of Birmingham, but it was more mobile as it didn't have to follow the tracks, was faster, and the fares were about the same. Apparently, it was also less safe, caused more accidents, and was less reliable in paying off claims resulting from accidents than the railed vehicle. By using the main thoroughfares, the jitney also contributed to congestion in the downtown areas.

Birmingham and Jefferson County had 310,054 inhabitants and about 16,000 motor vehicles in 1920 (about one for every 19.4 people). But at the end of the '20s, there was an estimated 70,000 vehicles (one per 6.6 persons). By modern standards this is not many automobiles, but, considering the concentration in downtown streets during rush hours and the lack of today's traffic control methods, the private automobiles and the jitneys perhaps did contribute to congestion. More important, the jitney took away enough potential street car fares to arouse the local street car company, the Birmingham Railway Light and Power Company, to mobilize its political forces and influence the City Commissioners to effectively legislate the jitney out of business in 1923.

Jitney travel may have been hazardous, but early automobiles also had hazards and their share of accidents — whether due to the vehicles or the drivers. Northwest Alabama historian and ex-Congressman, Carl Elliott, related one such accident. Appropriately occurring on a May day in 1917, it involved two Jasper residents, the mayor and a well-known lawyer, returning from Birmingham to Jasper. Leaving the "Magic City" at 10 o'clock to be home for lunch, they arrived at the midway point near West Sayre about 11 o'clock, upon which the lawyer offered to relieve the mayor of the task of driving the remaining distance. The mayor, "then and there:"

stood straight up on the floor board of the front seat, all the while gripping the car's steering wheel so as to allow his friend ... to slide under him into the driver's seat ... while the maneuver of swapping drivers without stopping the car was underway ... (the mayor) somehow lost control of the car ... (He) attempted to resume the driver's normal position and made a desperate effort ... (but) the car slowed down, and for one full second stood absolutely still. Then it started, slowly at first, to roll over and over down the high embankment. When it reached the bottom of the hill, the car stood upright again.

Doctors from Sayre and Jasper were summoned and they dispatched the victims to the Birmingham Hospital. The mayor had a broken collar bone and head cut and the lawyer had a deep chest bruise. Apparently their many friends were so overjoyed to see them well that no one asked why they didn't stop the car before they attempted to change seats. It was fortunate that automobile speeds were as low as they were in 1917.

Auto breakdowns led to many jokes. Alabama Roadbuilder editor, Ed Rodgers, collected the following ones. An early Buick ad read: "Built to Run and Does It," which a dissatisfied customer edited to: "Built to Run and Does It?" An Oldsmobile ad — "Nothing to Watch But the Road" — promoted an owner's complaint that he was tired of watching the same stretch of road. One widely advertised low-cost car, the Bush, had wooden wheels, a wooden axle, and a wooden frame, to which a critic added: "it wooden run."

In the end, the skeptics were silenced and the entrepreneurs proved the worth of the new transportation device. The automobile transformed Alabama society. By bringing farmers to the city and city-dwellers to the farm, it homogenized the rural-urban population. It caused cities to expand into suburbs and, through shopping centers and thoroughfares, made the suburbs more city-like. Superhighways, motels, drive-ins, parking areas, service stations and garages "automobilized" the Alabama landscape.

Reform and Reaction: Progressivism and the 1920s/1930s

The Civil War proved that a federal government could enforce the will of the nation over that of individual states. Before the war when Alabamians referred to "the government" they meant state government. By the end of the Progressive Era "the government" was understood to be the federal government. The industrial growth of the late 19th century was accompanied by social problems. People looked to the national government to correct the abuses of this rapid urbanization and industrialization. There was a wide gap between social progress and technological progress. The reformers of the Progressive Era hoped to narrow the gap. Among the strongest campaigns for social reform were those for child labor laws, the temperance movement, women's suffrage, and the fair treatment of workers, especially convict labor. And on the eastern shore of Mobile Bay, the "Fairhope Experiment" in progressive education was in its heyday (See the sidebar by Amelia Bartlett-Dodd).

Child Labor

With the growth of textile mills in Alabama and the need for cheap labor, exploitation of children became a common practice. Mill workers were not paid much, and young children were often put to work in the mills to add to

'Foolish and Useless Sport': The Southern Evangelical Crusade Against College Football

By ANDY DOYLE, Ph.D. student, Emory University, and adjunct faculty, Auburn University at Montgomery

College football has long served as a complementary bulwark of evangelical Protestantism in the South. Nonsectarian pregame invocations by Protestant ministers and postgame prayers by members of Fellowship of Christian Athletes unite players and fans in a ritual of fealty to the values and beliefs that form the southern evangelical consensus. Many southern coaches have said that their work reinforces the Christian values that their players begin to learn at home and at church. Southerners gather together for college football on Saturday afternoons and for church on Sunday mornings with a similar spirit of respect for the traditions and values that shape and define southern identity.

Today's amicable relationship strikingly reverses the intense hostility that an earlier generation of pious southerners felt for football. When Auburn (Auburn University was officially known as the Alabama Agricultural and Mechanical College between 1876 and 1901, and as Alabama Polytechnic Institute from 1901 until 1960, when it acquired its present name) defeated Georgia 10-0 in a cold rain in Atlanta in February, 1892, in the first intercollegiate football game in the Deep South, evangelical divines loosed a torrent of fierce jeremiads against this "theater of mud and blood" that continued intermittently for the next 40 years. Leaders of the three major evangelical denominations joined in denouncing football. The Southern Methodist Church, the largest and the one most involved in higher education, eagerly led the charge, but southern Baptists and Presbyterians participated as well.

The southern evangelical critique of college football advanced five major themes. The first two themes evoked practical rather than strictly religious objections. Football was a brutally violent endeavor during the era of flying wedges and mass momentum plays, and southern evangelicals joined a chorus of secular critics in denouncing the flood of serious injuries and occasional deaths. They also bemoaned the energy wasted on this "foolish and useless sport." Football consumed so much of the time and attention of players and student spectators that their studies inevitably suffered. The minister of the First Methodist Church of Auburn complained that "here in Auburn, football is the one engrossing theme during the season .... The whole thing is a travesty upon higher education."

The third aspect of the evangelical critique concerned specific moral issues. Southern evangelicals emphatically and unanimously denounced the drinking, gambling, and general dissipation that inevitably accompanied off-campus games played in southern cities. Southern colleges and universities all enforced rigid standards of discipline and public piety on their campuses in the late 19th century, so many students misbehaved with gusto when they attended football games in Atlanta, Montgomery, Birmingham, or Nashville. Prior to World War I, Auburn students lived under a highly regimented system of military discipline from their 7:30 a.m. roll call until lights out. The college president or a faculty member began each weekday with a reading of Scripture, Sunday church attendance was mandatory, and students could be expelled for drinking or for leaving the campus without the permission of both their parents and the college president. Thus, when Auburn students escaped this rigid discipline, a number of them unleashed their pent-up energy in ways that outraged the sensibilities of the devout.

The behavior of students at the annual Thanksgiving Day games between Auburn and Georgia and later Auburn and Georgia Tech invited such criticism. At the very moment some Auburn students paid the three dollar fare and boarded the 7:00 a.m. passenger train to Atlanta on Thanksgiving morning, a group of their more adventuresome classmates were about to step onto the streets of Atlanta from the boxcars of the freight train they had boarded at 3:00 a.m. Many had begun their big football weekend by purchasing a few bottles of white lightning from a local bootlegger. They bribed the train crew with a portion of their contraband, and they consumed the rest before, during, or after the game. Students and citizens alike gambled openly, a practice duly noted in the newspaper coverage of southern games. Exhausted and hung over students then boarded the same boxcars for the trip back to Auburn. A veteran of a number of those boxcar journeys recalls that when the train returned to Auburn, his comrades in revelry who had imbibed too freely were "passed out of the cars like sacks of meal" into the arms of fraternity brothers, who carried them back to the campus.

Southern evangelical leaders did not write off this behavior as mere youthful high jinks. Their expressions of outrage over the disorderly conduct of college football crowds began in 1892 and continued for the next four decades. In 1897, the *Alabama Christian Advocate* condemned football for its propensity to "convert a crowd of students, inflamed with liquor and excited by loyalty to their institution, into a howling mob of toughs, gamblers and drunkards." In 1900, the pastor of the First Baptist Church of Montgomery said that the behavior of Alabama and Auburn students in his city for a football game "is such as to startle and shock the community." In a 1920 Sunday sermon, the pastor of Birmingham's leading Presbyterian church denounced the drunken misbehavior of the Auburn team on the streets of his city after they had badly whipped archrival Vanderbilt. These complaints troubled college administrators and trustees, but city games continued to outrage pious southerners because gate receipts were exponentially greater at city stadiums than at the uniformly more primitive campus venues.

A fourth critique by the conservative southern divines was that football was of questionable morality because it exalted the innately corrupt human body. Drawing heavily from the writings of St. Paul and St. Augustine, orthodox southern evangelicals expressed grave moral and theological reservations about the glorification of the inherently corrupt and sinful temporal body by competitive sports in general and football in particular. They believed that football fostered an unhealthy obsession with the body and thus was a brazen ritual repudiation of Christian self-restraint and otherworldliness. Young men who possessed a narcissistic infatuation with "carnal sports" were likely to lose sight of spiritual matters. Evangelical divines sought to keep faddish physical pastimes like football from becoming an overriding concern among restless and impressionable college students. The *Wesleyan Christian Advocate*, the official organ of Georgia Methodism, called for the abolition of football because "the Apostle Paul teaches us that bodily exercise profiteth little." The WCA denounced football as a neo-pagan ritual before the bruises had faded from the initial game between Auburn and Georgia. "And so the sacred altars, whose incense has been so inspiring to our people in the past, are broken down, and these gods of the sensual and material man have set up their altars instead."

The Alabama Christian Advocate advised the state's Methodists to shun both the University of Alabama and Auburn and instead to send their sons to the Methodist-run Southern University, "where the YMCA takes precedence over the football team, and where the legs and head are not developed at the expense of the soul." The pastor of the First Methodist Church of Auburn denounced intercollegiate football because it "unduly exalts and cultivates the animal" in young men. He grudgingly allowed that a degree of exercise and physical development was necessary, but declared that "any young man can acquire that at home in the useful emoluments of cutting his mother's yard or driving his father's plow."

The fifth and final argument against football employed by orthodox Southern evangelicals extended the theological dispute between orthodoxy and liberalism. Football was a powerful symbol of the larger national culture to both progressives and traditionalists in the late 19th and early 20th century South, and a Southerner's attitude toward football generally mirrored his attitude toward the emerging regime of the New South. Culturally conservative Southern divines accused Northern progressives and their traitorous Southern allies of foisting an irreligious, materialistic, Mammon-worshiping culture upon a prostrate and defeated South. The Presbyterian theologian Robert Dabney admonished the postbellum Southerners to avoid the temptation to "become like the conquerors ... and to share, for a few deceitful days, the victor's gains of oppression."

Football thus became a flash point in the larger war between traditionalists and modernizers. The fashionable sport of the northeastern bourgeoisie symbolized the new regime of industrial capitalism, popular mass culture, and consumerism to both proponents and opponents of this new order. Southern progressives adopted the sport as a self-conscious declaration of independence from what they saw as the oppressive and dogmatic Puritanism of orthodox evangelicals. The power and regenerative capacity of the human body as displayed on the gridiron was a metaphor for the vigor, and ambition of the apostles of the New South. Their lionization of youth, their indulgence of the misbehavior of the college boys, and their almost homoerotic obsession with the physical prowess of the football players stands in sharp symbolic contrast to the defeatist, anti-progressive, otherworldly, defiantly backward-looking worldview of orthodox evangelicals.

Southern evangelicals in the 1890s and early 1900s saw football as a brutal, time-consuming sport that emphasized the earthly body over the heavenly spirit, and fostered drinking, gambling, and hell-raising among student spectators. They saw the sport as an encroachment by the materialistic northern Babylon into the serene South and as a manifestation of the irreligious, permissive, and generally decadent culture of mainstream America.

Sources: Alabama Christian Advocate; Wesleyan Christian Advocate; Alabama Baptist; Charles C. Thach Papers, Auburn University Archives; Scrapbook of Mrs. P. H. Mell, Auburn University Archives; Jim L. Sumner, "John Franklin Crowell, Methodism, and the Football Controversy at Trinity College, 1887-1894," Journal of Sport History, 17 (Spring 1990) pp. 5-20; Michael Oriard, **Reading Football: How the Popular Press Created an American Spectacle,** Chapel Hill, University of North Carolina Press, 1993.

the family income. Before 1887 no laws prevented mill owners from hiring even very young children. Under pressure from ministers and others concerned about the children, the state passed a law in 1887 setting eight hours as the longest work day for a child under 14. Children under 15 could not be hired to work in the mines.

Prompted by a New England firm which was considering an Alabama venture, the legislature repealed its child labor law in 1894. The Reverend Edgar Gardner Murphy, an Episcopal minister from Montgomery, organized a committee to work against child labor. He circulated photographs showing Alabama children working in the mills, one of a 6-year-old boy who worked 12 hours for 15 cents a day. Another showed three 7- to 9-year-old boys who worked up to 16 hours a day.

Murphy helped to persuade the legislature to pass a new child labor law in 1907 raising the minimum age of child workers to 12, forbidding those under 16 to work an all-night shift, and limiting the work week of children to 60 hours. In 1915 the legislature passed a law raising the minimum age of workers to 14, but child labor did not end until the 1930s.

The Temperance Movement

One of the most successful organized attempts at reform during the Progressive Era was the temperance movement. The Women's Christian Temperance Union (WCTU) encouraged pastors to preach against the use of alcohol. And, as if Demon Rum flowing freely on Saturday nights didn't create enough sins for the preachers to lament on Sunday mornings, Auburn University students found a way to begin the frivolity on Saturday afternoons. (See the "Foolish and Useless Sport" sidebar.)

The constitutional amendment for prohibition failed to pass in 1909, and Emmett O'Neal of Florence (son of the 1882-1886 Bourbon Governor Edward A. O'Neal) used it as an issue for his campaign for governor in 1910. His slogan was "Every man his own prohibitionist," and he supported a county-option liquor law. The victory of the "wets" was shortlived however as O'Neal only served one term and the legislature during his successor

Two Alabamians in the Spanish-American War: Joe Wheeler and Richmond Hobson

By Dr. WALTER EARL PITTMAN, History Department, Livingston State University

Alabamians were quick to volunteer their services when the Spanish-American War broke out in 1898. However, the "Splendid Little War," ended so quickly that few were able to play an active role. Some Alabamians, already in the military services when the war started, took part in active operations. Two, Gen. Joseph Wheeler and Lt. Richmond P. Hobson, played critical roles and achieved great fame in America's little adventure.

Fighting Joe Wheeler was a genuine hero of the "Lost Cause;" a dashing cavalry commander who became a Confederate major general at the age of 26. After Appomattox, Wheeler served eight terms in the U.S. Congress, resigning in 1898, to accept an appointment as a major general of U.S. Volunteers. He was the only ex-Confederate general to fight in the Spanish-American War. During the Cuban campaign, Wheeler commanded a division of cavalry which fought dismounted and which included the famous "Rough Riders" of Theodore Roosevelt. A tough, wiry, little man, Wheeler was noted for his personal courage and proved to be an outstanding tactician and an inspirational battle leader. However, he was reported as encouraging his men in one particularly tough fight to "Git them damn-Yankees, boys!" Wheeler's troops were the spearhead of General William Shafter's army as it drove inland toward the campaign's objective, the port city of Santiago. In the decisive battle of the San Juan Ridge, which broke Spanish resistance, Wheeler's forces did most of the difficult fighting. After the war, Wheeler accepted a commission as brigadier general in the regular U.S. Army and died in service in 1906. Many of his old Rebel comrades feared that Wheeler would never reach heaven after he was buried in his blue uniform.

Richmond P. Hobson of Greensboro graduated first in his class at Annapolis after being ostracized by the entire student body in retaliation for his zealous reporting of fellow midshipmen for rules infractions. A remarkably handsome and intelligent man, Hobson was selected by the Navy for post-graduate training as a naval architect in France. In 1898, he secured a position on Admiral William Sampson's flagship. When Sampson called for volunteers for a dangerous mission, Hobson was the first to step forward. The mission required the scuttling of a large collier, the Merrimac, across Santiago harbor, thereby sealing up Spanish Admiral Pascal Cervera's small fleet. With a volunteer seven-man crew Hobson sailed into fame before daylight on the morning of June 3, 1898. Explosive charges were rigged to scuttle the ship quickly when it was across the narrow harbor mouth. But in the actual event, some of the charges failed to fire and others were shot away by the intense Spanish crossfire. Merrimac's steering was also shot away, and in the pre-dawn darkness, the old ship drifted with the unexpectedly strong current into the harbor where it sank. Hobson and his crew, miraculously unhurt by the heavy fire, escaped by clinging to a small boat. Captured at daylight, Hobson, and his crew were treated as heroes by the Spanish. When he was exchanged some weeks later Hobson found that he had become an American national idol. He and his crew were awarded the Medal of Honor. A national tour was quickly arranged and a wave of "Hobson mania" swept the country which included marketing a best-selling candy called "Hobson's Kisses." Hobson used his new fame to enter politics. He served in Congress from 1906 to 1914 and emerged as a major (and very controversial) figure, becoming the most important spokesman for an enlarged Navy and the Congressional leader of the Prohibition Movement. After 1914, Hobson became the highest paid lecturer in the nation. His final crusade was the successful effort to persuade the League of Nations to prohibit the international narcotics trade. Hobson died in 1937 in New York City.

Sources: Walter E. Pittman, **Richmond P. Hobson, Progressive Crusader,** Manhattan, Kansas: American Military Institute, 1982;

G.J.A. O'Toole, **The Spanish War,** New York: W.W. Norton and Co., 1984.

Charles Henderson's administration passed a statewide prohibition law to replace the county-option law.

The temperance movement was strong nationwide. In his last year in Congress (1914), Alabama Congressman Richmond P. Hobson of Greensboro proposed an amendment to the United States House of Representatives to make the sale of alcohol illegal throughout the country. Hobson's proposal did not receive the two-thirds majority needed to pass an amendment, but it did draw attention to the temperance movement.

Hobson's political career, and that of the Tennessee Valley's Joe Wheeler, was expedited by successful military careers — Wheeler in both the Civil War and the Spanish-American War and Hobson in the 1898 venture. (See the sidebar.) While wars produce heroes and politicians, they also distract the public from domestic reforms. Just as the Spanish-American War interrupted the farmers' movement, World War I took the focus off progressivism.

World War I

The United States declared war on Germany in April, 1917. Alabama furnished about 95,000 men and sustained 6,262 casualties. Alabama's generals included Lee County's Robert Lee Bullard, commander (CO) of the Second Army, nicknamed "Counterattack Bullard" for his heroics in the 2nd Battle of the Marne, and Etowah County's William Luther Sibert, CO of the 1st Infantry Division (the "Big Red One"). Sibert had been earlier promoted to brigadier general by a special act of Congress for his engineering feats in building the Panama Canal under the command of Major General George

The Montgomery Advertiser

Montgomery victory parade celebration upon the return of the 167th Regiment from Europe in 1919.

Goethals. After his retirement in 1920, he became the first chairman of the Alabama State Docks Commission.

Alabama's "Fighting Fourth" National Guard regiment fought Pancho Villa with "Black Jack" Pershing in Mexico before the war and was called back into federal service to go "Over There" with the doughboys of the Rainbow Division as the 167th Infantry regiment during World War I. The Rainbow Division participated in Chateau-Thierry, St. Michiel, and Argonne Forest. Gordon Johnson, a cavalry colonel from Birmingham who had won the Medal of Honor in the Philippine Insurrection (1906), won the Distinguished Service medal for Argonne Forest fighting. Osmond Kelly Ingram died trying to release depth charges about to be struck by a German U-Boat torpedo. He was the only Alabama naval man to receive the Medal of Honor, America's highest award. Corporal Sidney E. Manning of Flomaton (Escambia County) became the only Alabama Army man in World War I to receive the Medal of Honor. Despite seven wounds, he led his platoon in a charge that took a strong enemy position. Twenty-eight of the 35 men in the platoon were killed; Corporal Manning received two more wounds holding his newly won position.

World War I had a major impact on the Alabama home front from the Tennessee River to Mobile. Wilson Dam was built near Muscle Shoals with

Photos courtesy of the Fitzgerald Museum

Fitzgerald Museum, Montgomery, Alabama; Zelda and F. Scott Fitzgerald in the 1920s.

power and nitrate plants nearby to produce munitions (and fertilizers after the war). The Tennessee Valley Authority (TVA) developed from these World War I works. Maxwell Field, Montgomery became a center for Army aviation. Camp Sheridan, a mobilization center in northeast Montgomery, brought Scott Fitzgerald and other troops to town for temporary duty. (See the Zelda Fitzgerald sidebar.) Shipbuilding and trade at the Mobile Docks flourished.

Alabamians at home supported the war effort. Farmers planted more crops and others had "victory gardens" to grow food for their own family. Food was conserved by having "wheatless Mondays" and "meatless Tuesdays." Citizens helped finance the war by buying Liberty Bonds. Suffragists put their major goals of securing the vote for women on hold to assist in draft registration, volunteer home service enlistments, loan drives, and Red Cross projects.

Prohibition and Women's Rights After the War

After World War I, a new Congress passed the 18th Amendment to the Constitution, which was ratified by the states in 1919. This amendment made it illegal to manufacture, sell, and transport "intoxicating beverages." For the next 14 years the nation was legally dry. Of course, on a local level, moonshiners continued selling illegal booze.

The 21st Amendment, passed in 1933, ended national prohibition. The fight over wet or dry in Alabama is still an issue in many local elections since county voters can choose whether to allow the sale of alcohol in their counties.

Zelda Sayre Fitzgerald

By DR. ANNE LITTLE, English Department, Auburn University at Montgomery; Representative of the Fitzgerald Museum at the International Hemingway/Fitzgerald Conference in Paris, July 1994

Zelda Sayre was born on July 24, 1900, the youngest of five children, to Minnie Machen Sayre and Judge Anthony D. Sayre, of the Alabama Supreme Court. Growing up with fewer restrictions than other girls of her time, Zelda was unconventional and sometimes daring. Once she called the fire department to rescue a child and then climbed onto her roof and waited for the truck to come. As a feisty teen-ager, she swam in a flesh- colored bathing suit, causing many a raised eyebrow from those who supposed she was nude. Considered a beauty with her long golden hair and peaches-and-cream complexion, she was a belle with many beaus. When World War I brought soldiers from all over the country to Montgomery, her circle of admirers grew larger and included F. Scott Fitzgerald, a handsome infantry lieutenant stationed at nearby Camp Sheridan. The two met at a Montgomery Country Club dance and, although immediately attracted to each other, had a rocky courtship of almost two years as Zelda refused to give up her dance dates and college weekends to marry Scott, an aspiring writer with limited prospects as a husband. Finally, eight days after publication of Scott's first novel, **This Side of Paradise,** in 1920, they were married in New York City. The novel, depicting college life as it had never been shown before, brought the Fitzgeralds fame and fortune. With their striking good looks, glamorous lifestyle, and uninhibited behavior, they were the darlings of the Jazz Age and became one of the most celebrated couples of the century. Whether in taxicabs in New York City with Zelda on the hood and Scott on the roof, extended weekend parties at their home in Westport, Connecticut, or living as expatriates on the Riviera, their antics were legendary. But the excitement was brief. After 1930, Zelda spent much of her time in mental institutions, treated for schizophrenia. In 1940, battling alcoholism and desperately trying to finish **The Last Tycoon,** Scott died of a heart attack at age 44. Zelda perished eight years later in a fire in an Asheville, North Carolina, sanitarium.

Despite the brevity of their lives, Zelda and Scott Fitzgerald left a versatile legacy. Zelda's heritage includes a number of paintings, an evocative novel, **Save Me the Waltz,** a farce, Scandalabra, and some short stories published in 1991 as **Zelda Fitzgerald: The Collected Writings.** Scott wrote six novels, two of which, **The Great Gatsby** and **Tender Is the Night,** rank among the best in American literature. Although this daughter and adopted son of Alabama spent most of their married life outside of Montgomery, the city and the South in general shaped the work of both writers. A memorial to their Alabama tenure is the Scott and Zelda Fitzgerald Museum on Felder Avenue in Montgomery — the only museum in the country devoted to the Fitzgeralds — located in the last remaining house in Montgomery in which either of them lived.

Sources: Bruccoli, Matthew J. **Some Sort of Epic Grandeur: The Life of F. Scott Fitzgerald** (New York: Harcourt Brace Jovanovich, 1981).

Milford, Nancy. **Zelda: A Biography** (New York: Harper & Row, 1970).

Photo courtesy of the Fitzgerald Museum

Portrait taken for the dust jacket of Zelda's novel, ***Save Me the Waltz,*** *1932.*

Women's Suffrage

Priscilla Holmes Drake of Huntsville began work for women's suffrage in the late 1870s. By 1893, a state organization developed a branch of the National American Woman's Suffrage Association. Women in Decatur,

The Montgomery Advertiser

*The Margaret Booth School, 117 Sayre Street, Montgomery, Alabama, operated from 1914 until its closing in 1953 as a college preparatory school for young daughters of Montgomery's finest families. One of the more distinguished graduates, Sara Powell Haardt, wrote the novel, **The Making of a Lady** (Doubleday, 1931). Now a half-way house, the building still fulfills the school's cardinal virtue (from Robert Browning): "Only grant that I do serve." (See the sidebar by Tom Bartlett.)*

Verbena, Huntsville, Gadsden, and Calera began local groups. In the 1901 constitutional convention that took the vote away from blacks, suffragists managed to get a proposal for womanhood suffrage before the convention but 80 percent of the 109 delegates, all men, voted against it.

Mary Winslow Partridge organized a women's suffrage group in Selma in 1910, and two years later Patti Ruffner Jacobs founded the Alabama Equal Suffrage Association. Miss Amelia Worthington edited a suffrage column for the *Birmingham News* in 1913, and by 1915 there were similar columns in 14 Alabama newspapers. Another amendment to the state constitution for women's suffrage was proposed and defeated in 1915, although the House members voted for it 52 to 42. Meanwhile, some young, independent, and spirited Alabama women left the state to develop their potential in more receptive settings. (See the feature on Sara Haardt Mencken, Zelda Sayre Fitzgerald, and Tallulah Bankhead.)

In 1919, the United States Congress passed the 19th Amendment stating that the right to vote would not be denied based on gender. An Anti-Ratification League was formed in Montgomery led by Marie Bankhead

Owens and Lister Hill, and the Alabama Legislature refused to ratify the amendment. Three-fourths of the other states did. Alabama women voted for the first time in the presidential election of 1920.

Convict Leasing

Private citizens could lease prisoners from the state of Alabama for about 18 dollars a month to work in coal mines or other industries. Treatment of convicts was often inhumane.

Prison reformer Julia Tutwiler, president of Livingston University and founder of Montevallo, pronounced the system worse than slavery because a slaveholder had a permanent investment to protect, and one who leased convicts did not. As convict leasee guard Jim Saunders noted in interviews in the Alabama Writers' Project during the depression, the operators of the Red Diamond mine near Birmingham encouraged guards to "shoot quick as hell if anybody got rough, or tried runnin' off ..." because there ... "was lots more whar these come from." Another guard observed that the company preferred guards to shoot to kill rather than wound "fer a dead convict didn't cost nothin' fer medicine."

Alabama Department of Archives and History

Julia Tutwiler (1841-1916). Educated at Vassar and in Germany and France, Tutwiler was the president of Livingston State College and founder of Montevallo State College. She was called the "Angel of the Prisons" for her life's work in prison reform.

Reformers wanted the legislature to end the leasing of prisoners, but few leaders of government were interested in listening to the reformers. From 1922 to 1926, prisoner leases brought $3 million into the treasury of Alabama. Convict leases ended when Bibb Graves became governor in 1927. After that, prisoners worked on state-owned farms or in factories on prison grounds.

The movements for social reforms and the industrial and demographic surge of Birmingham and North Alabama by the turn of the century also affected Alabama politics. The five governors elected from 1907 to 1927 were more progressive in outlook than their Bourbon predecessors.

Braxton Bragg Comer of Jefferson County (governor, 1907-1911) began the "Progressive Movement" in Alabama. His administration regulated railroads, established high schools, and passed prohibition laws and the 1907 child labor law.

Alabama Women Who Made the Twenties Roar: Sara, Zelda, and Tallulah

By TOM BARTLETT

Stars not only fell on Alabama, stars were born and raised in Alabama. Stars, that is, of the literary, theatrical, and social worlds. In the 1920s a remarkable trio of ladies from Alabama — all of whom were acquainted with each other — presented a far different picture from the stereotyped Southern female.

In the literary world, a native of Montgomery, Sara Haardt sat at the throne of the dean of American letters. She had journeyed north to attend Goucher College in Baltimore. She so impressed the faculty there that she was invited to teach after graduation. Her literary efforts and her attractive features caught the eye of the premier magazine editor of the era, H.L. Mencken, whose office was in Baltimore.

Mencken was at that time starting the publication that would give him his widest audience, "The American Mercury." Although Mencken rejected Sara's first submission, he recognized her obvious talent for writing. Over the next seven years he wooed Sara and published her work. Finally they were wed in 1930 and Sara joined the dizzying world of writers, characters, and statesmen who journeyed to Mencken's dinner table. Virtually every major American author of the time, from John Dos Passos to Sinclair Lewis to Scott Fitzgerald, came to pay homage to Mencken's powerful literary influence. Mencken respected Sara's literary judgment and was devoted to her. Sara's declining health led to her death of tubercular meningitis in 1935, devastating Mencken.

But far more flamboyant was the daughter of a U.S. Congressman from Jasper, Alabama. Will Bankhead's youngest daughter, Tallulah, was named for her grandmother. Tallulah's mother died shortly after Tallulah was born, so the child was raised partly by her grandmother in Jasper, Alabama and by her aunt, Marie Bankhead Owens, in Montgomery.

When Tallulah was 15, she answered an advertisement in a popular magazine calling for photographs of aspiring actresses. In her haste, she sent in a photograph but forgot to add her name and address. When her photo was published as one of the winners selected, she quickly sent along proof that she was "Cinderella." Tallulah obtained her father's permission — Congressman Bankhead could never say "no" to his daughters — to journey to New York with her aunt as chaperone. They found rooms near the famous Algonquin Hotel and Tallulah entered the fast-paced world of Broadway.

Amazingly, she found parts. With her beautiful looks, husky voice and quick wit, she charmed directors, producers, and writers. Her parts grew from walk-ons to speaking roles as she grew in confidence and skill. Even in mediocre plays she received excellent reviews from the New York critics.

Tallulah quickly became part of the trendy "Big Apple" scene. She partied with the Fitzgeralds, Zelda and Scott, who lived nearby. Tallulah had known Zelda in Montgomery (see the parallel article on Zelda) and both exulted in the new freedom that females were finding in the Flapper Age.

But her greatest successes lay in London. She went there in 1922 and quickly became the talk of the town. She mixed easily with both royalty and theatre hangers-on. For eight years she earned her own way and gained a fanatical following of worshippers. She returned to the United States for a lucrative offer to make movies in Hollywood.

Tallulah's real love, however, was Broadway, and so to New York she returned. Her roles brought her fame and fortune and allowed her to mingle with the famous, including Eleanor Roosevelt, Harry Truman, and Tennessee Williams. She was outrageous, outspoken, and out to be remembered. Reporters hungry for a story loved her for quotes such as "Don't talk to me, I've got laryngitis" or "I have no sense of direction — I don't know my left from my right, except politically." Her mannerisms, her style, and her outspokenness made her distinctly an American original. Her death in 1968 closed a chapter on one of Alabama's most colorful characters.

Sources: Tallulah Bankhead, **Tallulah: My Autobiography** (N.Y.: Harper, 1952).

Lee Israel, **Miss Tallulah** (N.Y.: G.P. Putnam & Sons, 1972).

Sara Mayfield, **The Constant Circle: H.L. Mencken and His Friends** (N.Y.: Delacorte Press, 1968).

————, **Exiles from Paradise: Zelda and Scott Fitzgerald** (N.Y.: Delacorte Press, 1971).

Nancy Milford, **Zelda: A Biography** (N.Y.: Harper & Row, 1970).

His successor, Emmett O'Neal of Florence, allowed cities to adopt commission governments, made prohibition a local issue via the county-option system, created the State Highway Commission, and passed the 1915 child labor law. Charles Henderson of Pike County organized the Alabama Railroad Commission and a Child Welfare Department, and passed a Workmen's Compensation law. Anniston's Thomas E. Kilby created a budget commission and passed an income tax (ruled unconstitutional by the State Supreme Court but later passed as a constitutional amendment during the Miller administration), a new Workmen's Compensation Act, and a new child labor law. Kilby also created a State Board of Education, got a $25 million bond amendment for dollar-matching with the national government on road building, and effected considerable prison reform including the construction of Kilby Prison in Montgomery. William "Plain Bill" Brandon of Tuscaloosa returned Alabama to the "Age of Normalcy" with his gubernatorial tenure from 1923 to 1927 but retained some of the progressive tendencies with an old age assistance law, the continuation of Kilby's road program, and the creation of the Alabama State Docks Commission.

Photo courtesy of Alabama Department of Archives and History

Marie Bankhead Owens, Alabama state archivist, with her niece, Tallulah Bankhead.

The senatorial seats from 1907 to 1930 were also dominated by Alabamians with a generally progressive outlook. Edmund Pettus and John Tyler Morgan, both conservative senators from Selma, were succeeded by John Hollis Bankhead, Sr., from Jasper and Joseph F. Johnston of Birmingham (a lawyer in Selma for 17 years). Bankhead was instrumental in securing federal money to dredge Mobile Harbor and improve navigation on the Tombigbee River, leading to the Mobile to Birmingham Port navigation, and, as noted earlier, the Federal Good Roads Act of 1916. Bankhead also had two sons who played a major role in New Deal legislation. After Johnston died in 1913, Oscar Underwood of Birmingham (Democratic floor leader in the U.S. House for Wilson and a major force in the passage of the Federal Reserve Act and the Underwood-Simmons Tariff) was elected Senator. Underwood's senatorial career was highlighted by his opposition to prohibition and the Ku Klux Klan, both positions partially responsible for the failure of his plans to secure the Democratic Presidential nomination in 1924. Bankhead died in 1920 and was succeeded by "Cotton Tom" Heflin of Lafayette, who served until defeated by John Hollis Bankhead, Jr., in 1930.

Thus progressivism dominated the Alabama economic, demographic, and political life in the first three decades of the 20th century. The state became accustomed to providing greater services for its people, and a beginning was made in improving the socio-economic status of the residents — an effort which was continued in the post-1927 period by the progressive administration of Bibb Graves.

One newspaper editor called Graves "a good, but expensive governor." After his inauguration in 1927, Graves pushed for $25 million in road building. He set aside an emergency educational appropriation of $600,000 and greatly increased the annual education budget. The elderly, sick, young, and unemployed obtained additional aid. The Talladega Deaf and Blind School and vocational education received generous grants. A new state health program provided medical facilities that were accessible to 90 percent of the people.

Alabama Department of Archives and History

Bibb Graves, Alabama's governor, 1927-31 and 1935-1939.

Governor Bibb Graves was an honor graduate of Yale Law School. He was also a tobacco-chewing member of the renewed Ku Klux Klan. Alvin Horn, former KKK grand dragon of Alabama, recalled that the day his father-in-law was initiated into the Klan at East Lake Park in Birmingham was the day "the Klan gave Colonel Bibb Graves and Hugo Black a lifetime gold card." Horn said he regretted the lifetime membership given fellow Clay Countian Black because he subsequently favored kicking him out of the Klan. Of course Black's Klan tenure was shorter than Horn's admiration of him.

John Hollis Bankhead, Jr., served from 1930 until 1946 when he was succeeded by John Sparkman of Huntsville. J. H. Bankhead, Jr., and his younger brother, Will B. Bankhead (U.S. House of Representatives, 1916-1940) were prominent members of the New Deal administration of President Roosevelt. John Hollis coauthored the Bankhead- Jones Farm Tenant Act of 1937 to reduce farm tenancy, authored the Bankhead Cotton Act establishing a quota system for cotton production (to increase the price), and played a major role in developing the Agricultural Adjustment Acts. William (the father of Tallulah) was Speaker of the House from 1936 to his death in 1940. Bankhead Forest, just northeast of William's hometown of Jasper, was named for him. West of the forest was the small, rural town of Haleyville.

Haleyville, in northwest Alabama, was probably better off than most Alabama towns in the 1920s and 1930s. Already on the Illinois Central (Mobile to Chicago) railroad, the addition of Alabama Power Company service in 1925 fostered the building of a cotton mill in 1928. Extensive

Photo courtesy of Carl Elliott

Former Congressman Carl Elliott, Sr., at an October 4, 1993, University of Alabama reception in his honor. With him are former state Senator Tom Radney of Alexander City and his son, Thomas Anderson Radney, a law student at the university.

forests (almost 200,000 acres of which was eventually consolidated into Bankhead Forest) made possible a market for selling crossties to the railroad for $1.65 each. On some Saturdays wagons loaded with crossties would be lined up for a mile. Hickory for ax handles, hand-cut shingles, furs, hides, and star root ginseng, could also be marketed. In 1930, the *Advertiser-Journal* newspaper estimated that 40 percent of Haleyville's income came from cotton, 40 percent from railroad and industrial interests, crossties and lumber 10 percent, and 10 percent from chickens, eggs, and other produce. With cotton 5 cents and 6 cents per pound, conventional wisdom and national statistics suggested switching to livestock-raising. Although cotton prices went up to 12 cents a pound, the largest farm operator in the county, Crittenden of Ashridge, still made the switch . Senator Bankhead, in a fall 1934 speech at the Haleyville Courthouse, attributed the cotton price increase to crop planning, one of his major senatorial accomplishments. In the mid-30s, the cotton mill paid a minimum of $12 for a 40-hour week (or 30 cents an hour). The minimum increased to 35 cents an hour by 1941 and the mill employed 276. The ownership survived a major unsuccessful attempt to unionize in 1934.

A major problem was bad roads. To travel to Birmingham on a paved road in the 1930s, Haleyville residents had to travel north to Russellville, east to Moulton and Decatur then south to Birmingham, a distance of about 160

Alabama Department of Archives and History

Hugo Black of Clay County was U.S. senator, 1927-1937, and a U.S. Supreme Court justice, 1937-1971.

Alabama Department of Archives and History

Lister Hill served in the U.S. Senate, 1938-1968.

miles. With the completion of the paved road through Double Springs to Jasper in 1940 the distance was almost cut in half.

Salaries were low in the 20s and 30s but so were prices. One could buy a Chevrolet Coach for $595 in 1929 and gas for 19 cents a gallon. And after the city swimming pool opened in 1935, residents could swim for 10 cents (15 cents if suits were furnished).

Long-time northwest Alabama Congressman Carl Elliott represented the same 7th district of Congress as had William Bankhead (after four intervening terms by Carter Manasco). Elliott grew up on Gober Ridge (named for his grandmother's side of the family) one mile from Coker Spur. It was on the same railroad that connected Haleyville with Red Bay, the largest town near the Elliott homestead. Elliott remembers Red Bay as a similar town to Haleyville and his favorite memories are of hearing the prominent politicians of the day make speeches there and at Vina, three miles away, where Carl attended public school. Will Bankhead spoke at Vina on a rainy fall day in 1922 and after his speech Carl met him. When Bankhead asked Carl what he wanted to be when he grew up, Carl replied that he wanted to have a political career like him. Carl, 8 years old at the time, was thrilled when Bankhead told him that he had served a while and by the time he got ready to step aside there was no reason Carl could not succeed him. At age 12, Carl rode a horse 30 miles to Russellville to hear "Cotton" Tom Heflin speak. Heflin had striped trousers, a double-breasted waistcoat, bow tie, and spell-binding power over his audience. He ridiculed blacks, Catholics, and Jews while extoling the virtues of cotton. "Cotton is a child of the sun. It is kissed by the silvery beams of a Southern moon and bathed in the crystal dewdrops that fall in the silent watches of the night." He used fire and brimstone rhetoric in the best tradition of backwoods revivalism giving Wall Street hell and playing all his symbols of hate like the keys of an organ. He hypnotized the crowd and demonstrated the power of hate. Young Carl was impressed — and frightened.

But Carl Elliott learned the politics he was to practice from a politician who arrived in Vina in 1926 at the wheel of a new Ford roadster. His name was Black but he was dressed in white — white linen suit, white necktie, and white shoes with a streak of black around the toes. With a conversational style he worked "the crowd with care, every sentence with a strategy to it. When he was done, I felt I'd seen a smart man, a real smart man. Almost a scientist." Twenty years later Elliott, as a freshman Congressman, met Supreme Court Justice Black in Washington, D.C., Black asked Elliott where he was from and narrowed him down to Gober Ridge. Black then asked if Carl's father was G.W. Elliott. When Carl said yes, he asked Carl to name all the other Black supporters on Gober Ridge. Carl did. Black then showed Carl all their names in his black book where he had written them in 1926. Black was smart but also a very thorough politician who knew the importance of identifying with individual voters to consistently win elections in rural Alabama. Mr. Elliott, in his time, refined the technique by knowing his own genealogy and that of his neighbors well. When a potential voter's knowledge of his own genealogy ran out, Mr. Elliott would supply missing links. Before Elliott left, the voter was convinced he and Carl were kinfolks. And Mr. Elliott's cousins, three times removed, elected him to Congress eight times. He had learned a lot from a man named Black who wore white.

Black of Birmingham followed Underwood as U.S. Senator and served until President Roosevelt appointed him to the Supreme Court in 1937. Governor Bibb Graves appointed his wife Dixie to take Black's seat in the Senate, but shortly before the 1938 election he appointed Lister Hill of Montgomery to the seat. Hill was a very progressive Senator who, in his 30 years in the Senate (1938-1968), was known for legislation supporting labor, TVA, and federal aid to education, health, and hospitals, including the Hill-Burton Act, which made federal funds available for the building of hospitals.

The Klan in the Twenties

The Harpersville, Alabama, native and former Methodist minister William J. Simmons revived the Klan on Thanksgiving eve, 1915. He and some companions burned a fiery cross on the top of Stone Mountain while "The Birth of a Nation" movie glorifying the Reconstruction Klan was being shown in nearby Atlanta. The next year the Robert E. Lee Klan, No. 1 (Birmingham), was organized, apparently the first klavern in Alabama. By 1924, the Lee klavern had over 500 members and Birmingham was the center of Klan activity in Alabama. Three 1923-1924 rallies there attracted 50,000 visitors — Edgewood Park in September, 1923 when Hugo Black and more than 1,000 other "aliens" were "naturalized" into the Klan; East Lake Park soon afterwards when 2,000 were initiated; and a 2nd East Lake Park rally in June, 1924 with more than 4,000 initiated as a part of the largest

Alabama Department of Archives and History

Ku Klux Klan parade in downtown Montgomery.

Klan rally in the Southeast. Ten thousand spectators attended a 1924 rally south of Montgomery at Snowdoun, the largest Klan ceremony in central Alabama, although almost as many attended a Clanton ceremony the same year.

And a Klan ceremony was something to behold. The *Birmingham Age-Herald* described the first East Lake Park spectacle: "There was a parade of thousands of white-robed figures moving in a steady line with their robes standing out in bold outline against the landscape ... a part ... was lighted by red torches ... lending a somber light to the whole scene."

The Klan of the twenties was initially dedicated to 100 percent Americanism, Caucasian supremacy, and the promotion of Protestant morality. And on the prohibition issue, the Klan's appeal overlapped with that of the Anti-Saloon League and its ally, the Women's Christian Temperance Union (WCTU). With the demise of the farmers movement of the 1890s and Progressivism in the early 20th century, reform-minded north Alabamians turned to the League for a quasi-political faction within the Democratic Party. By the 1920s the League's strongest section was north Alabama. And the Klan picked up considerable north Alabama support too, especially in Birmingham. Thus, by the 1926 elections, the Black Belt Bourbons, traditionally wet, were opposed by the Progressives' Bibb Graves in the Governor's race and Hugo Black in the Senate race. Both were supported by the drys, north Alabamians, and the Klan. The Bourbons were white supremacists and no friends of blacks, yet in the twenties they were cast as anti-Klan and anti-prohibition "good guys." Politics does yield some strange bed fellows, and, for north Alabamians, sheets to match!

In the social and moral arena, the Klan particularly reacted to the perceived moral decay associated with the Jazz Age — hip-flasked youngsters cruising the highways and byways in the new-fangled automobiles, dubbed by moralists "houses of prostitution on wheels." Robed Klan bands took tag numbers of parked cars for the Sheriff's Department in

Causes Won, Not Lost: The Crimson Tide, the Rose Bowl and the Modernization of the South

By ANDY DOYLE, Ph.D. student, Emory University, and adjunct faculty, Auburn University at Montgomery

The Southern poet and critic Donald Davidson asserted that the American South during the 1920s "disproved the axiom that two bodies cannot occupy the same space." An emerging urban society built upon the secular gospel of progress and innovation coexisted uneasily with an agrarian society wedded to the outlook and more of evangelical religion and a rural folk culture. A region beset by these fundamental conflicts used college football as a symbolic reconciliation of progress and tradition. The Rose Bowl appearances by the University of Alabama in 1926 and 1927 reveal how football reassured white Southerners that their distinctive cultural identity and bedrock traditions could flourish in a society undergoing the process of modernization.

The 1926 Rose Bowl contest between Crimson Tide of the University of Alabama and the University of Washington Huskies marked the first time that a Southern team had ever competed in this prestigious post-season event. Since the sectional crisis leading to the Civil War, Southerners had regarded the rest of the nation with a complex mixture of assertive pride and defensive hostility, and intersectional football gave full rein to both sentiments. For more than 30 years, Southerners had regarded intersectional football games as symbolic assertions of Southern honor. Southern colleges and universities belatedly adopted football in the early 1890s, and this late start combined with the endemic poverty and tiny enrollments of Southern schools to render Southern football decidedly inferior to the rest of the nation. Southerners took to the game with a passion that belied the perennial inferiority of their teams, and they spoke longingly of the day when Southern teams would cease to take regular drubbings from Northern counterparts.

Southern football improved dramatically in the years after World War I, but the Northern sportswriters and coaches who dominated the college football establishment continued to ignore developments south of the Mason-Dixon Line. The Rose Bowl committee tendered a reluctant, last-minute invitation to Alabama in December 1925 — only after several Northern teams declined invitations. The Rose Bowl agent charged with finding an opponent for Washington initially refused to consider extending an invitation to Alabama, and worried that by doing so he was "mixing a lemon with a rose." A victory by Alabama would not only diminish the stigma of Southern football inferiority, it would be a sublime tonic for a people buffeted by a historical legacy of military defeat, poverty, and alienation from the American political and cultural mainstream.

On New Year's Day, 1926, nervously hopeful crowds of Alabamians assembled in theaters, auditoriums, and on windswept city streets to follow a play-by-play account of the game flashed over a special Associated Press wire. In Montgomery, a free football matinee sponsored by the *Montgomery Advertiser* filled that city's Grand Theater to standing room capacity while hundreds more clamored at the doors for admission. *Advertiser* officials quickly arranged a second free presentation from the balcony of the newspaper office two blocks away, and police roped off a block of Dexter Avenue for those willing to stand there for two hours in cold winter weather. A more affluent crowd attended a football matinee sponsored by a private promoter at the Municipal Auditorium, thus avoiding both the mobbed theater and the chilly street. Alabamians sweated out the final minutes before the kickoff balanced on a razor's edge between anxiety and enthusiasm. The tension was unbearably high, the psychic stakes enormous.

The first game details that flashed over the telegraph lines shattered the anxious optimism of the Alabama faithful. George Wilson, Washington's All-American halfback, intercepted a pass on Alabama's first possession, and the Huskies marched 85 yards through a porous Alabama defense for a touchdown. In the second quarter, Wilson tossed a 20-yard touchdown pass that put the Huskies ahead 12-0. The vaunted Alabama defense, which had surrendered only one touchdown in nine regular season games against Southern opponents, floundered helplessly.

During the halftime intermission, the forlorn and joyless crowd on Dexter Avenue milled about quietly as the short winter afternoon waned into evening. Some fans stopped for a wistful glance at the front window of the Rosemont Gardens florist shop, which proudly displayed an Alabama team photograph inside a huge, horseshoe-shaped arrangement of red roses. In the same Court Square in which Montgomery citizens had celebrated the news of South Carolina's secession 65 years earlier, city fathers had planned a similar demonstration if Alabama could successfully defend the honor of the region on the gridiron. The crowd on Dexter Avenue and their counterparts throughout the state faced the painful realization that the Yankee sportswriters who had long dismissed Southern football as hopelessly inferior and smugly questioned the wisdom of inviting Alabama to the Rose Bowl might have been right after all.

Then, in the third quarter, the Crimson Tide mounted a dazzling comeback that confounded the critics and brought joy to the believers. Alabama's rugged quarterback, Pooley Hubert, cut the Washington lead to 12-7 with a one-yard plunge that capped a 42-yard touchdown drive. Pandemonium reigned on Dexter Avenue when Alabama halfback Johnny Mack Brown put the Tide ahead 14-12 with a 63-yard touchdown reception. Brown, a speedster described as "slicker than an eel in a sea of stewed okra," then made a spectacular over-the-shoulder catch of a Hubert pass, eluded one tackler, stiff-armed another, and crossed the goal line with Alabama's third touchdown of the quarter. The stunned Washington squad regrouped and scored a fourth quarter touchdown, but Alabama killed a final Huskie drive with an interception and held on for a 20-19 upset victory. Stanford Coach Pop Warner, who had predicted a Washington victory, reflected the surprise of the national sporting establishment when he called the Alabama victory "a shock to everybody."

When the words "Alabama Wins" flashed over the wire, the crowd on Dexter Avenue exploded into a joyful frenzy and began to light torches and set off fireworks. A crowd of between three and four thousand laughing, shouting citizens led by Alabama Governor William W. Brandon and Montgomery Mayor William A. Gunter marched by flickering torchlight through the central business district of Montgomery. Similar demonstrations lasted into the early morning hours in Tuscaloosa and Birmingham.

Southerners were united by this glorious victory that transcended the realm of football. "Alabama was our representative in fighting for us against the world," declared Vanderbilt coach Dan McGugin. "I fought, bled, died and was resurrected with the Crimson Tide." The *Atlanta Georgian* called the 1926 Rose Bowl "the greatest victory for the South since the first battle of Bull Run.' The *Atlanta Journal* announced, "The Crimson Tide no longer belongs exclusively to Tuscaloosa and the state of Alabama. It belongs to the whole South, just like the Stone Mountain Memorial."

New Orleans residents lavished an ecstatic reception on the Tide as they passed through that city on their homeward journey, but an even more frenzied welcome awaited them back home in Tuscaloosa. In a scene that resembled the return of a Roman legion from a war of conquest, the team rode in a procession of decorated wagons pulled through the crowded streets by University freshmen. Euphoric citizens surged forward to congratulate the players, and the caravan took an hour to inch along the three-quarter mile route from the train station to downtown. A local attorney and civic leader told the jubilant crowd, "When the band plays 'Dixie' over this team, it can whip eleven Red Granges." He also chortled that the members of the Washington team and several generations of their descendants would henceforth "speak with a soft Southern accent."

The Crimson Tide followed this triumph with another undefeated season in 1926, and Alabama was invited back to defend its Rose Bowl title on New Year's Day, 1927. The pundits who had been embarrassed the previous year confidently predicted that Pop Warner's powerful Stanford Cardinals would give these Southern upstarts their comeuppance. Stanford dominated the game statistically, but Alabama converted a blocked punt into a touchdown in the final minutes of the game and came away with a 7-7 tie. Southern editorialists, politicians, and business leaders led a reprise of the hallelujah chorus that followed the victory over Washington. They crowed over how foolish the self-proclaimed experts who had dismissed the 1926 victory as a fluke now appeared, and they celebrated the tie game as a "moral victory" for "our boys" and the "Solid South" that had faithfully backed them. At the homecoming celebration in Tuscaloosa, Governor-elect Bibb Graves, himself a former Alabama football player, declared that "the hearts of all of Dixie are beating with exultant pride." The Crimson Tide, declared Graves, had "upheld the honor of the Southland and came back to us undefeated."

This deluge of sectionalist passion indicated that the passion of the Lost Cause was still alive two generations after Appomattox. Yet while Southerners embraced these Rose Bowl champions as instruments of glorious vengeance unleashed upon ancient enemies, they also saw them as proof that the South could prosper in the highly competitive modern world. Since the 1880s, Americans had viewed football as a metaphor for the Machine Age. They commonly referred to football teams as "machines," and hailed the game as the ultimate in "scientific" sport. Like a modern factory, a football team depended on precise planning, intricate teamwork, split second timing, and a complex division of labor to produce results. The triumphs of the Alabama "machine" in these Rose Bowls implied that the South could indeed rise to the challenge posed by the industrial era.

The Business Progressives who dominated the South in the 1920s sought to maintain the cultural traditions that bolstered the rigid Southern social order, but they also wanted to integrate the region into the national economic mainstream. Southern college football served as a symbolic reconciliation of progress and tradition. It evoked the timeless spirit of the Lost Cause while it embodied the competitive self-confidence so vital to 20th century capitalism. John Temple Graves, a Birmingham newspaper editor and leading Business Progressive spokesman, believed that the Alabama Rose Bowl teams played a key role in grafting this new ethos of victory onto the southern character. Writing in 1941, Graves declared:

> *For all the last stands, all the lost causes and sacrificings in vain, the South had a heart. And a tradition. But the South had a new tradition for something else. It was for survival, and for victory. It had come from the football fields. It had come from those mighty afternoons in the Rose Bowl at Pasadena, when Alabama's Crimson Tide had rolled to glory .... The South had come by way of football to think at last in terms of causes won, not lost.*

Yet the Southern progressive ideal of reconciling regional traditions and folkways with modern corporate capitalism proved illusory. Football symbolized the values and ideals of the Southern past, but it was itself a product of the mass culture that was systematically undermining the traditional culture. Southern college football helped to ease the cultural transition to modernity by providing a false reassurance that a reconciliation of progress and tradition was possible.

This essay is an abridgement of "Causes Won, Not Lost: College Football and the Modernization of the American South," International Journal of the History of Sport, 11 (August 1994), pp. 231-251.

Etowah County, in Troy the Klansmen reported names to parents and the police, and on Red Mountain the Klansmen flashed lights on the occupants of parked cars and ordered them to move on.

The Birmingham Klan came down on the roadhouses along the Montgomery highway and on houses of ill repute. These moralistic moves met with public favor as did some practical economic actions such as handbills in Dothan warning against loafing while "the fields are white with cotton." But by 1925, the Klan became more aggressive and more controversial. A cross was burned in front of St. Matthew's Catholic Church in Oakdale (Mobile). Then a series of floggings occurred in Birmingham and Jasper. In the latter town, northwest of the Magic City, a band of masked Klansmen led by Will Dupree took turns whipping an outspoken critic of the Klan, George Tallant. Five were convicted but the Alabama Supreme Court set aside the verdict on technical grounds. And in June, 1926, a robed band led by Avondale Klansman W.J. Worthington raided three Chinese restaurants in Birmingham. They searched the premises and the patrons. After a public outcry, four were convicted but eventually released as one member of the group was a deputy sheriff with a legal search warrant.

The crowning blow came in the summer of 1927 when three white-robed men who had just spoken from the pulpit of Antioch Baptist Church (near Oneonta), upon leaving, kidnapped and later flogged a 19-year-old orphan, Jeff Calloway. Calloway had a bottle and had been drinking. Attorney General Charles C. McCall, a Klansman himself, demanded the names of the three and the floggers from state Grand Dragon, James Esdale. Seven men were tried. Two men were found guilty and the others entered guilty pleas. Klan members were convicted of crimes by a local jury! The Klan's demise was apparent. The *Birmingham Age-Herald* compared the conviction to the fall of the Bastille in the French Revolution.

William Snell, in an Alabama Review article titled "Fiery Crosses in the Roaring Twenties," noted that the Klan destroyed itself by its own excesses. In 1925, the Alabama Klan had 115,000 members including the prominent politicians Graves, Black, and McCall. As unpopular violence increased, Klan membership decreased. By the end of the year following the Calloway incident in 1927, the Klan had shrunk to 10,000 and the membership was reduced by half each year until 1930 when a mere 1,349 remained — a far cry from the 115,000 of 1925 and the Birmingham Park rallies of 1923-1924 which attracted crowds of 50,000. Of course, by 1926-1927, Alabamians had a new way to vent southern nationalism. (See the Crimson Tide sidebar.)

As explained earlier the South Alabama Bourbons via political positioning were in steadfast opposition to the Klan. Montgomery's mayor throughout the 1920s to his 1940 death, William Adam Gunter, Jr. (Gunter Air Force Base's namesake), was an Episcopalian with planter-aristocratic roots. Gunter didn't care for legal prohibition or the Klan. Supported by the editor of the *Montgomery Advertiser*, Grover Cleveland Hall, Sr., and Montgomery's elite, Gunter controlled capital city politics. Thus Grover Hall could follow political pragmatism as a Bourbon opposed to Progressivism and reform and also become a decisive player in destroying the state power of the Klan. Hall's anti-Klan stance was publicized nationally by The *Baltimore Evening*

Alabama Department of Archives and History

Grover Cleveland Hall, Sr., (1888-1941) worked on newspaper staffs in Dothan, Enterprise, Selma, and Pensacola before joining the Montgomery Advertiser in 1910. He was the associate editor for 10 years before becoming editor. His editorials promoting racial and religious toleration won the Pulitzer Prize for Journalism in 1928.

Sun editor and renowned social critic, H.L. Mencken, whom Hall came to know through Mencken's Montgomerian wife, the former Sara Powell Haardt. As a result, Hall won the 1928 Pulitzer Prize for his anti-intoleration articles. A sample of Hall's prose is his reply to a tirade against him by the race-baiting and Klan-backed U. S. Senator "Cotton" Tom Heflin: "Sugar Babe Heflin! Darling of the Klan and beneficiary of its till! He has proven that ... patriotism pays good fees ... that virtue is its own (cash) reward, and ... hell hath no fury like a sweetened-coffee addict exposed!" When Heflin became a Hoovercrat in opposition to Democratic Party nominee Al Smith, a Catholic and wet, Hall and Gunter supported John Hollis Bankhead, Jr. of Jasper who won by 50,000 votes. Graves and Black survived their Klan identification by supporting the Democratic Party's choice in 1928. Al Smith was not elected but they were.

Alabamians in World War II and the Aftermath

More than 288,000 Alabamians served in World War II and 7,626 died. Many served in the 31st "Dixie Division" under General John Person of Birmingham. Major General Holland Smith of Russell County, a pioneer of Marine amphibious doctrine and technique, commanded the 1st Marine Division in the South Pacific. General Charles Scott of Uriah commanded the 1st Armored Corps and General James Persons of Rockford was the Commandant of the Fort Meade Tank School. Alabamians served in all services in all theaters.

More than a million black Americans served in World War II. In the Mediterranean Theater, the principal black combat unit, the 92nd Division, had been reactivated at Fort McClellan in 1942, and many Alabamians joined the 92nd, including Ernest Warren of Montgomery, who later taught history at Jefferson Davis High School and Auburn University at

The Tuskegee Pilots

The black pilots initially trained by black civilian pilots under "Chief" Charles Alfred Anderson at Moton Field were eventually a part of the 332nd Fighter Group, the "red tails," consisting of four fighter squadrons: the 99th; 100th; 301st; and 302nd. Commanded by Colonel Benjamin O. Davis, Jr., the 332nd changed from P-47 "Jugs" to P-51 "Mustangs" in June 1944 and flew escort for bombers of the 15th Air Force. The group received a Distinguished Unit Citation (DUC) for escorting B-17's on Berlin March 24, 1945. They successfully fought 30 Me-262 and Me-263 jet interceptors (the 100th Ftr Sq had four victories) and strafed transportation facilities en route back to their base in Ramitelli, Italy. It was a 1,600-mile round trip, the longest 15th AF mission of the war. The 99th Fighter Squadron also had DUCs for action over Sicily, June-July, 1943 and Cassino, May 12-14, 1944. The 332nd's top shooter was Lt. Lee A. Archer of the 302nd Ftr Sq, who had four confirmed victories, three on Columbus Day, October 12, 1944. The group had more than 100 confirmed aerial victories in the war. After the war the 332nd's CO, Benjamin O. Davis, Jr., a graduate of the first class at Tuskegee, became the 1st black general in the Air Force. His father, B.O. Davis, Sr., had been the first black general in the Army. Another Tuskegee pilot and Tuskegee Institute graduate, Chappie James, became a four-star Air Force general.

Sources: Benjamin O. Davis, Jr., **Benjamin O. Davis, Jr., American: An Autobiography** (Washington, D.C.: Smithsonian Institution Press, 1991).

Maurer Maurer, ed., **Combat Squadrons of the Air Force, World War II** (Maxwell AFB, AL: USAF Historical Division, Air University, 1969).

————, ed., **Air Force Combat Units of World War II** (Washington, D.C.: Office of Air Force History, 1983).

Col. Benjamin B. Williams, Col. Alfred W. Goldthwaite, Lt. Col. Forrest B. Dowdy, Lt. Col. Leigh Maier, and Maj. Donald B. Dodd, **USAF Credits for the Destruction of Enemy Aircraft, World War II,** USAF Historical Study No. 85 (Washington D.C.: Office of Air Force History, 1978).

Montgomery. But Alabama's main contribution in regard to blacks in World War II may have been the training of the Tuskegee pilots. (See the sidebar.)

Twelve Alabamians received the Medal of Honor:

Staff Sergeant Paul L. Bolden, U.S. Army, Madison
First Lieutenant Cecil H. Bolton, U.S. Army
Captain Charles W. Davis, U.S. Army, Gordo
Staff Sergeant Henry E. Erwin, U.S. Army Air Forces, Bessemer
Captain Howard W. Gilmore, U.S. Navy, Selma
Sergeant Ross Franklin Gray, U.S. Marines, Bibb County
First Lt. William R. Lawley, U.S. Army Air Forces, Leeds
Technical Sergeant Jake W. Lindsey, U.S. Army, Isney

Alabama Department of Archives and History

Major General Holland Smith of Russell County, a pioneer of amphibious warfare, commanded the 1st Marine Division in the Pacific Theater in World War II.

Alabama Department of Archives and History

First Lady Eleanor Roosevelt visits with "Chief" Charles Alfred Anderson at Moton Field, where black fighter pilots were trained.

Alabama Bureau of Tourism and Travel

Big guns of battleship U.S.S. Alabama.

Literature and War: Alabama Authors on the Two World Wars, 1917-1918, and 1941-1945

By DR. BENJAMIN BUFORD WILLIAMS

Professor of English, Emeritus, Auburn University at Montgomery, combat infantryman, World War II, and retired colonel, USAFR

When the United States entered World War I in 1917, the Fourth Infantry Regiment of the Alabama National Guard was called into federal service as the 167th Infantry Regiment of the 42nd (Rainbow) Division of the U.S. Army. The 42nd was commanded in combat by General Douglas MacArthur, of later World War II fame. In 1919, William H. Amerine published **Alabama's Own in France,** an account of the 167th Infantry's regimental actions.

William Edward Campbell of Mobile, Alabama, served with the Marine Corps in combat in France. He was decorated with the Navy Cross, French Croix de Guerre, and the Distinguished Service Cross. After the war, Campbell became vice-president of the Waterman Steamship Lines, but retired to write literature. In 1933, he published his first novel, **Company K,** one of the most powerful war stories ever written.

In **Company K,** Campbell, under the pseudonym William March, has each of the 113 members of his fictional company relate an impression of the war. Through these individual monologues the reader receives the total impact of war upon men of different temperaments and sensibilities. In **Company K,** the characters reveal the human strengths and weaknesses of men under the stress of combat, and illustrate the fine line between heroism and cowardice. March's fictional war in **Company K** was based on his actual experiences as a Marine sergeant in the trenches of World War I, and reinforces the factual but equally horrific account of **Alabama's Own in France** by Amerine.

The United States and Alabama were plunged into World War II, when the Japanese bombed Pearl Harbor in Hawaii on December 7, 1941. No fiction of the quality of William March's **Company K** has come out of World War II by an Alabama author, but two works based on war-time experiences have been recently published. Eugene Sledge of Mobile wrote of his combat in the Pacific with the 3rd Battalion, 1st Marine Division in **With the Old Breed** (1981). In **G Company's War** (1992), two soldiers of the 26th Infantry Division give almost daily accounts of the ground war in Europe in France and Germany in 1944 and 1945. The parallel combat diaries of Staff Sergeant Bruce Egger of Prineville, Oregon, and Lieutenant Lee M. Otts of Brewton, Alabama, recite the action of an infantry company in World War II. Both men were in G Company, 328th Infantry Regiment but were in different platoons and did not meet until they came together for the book publication almost 50 years later.

William Bradford Huie of Hartselle has two books on World War II. His first novel, **Mud on the Stars** (1942), is the story of a young soldier who entered the Army soon after Pearl Harbor. The bulk of the narrative depicts the narrator's pre-war life. It ends with the optimistic and patriotic statement: "I believe that in spite of all the mud that has been splashed across the stars, the sons of the men who fought at Bunker Hill know that the stars are still there." Huie's non-fiction war book is **The Execution of Private Slovik** (1954), the story of the only American soldier in World War II executed for desertion in the face of the enemy. Private Eddie Slovik was in Company G, 109th Infantry Regiment, 28th Division. He was executed on January 31, 1945, at the end of the Battle of the Bulge.

Lonnie Coleman published **Time Moving West** in 1947, a novel based on his service in the U.S. Navy, 1942-1946. The story is more a conflict of personalities than a story of naval warfare. Coleman, author of many novels, is best remembered for **Beulah Land** (1973), later dramatized on television. Robert O. Bowen's **The Weight of the Cross** (1951) is a fictionalized account of Bowen's three years in a Japanese prisoner of war camp in the Philippines. Joe David Brown from Birmingham was a paratrooper in the war and drew on his military background for the writing of his war novel **Kings Go Forth** (1956). This novel was made into a film as were his **Stars in My Crown** (1947) and **Addie Pray** (1971), retitled as the popular movie 'Paper Moon.'

Commander David McCampbell, U.S. Navy, Bessemer
Private First Class John D. New, U.S. Marines, Mobile
First Lieutenant Jack L. Treadwell, U.S. Army, Ashland
Private Wilson D. Watson, U.S. Marines, Russellville.

Politics During the War

Alabama's wartime governors, Frank M. Dixon (1939-1943) and Chauncey M. Sparks (1943-1946) were both lawyers educated out-of-state. Dixon, born in California and educated at the University of Virginia and Columbia, was a Birmingham attorney. While governor, he reorganized the executive branch with some departments directly under him, such as Revenue, Finance, Highway, Industrial Relations, and Conservation. Other departments, including the State Personnel Department administering the state merit system and the Department of Pardons and Paroles, were under boards whose members were appointed by the governor on a staggered basis (no one governor made all the appointments, thus yielding some independence).

Sparks, a native of Barbour County (the "home of the governors" — Shorter and Jelks before Sparks and George and Lurleen Wallace later), studied law at Mercer College in Georgia and practiced in Eufaula. Both Dixon and Sparks led the Southern Governors Conference's fight against discriminatory (against the South) freight rates resulting in favorable Interstate Commerce Commission (ICC) adjustments in 1945. Both also benefited from a booming war economy.

World War I facilities were expanded during World War II. Fort McClellan became the home of the Women's Army Corps (WAC) and the Chemical Center and School. Maxwell Field housed the Army Air Corps Tactical School and, with the Air Force establishment in 1948, the Air Force's professional military education complex. Now under Air University, the academic courses include Air War College, Air Command and Staff College, and Squadron Officer School, with professional military education for officers from lieutenants through colonels.

New military installations built during World War II were Redstone Arsenal near Huntsville and Fort Rucker Army Air Force Base near Dothan. DuPont maintained an Ordnance Works near Childersburg. Ingall's Shipbuilding Corporation built ships with welded hulls in Mobile Bay. Mobile's population increased from 78,720 to over 125,000. One hundred ninety-six ships were built and more than 2,000 repaired. Mobile became a major port on the Intercoastal Canal from Texas to Florida and up the East Coast.

In 1949, the Army transferred its guided missile research activities from Fort Bliss, Texas, to Huntsville, with the more than 1,000 German scientists brought to the United States by "Operation Paperclip" after World War II. Huntsville, a city of 16,437 in 1950, expanded to 123,000 in the fifties. In 1960, the National Aeronautics and Space Administration (NASA) located the George C. Marshall Space Flight Center in the "Rocket City" and Huntsville became known as "the Space Capital of the World." Four months after Sputnik (October 1957), Wernher Von Braun's scientists prepared Explorer I for launching. Explorer I, II, III and IV, launched into orbit from Cape Canaveral, Florida were carried by Jupiter I, the rocket developed at Redstone. Explorer II was unsuccessful.

World War II brought many changes. The war stimulated the economy and ended the Great Depression. With white males off to war, blacks and women had new opportunities in the workplace. The U.S. and U.S.S.R. emerged as the two major powers. The Cold War began. On the domestic front, Americans were eager to welcome their soldiers home and get back to more normal lives.

On the grassroots social level, especially to rural-raised white Southerners, there is nothing more normal than a steady diet of country music during the week culminating in a festive Saturday night and gospel music and redemption on Sundays. It is both an escape and a way to cope with rapid changes threatening traditional ways. And none captured it all better than Hank Williams.

Hank Williams (1923-1953)

To Southern historian Wayne Flynt, who has written so eloquently about the poor white, the most articulate spokesman of the Alabama rural whites in the post-World War II South was the plain folk's popular hero, Hank Williams. Born in the Mount Olive community near Georgiana in 1923, Hank was raised in lumber camps where his father Alonzo worked and his mother Lilly played gospel music on the Baptist church organ. At 6, young Hank sang with his mother, at 8 he got a guitar, and at 14 he had his own band. He dropped out of school and moved to Montgomery where he won an amateur night prize of $15 for "WPA Blues" and landed a job with radio station WSFA. He left Montgomery briefly for a shipyard job in Mobile. A young housewife refugee from the hills of Winston County, Charlene Wha-

The Montgomery Advertiser

Hank Williams (1923-1953). Williams's sad and lonely voice and manner, with lyrics to match, struck a responsive chord in the hardest of country hearts as his honky-tonk songs dominated the charts as no one else had in his five years at the top, 1949-53.

len, remembers Hank in Mobile as a never-do-well who was always dragging her husband, Howard Whalen, off for all-nighters at the port city's honky tonks.

After another stint in Montgomery, Hank was off to Nashville and by 1947 was a songwriter with Roy Acuff in country music's first music publishing firm. His heyday was 1949 to his death on New Year's Day, 1953. He dominated the charts with from three to seven hits per year including "Love Sick Blues" (1949), "Long Gone Lonesome Blues" (1950), "Cold, Cold Heart" and "Hey, Good Lookin" (1951), and "Jambalaya" and "Honky Tonk Blues" (1952). Buried next to his wife, Audrey Williams, in the Annex to Montgomery's Oakwood Cemetery, his marble shrine is emblazoned with cowboy hat, boots, guitar, and engravings highlighting big hits. But his epitaph is not at Oakwood but in the lyrics of his country music blues revealing shared perspectives with his rural southern listeners. Professor Flynt cites music critic D.K. Wilgus for one of these perspectives (in the spirit of Hank, Jr.'s "Family Tradition"): "He embodied drunken Saturday nights in the tavern and soul-saving Sundays in the country church ... he went 'honky-tonkin,' but knew he was 'Headed Down the Wrong Highway'; he cheated, was cheated on, cursed her 'Cheatin' Heart,' 'Dreamed About Mama Last Night,' and looked forward to the land 'Beyond the Sunset.' "

Hank's songs may not approach the complex legacy of the Southern family in the manner of Pat Conroy's **Prince of Tides,** but they touched the heart and nerves of the "poor but proud" unlettered masses, and more. As another country-music Williams, Don, related in "Good Ole Boys Like Me": "And those Williams' boys, they still mean a lot to me, Hank and Tennessee."

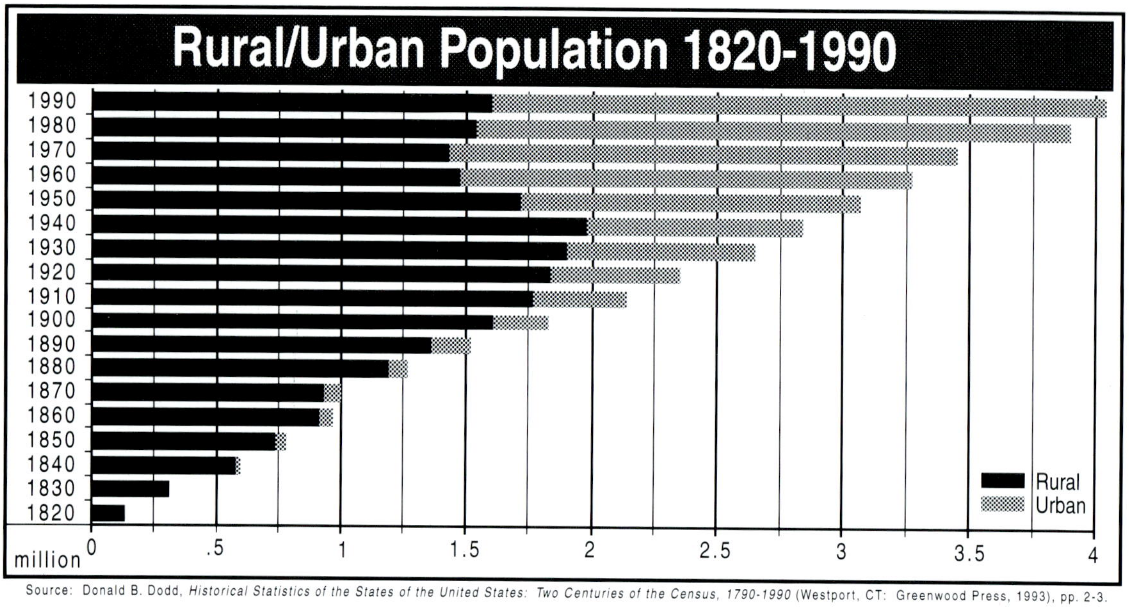

Source: Donald B. Dodd, *Historical Statistics of the States of the United States: Two Centuries of the Census, 1790-1990* (Westport, CT: Greenwood Press, 1993), pp. 2-3.

Photo by Don Newton, Jr., Birmingham Chamber of Commerce

Birmingham skyline at night

VII
Post-World War II Alabama

The Civil Rights Movement

Black churches and black ministers were the major forces behind the birth of the civil rights movement in Alabama and the nation. First Baptist Church (Colored), founded in 1867 as the first independent black Baptist church in Montgomery, was one which played a prominent role in the movement. A former slave, Nathan Ashby, was its first pastor. Over the years, this church, located across Ripley Street from the present Montgomery Police Station, became the church of the working class people and was traditionally dominated by its pastor. By the early 20th century it was the largest black church in the United States. In the 1950s, the Rev. Ralph D. Abernathy was its pastor.

Montgomery's wealthier black Baptists founded the Second Baptist in 1877 and shortly afterward renamed it Dexter Avenue Baptist Church. Shadowed by the state capitol, one block away atop Goat Hill, Dexter Avenue experienced a high turnover of pastors for their deacon-dominated congregation.

Into this post-World War II environment, as documented by Taylor Branch's **Parting the Waters,** entered one of the most brilliant scholar-preachers of the modern age, Vernon Johns. Raised in Farmville, Virginia, near Williamsburg, Johns relished tilling the soil almost as much as reciting poetry and studying the scripture in the pre-English versions. Self-educated, he was admitted to Oberlin College for his aptitude in German and Greek and became the top student, displacing Robert M. Hutchins, later longtime president of the University of Chicago. After graduation from Oberlin, Johns studied at the University of Chicago's School of Theology. His sermon "Transfigured Moments" in 1926 became the first sermon by a black minister in the prestigious **Best Sermons.** He subsequently succeeded Mordecai Johnson as pastor of the First Baptist Church of Charleston, West Virginia.

Like Johnson, Johns was a scholar comfortable with universities, but he also worked the soil and sold his farm produce on the street. He agreed with W.E.B. DuBois that blacks should seek political rights as well as the economic rights stressed by Booker T. Washington but, like Washington, Johns believed that the dignity and security of a people derived from its masses. Johns' sermon, "Mud is Basic," confirmed this roots identity and his "Segregation After Death" sermon referred, not only to racial segregation, but economic class segregation practiced by black elites such as those regularly participating in what Johns called the "fashion show" at Dexter.

Johns agreed with the Dexter deacons on excluding emotionalism from church, but he loved black spirituals. He was not happy when he was stopped from using them in services by the deacons who informed Johns this was "not done at Dexter." In response, Johns lectured the congregation on the significant distinctions between dignity, pride, and vanity.

Unsuccessful in reversing Dexter's social elitism, Johns turned his attention to the racial climate in Alabama's capitol city. Johns got charges filed in two cases of white men raping young black girls and one case to trial before acquittal. The other involved six white policemen and never got to

The Montgomery Advertiser

First Baptist Church, 347 North Ripley Street, was established in 1867 as the Columbus Street Baptist Church, a wooden structure that burned in 1912. Its third pastor, Andrew Stokes, a great orator and organizer, baptized 1,100 new members his first year and made First Baptist the largest black church in the United States until the great migration of 1917 created larger Chicago congregations. Stokes could also be a little high-handed, especially on money matters, and his proposed property exchanges in regard to rebuilding the new First Baptist Church caused some wealthier members to transfer to Dexter. Undaunted, Stokes asked the poorer members who remained to bring a brick a day to the new site and the "Brick-A-Day" church was dedicated five years later. By the time the Rev. Ralph Abernathy (inset) became pastor in 1952 (serving until 1961), Dexter-First Baptist relationships were cordial and cooperative with the more spacious First Baptist Church hosting particularly huge gatherings. One of the largest followed the freedom-rider beatings on May 21, 1961. Source: Branch, ***Parting the Waters*** *3-4, 25.*

Photo by Frank C. Williams Jr.

Dexter Avenue-King Memorial Baptist Church, 454 Dexter Avenue, is probably the best-known church in the United States. Land for the church was purchased in 1879 and the church opened in 1889, two years after the Normal School in Marion had moved to Montgomery to eventually become Alabama State University. Dexter emerged as the Alabama State faculty's primary church, thus Dexter became the most intellectual and least emotional of Montgomery's black churches. It was also politically active — notably so from the NAACP's early organizing efforts in Alabama through the pastorships of Vernon Johns (1948-1952) and Martin Luther King (1954-1960). The terrain between the church and the Capitol became especially explosive during the sit-in crisis on March 6, 1960, when 700 blacks from the church sought to pray on the Capitol steps and their route was blocked by about 5,000 angry whites. More than 400 law enforcement personnel separated the groups and pushed the blacks up the steps into the sanctuary. Governor Patterson watched from his Capitol office window. He was more involved in a similar occurrence at First Baptist after the freedom-rider beatings. Source: ***Touched by History,*** *5-6.*

trial. He also challenged segregation laws on the city buses and in a white restaurant without support although when exiting the restaurant ahead of the guns of customers he did retain the sandwich that he went in the place to get!

When the Montgomery Police Department strung together a series of beatings and killings of blacks, Johns delivered his sermon, "It's Safe to Murder Negroes in Montgomery," years later made famous by a TV special and a movie on Johns. The sermon was preceded by a KKK cross-burning the night before. Johns followed with the sermon, "When the Rapist is White." More to the chagrin of the Dexter deacons, Johns continued to sell farm produce and fish — finally doing so in the basement of the church after announcing his bargain prices from the pulpit! But his crowning insult was carrying a truckload of watermelons to the heart of his elitist detractors' homeland, the campus of Alabama State. After a stormy session, the Dexter deacons accepted Johns' resignation.

The deacons took their time in finding a replacement for Johns. They sought a traditional Dexter pastor, educated and trained, less controversial, and more conventional in dress, manner, and behavior than Johns. They decided to find a younger and less established man who could not give them such a battle. They found who they thought was the ideal man — Martin Luther King, Jr., son of the pastor of Ebenezer Baptist in Atlanta, and a graduate of Morehouse College in Atlanta, Crozier Theological Seminary in Chester, Pennsylvania, and who was pursuing a Ph.D. at Boston University. In Boston, King met and married Coretta Scott who grew up at Marion in rural Perry County, Alabama. Scott graduated from Antioch College before entering Boston's New England Conservatory of Music.

The Montgomery Bus Boycott, 1955-1956

"Jim Crow" — or legal segregation — laws developed in the antebellum north but spread to the south after the end of slavery as documented by Comer Vann Woodward in his well-titled book, **The Strange Career of Jim Crow.** The south may have gotten into legal segregation later than the north but made up for it by holding on to Jim Crow laws longer. In the 1950s, the laws still dominated everyday racial relations. A black person could not drink from a public water fountain unless it was especially marked "for colored only." Some states even required separate Bibles for the swearing in of witnesses in court.

Every day on Montgomery city buses, 40,000 black passengers put their dimes in the collection boxes next to the driver up front, got off the bus, and reboarded in the back to sit in the segregated black sections. Whites boarded from the front and took the front seats. If all seats were filled, the driver normally required blacks to stand and whites to take their seats. Some drivers enforced the rules with zeal. Almost all of the leaders of the thirteen-month Montgomery bus boycott, 1955-1956, were victims of such abuse. Vernon Johns indignantly left a bus after driver abuse but was unsuccessful in getting other passengers to join him. Alabama State English professor, Jo Ann Robinson, excited about going to Dannelly Field for a flight home to Cleveland for Christmas holidays, absentmindedly sat in the front section of a nearly empty bus. Suddenly the driver appeared

Photos from the Montgomery Advertiser

The Dexter Avenue-King Memorial Baptist Church Parsonage, 309 South Jackson Street. Martin Luther King, Jr., residence, 1954-60. On Monday, January 30, 1956, Coretta Scott King and a friend, Mary Lucy Williams, heard a heavy thump on the front porch and immediately moved to the back of the house. Coretta recalled they were in the middle of the guest bedroom "when there was a thunderous blast. Then smoke and the sound of breaking glass." Yolanda Denise "Yoki," then 3 months old and asleep in another bedroom, was unhurt. The porch was split and front windows blown out. Broken glass was scattered throughout the front of the parsonage, but the bus boycott's record of no one dying was preserved. Coretta Scott King, ***My Life with Martin Luther King, Jr.*** *(N.Y.: Avon Books, 1969, 1969), 118, 138.*

hovering over her with his hand drawn back as if to hit her saying "Get up from there! Get up from there!" Startled, she stumbled from the bus sobbing and stayed upset all the way to Cleveland. And Rosa Parks, whose December, 1955 arrest triggered the boycott, had been evicted by the same driver, James P. Blake, a decade earlier.

But the Rosa Parks of 1955 was not just another abused passenger. Described in **Eyes on the Prize** as "a quiet but strong-willed woman," she was a long-time NAACP Montgomery chapter secretary and the previous summer she had also attended a racial relations workshop at the Highlander School in Tennessee, infamous to conservatives as a training center for labor union and civil rights activists. Virginia Durr, wife of white attorney and former New Deal Administrator Clifford Durr, financed Parks'

Associated Press Photo

Coretta Scott King with her four children (L-R: Yolanda, Bernice Albertine, Dexter Scott, and Martin Luther King, III). Yolanda "Yoki" and M.L. King, III, "Marty" were born in Montgomery during Dr. King's tenure as pastor of Dexter Avenue Baptist Church. Yolanda Denise was born on November 17, 1955, less than three weeks before Rosa Parks was arrested in front of the Empire Theater for refusing to give up her bus seat. Martin Luther King, III, was born almost two years later, on October 23, 1957. On the fourth Sunday in January, 1960, when Yoki was 4 and Marty 2, Dr. King gave his final sermon as pastor of Dexter. His next child, a son, was born in the family's new home in Atlanta, and his name, after his dad's Montgomery church, was Dexter. Coretta Scott King, ***My Life with Martin Luther King, Jr.*** *(N.Y.: Avon, 1969), 118, 170, 190-191; Taylor Branch,* ***Parting the Waters*** *(N.Y.: Simon & Schuster, 1988), 385.*

Highlander education. It was a liberating experience for Parks: "I gained there strength to persevere in my work for freedom, not just for blacks but all oppressed people."

Montgomery's black leadership had been waiting for the right moment and the right person to protest mistreatment on the buses. Edgar Daniel Nixon, former head of the local NAACP chapter, had opposed protests based on earlier victims he considered unsuitable. He approved of Rosa Parks. The woman and the hour had met.

After Parks' arrest, Nixon moved quickly. Unable to reach black attorney

The Montgomery Advertiser

Holt Street Baptist Church, 903 South Holt Street, was the site of the first mass meeting on the Montgomery Bus Boycott. The night of December 5, 1955, about 5,000 black Montgomerians met in and around the church to pledge their continued support for the day-old boycott. Some of the crowd heard Dr. Martin Luther King for the first time. They were not disappointed. He praised Mrs. Parks and "the depth of her Christian commitment," and spoke of the injustice on the buses and how tired the people were of it, the moral and legal righteousness of their non-violent protest, and the "grim and bold determination" of the people "to gain justice on the buses in this city." From the Bible, King added his favorite quote on justice from the lowly herdsman Amos: "We are determined here in Montgomery to work and fight 'until justice runs down like water, and righteousness like a mighty stream!' " The Civil Rights Movement had found a leader, and later Maya Lin and the Southern Poverty Law Center a theme for a Civil Rights Memorial. Source: Taylor Branch, ***Parting the Waters*** *(N.Y.: Simon & Schuster, 1988), 138-141.*

Fred Gray, he called Clifford Durr and arranged for Mrs. Parks' bail. Nixon conferred with Ralph Abernathy, pastor of the First Baptist Church, after which he called 18 other black ministers to arrange a meeting. Meanwhile,

Jo Ann Robinson, in consultation with other leaders of the Woman's Political Council, decided to call a one-day bus boycott on the next Monday, December 5, 1955. Robinson worked all night running off 35,000 handbills on a mimeograph machine at Alabama State. The handbills were distributed to students in the all-black public schools, to be carried home to their parents. E.D. Nixon got one in the hands of *The Montgomery Advertiser's* Joe Azbell. Azbell's story, "Negro Groups Ready Boycott of Bus Lines," appeared Sunday, December 4, the day before the boycott was to begin. The word was out.

Early Monday morning, Coretta King interrupted her husband Martin's coffee to call him to the front window to see a slow moving bus: "Darling, it's empty!" The 26-year-old new pastor of Dexter Baptist drove around town to check other buses until he was satisfied the boycott was completely successful. Shortly thereafter, King was nominated to the leadership of the organization created to run the boycott, the Montgomery Improvement Association. Within hours, the young MIA leader addressed a crowd of more than 5,000 in and around the Holt Street Baptist Church:

> *... you know, my friends, there comes a time when people get tired of being trampled over by the iron feet of oppression ... we are here because we are tired now ... and we are not wrong in what we are doing ... If we are wrong — the Supreme Court of this nation is wrong ... if we are wrong — God Almighty is wrong! ... And we are determined here in Montgomery — to work and fight until justice runs down like water, and righteousness like a mighty stream!* (The last line is etched on the marble wall behind the Civil Rights Memorial on Washington Avenue in Montgomery.)

The civil rights movement had found a leader.

The movement to get better treatment on Montgomery buses was soundly defeated locally by Mayor "Tacky" Gayle and Police Commissioner Clyde Sellers — both of whom publicly joined the White Citizens' Council and refused to negotiate even minor concessions. Forced to "make a federal case out of it," the MIA had to pursue full desegregation of the buses to have a constitutional issue.

It was rough times for the boycotters. Initially, 325 car owners gave free rides to persons journeying too far to walk. As outside contributions permitted, the MIA bought station wagons and paid gas bills. Police harassment was continual. In one two-week span, 64 black drivers were put in jail for minor traffic violations. Jo Ann Robinson, in her book, **The Montgomery Bus Boycott and the Women Who Started It** (1987), noted that she received 17 traffic tickets during the boycott. Her picture window was shattered by a rock and her car splattered with acid — both by men dressed in Montgomery Police Department uniforms and driving marked squad cars. The homes of Dr. Martin Luther King and other MIA leaders were bombed. And the boycott dragged on.

In June 1956, a three-judge federal court voted two to one that segregation of city buses violated the equal protection clause of the 14th Amendment. Judges Richard Rives and Frank M. Johnson, Jr. voted in the majority. Five months later, the Supreme Court upheld their ruling. On December 21, 1956, the boycott ended and Mrs. Parks, Dr. King, and Rev. Abernathy boarded a city bus and sat in the front. The boycotters had won.

Montgomery's buses were desegregated. The civil rights movement was taking shape.

The Montgomery Bus Boycott propelled Dr. Martin Luther King, Jr. into national prominence. The 13 months of countering all the local power structure could throw at them also produced a network of financial and personnel support that transcended Montgomery and the boycott. Black ministers from 11 southern states met at Dr. King's father's church, Ebenezer Baptist, in Atlanta to consolidate their gains and decide on future plans. The Southern Christian Leadership Conference (SCLC) emerged from the meeting with Dr. M.L. King, Jr., as its president. Dr. King moved to Atlanta in early 1960. But the Civil Rights Movement did not leave Alabama.

The Freedom Riders

Although a 1946 Supreme Court case had ruled that segregated seating in interstate buses was unconstitutional, it was not carried out in the South. The Congress of Racial Equality (CORE) challenged state segregation laws in 1947 but the riders were arrested in North Carolina and served time. When James Farmer, a Howard University graduate and an advocate of Gandhian non-violence, became head of CORE in 1961, he thought it was time for the 1946 decision to be carried out. The CORE plan was to have an interracial group of "Freedom Riders" travel through the South. The blacks would sit in the front and whites in the back. At every rest stop, blacks would use the whites-only waiting rooms and try to use all the facilities.

On Mother's Day, 1961, two buses, a Greyhound and a Trailways, carrying Freedom Riders, left Atlanta for Birmingham. The Greyhound was attacked by a mob of 200 at the Anniston bus depot. The driver pulled away but the tires were slashed and flats forced the bus to stop just outside town. The mob, in hot pursuit, spilled out of some fifty cars to surround the bus and knock out several windows. A firebomb was tossed in the back while members of the mob barricaded the front door. Fortunately, a plainclothes state investigator, E.L. Cowling, pulled his revolver and got the door opened. Passengers exiting the smoking bus were beaten until arriving state troopers stopped it by firing warning shots. The injured passengers were ferried to the Anniston Hospital. Meanwhile, photos of the burning bus were distributed worldwide.

The Trailways bus pulled into Anniston an hour after the Greyhound had left. The riders bought sandwiches in the whites-only restaurant before reboarding the bus. Two black students sat in front seats. After conferring with Anniston policemen, eight white men boarded the bus, beat the two blacks on the front seat and two white Freedom Riders who came from the back to protest. The front spaces cleared, the eight whites sat in the middle of the bus and the driver pulled out for Birmingham.

In Birmingham the Klan was waiting in the terminal. By prior agreement with local authorities, they had 15 minutes to do their dirty work before the Birmingham police would be committed. On arrival, the eight Anniston whites lost themselves into the milling crowd. The Klan went to work with enthusiasm — to the point of hospitalizing seven bystanders. The Freedom Rider leader, Jim Peck, required 53 stitches to patch his head wounds. Interviewed at Hillman Hospital, he astonished reporters by declaring he intended to resume the ride the next day on the bus for Montgomery.

Meanwhile, in faraway Tokyo, the incoming President of the Birmingham Chamber of Commerce, Sidney Smyer, saw in the Japanese morning paper photographs of the Birmingham bus station carnage. The Japanese suddenly lost interest in Birmingham investments. Smyer, a stout segregationist, told his Birmingham colleagues that something must be done about Bull Connor.

The riders spent the night in the home of Rev. Fred Shuttlesworth and the next day he led them, 10 strong, to the Greyhound terminal across the street from Bull Connor's jail to catch the bus to Montgomery. Now protected by the Birmingham policemen, the riders were besieged for three hours by angry whites. Then Connor arrived to arrest them and put them in jail. Three riders were released separately and Connor came up with a cure for the other seven. He escorted them in unmarked cars to the Tennessee line and left them on the side of the road. The Justice Department, Governor John Patterson, and Birmingham city leaders, all walking political tightropes, were relieved. They underestimated Freedom Rider resolve. While Connor's convoy was moving north, 11 more riders were coming south from Nashville and the seven riders stranded on the Alabama-Tennessee line got automobile transportation — and promptly headed back south!

When the bleary-eyed riders finally got ready to be bused to Montgomery, the Greyhound driver, Joe Caverno, made a speech. Paraphrasing revolutionary era patriot Nathan Hale, Caverno announced: "I don't have but one life to give. And I don't intend to give it to CORE or the NAACP." He departed and the riders sang "Oh, Lord, Keep Your Eyes on the Prize." The riders were stranded again.

A distraught Attorney General Robert Kennedy sought unsuccessfully to get a Greyhound official to find a driver. He finally demanded to talk to "Mr. Greyhound" or whoever could secure one. An unhappy Caverno shortly reappeared at the terminal. Escorted by police and then state troopers, he roared for Montgomery at speeds close to ninety miles per hour. Montgomery Police Commissioner Sullivan reassured both the FBI office in Montgomery and the head of Alabama's highway patrol, Floyd Mann, that the riders would be protected by police in Montgomery and especially at the bus terminal.

On arrival in Montgomery, John Lewis, the leader of the riders, was being interviewed by the media when a dozen white men with baseball bats and lead pipes attacked. The media went down with the riders. Norman Ritter, the Time-Life bureau chief from Atlanta, was clubbed to the ground. Moe Levy of NBC News was slapped around and his camera smashed. Life photographer, Don Urbrock, was beaten in the face with his own camera. Bobby Kennedy's administrative assistant, John Seigenthaler, saw Susan Wilbur, a white woman rider, being pulled from a taxi and beaten by white women and a teen-ager and, announcing he was a federal agent, tried to get her in his car. He was hit in back of the head by a lead pipe and knocked unconscious. Two black men, Lewis, and William Barbee, were carried to a hospital by a black taxicab driver but a white male rider, Jim Zwerg, wasn't allowed to accompany them because of segregation laws. Lewis and Barbee were saved by Floyd Mann, who put a pistol to the head of a man with a baseball bat to stop the beating. After Commissioner Sullivan told reporters all white ambulances were out of service for repairs, the police allowed Zwerg to be taken by a black taxi to a Catholic hospital. The two white women riders escaped to a church where they phoned the police. The police put them on a train to Nashville. The scattered riders began showing up at the home of Rev. S.S. Seay, an active boycott leader five years earlier. Meanwhile, Jim Zwerg announced from St. Jude Hospital, as Peck had earlier in Birmingham, that the riders would continue the journey and they were "prepared to die."

Anniston, Birmingham, and Montgomery had a common theme — the police departments allowed white mobs to beat the Freedom Riders hoping this would discourage their continued journey and, when this failed, there was an attempt to get them out of town as soon as possible. After the beatings, in the latter two cities, the police arrived to restore order. If arrests were made, the riders were the ones arrested, apparently to appease the angry mobs. The riders were bloodied, an unsuccessful attempt to silence the media was made, and segregation laws were enforced. Except for the burning of the Anniston bus, the riders were protected by the state highway patrol between cities. The nation and world learned of two strong forces — local segregationists and determined civil rights activists. And local, state, and federal authorities learned what to expect from each other. The riders got the attention of the nation and taught the federal government that they expected them to enforce federal law and, in fact, if it was enforced, certain federal agencies would have to take the lead. Obviously the fight had just begun.

And it was not over in Montgomery. Despite promises to the contrary, the Montgomery police had disappeared as state and federal sources had predicted. Floyd Mann personally intervened and called in his state forces. Kennedy, at the Justice Department, closely followed the events after Anniston and assembled a hodgepodge of federal law enforcement officials to commit if all else failed. Alabama's Governor, John Patterson, had supported President Kennedy and both wanted to continue good relations. However, Patterson was acutely aware he was elected in 1958 because he "outsegged" his opponent, George Wallace, and his public statements followed his 1958 campaign rhetoric. President Kennedy had given lip service to black civil rights but was not ready to forfeit Southern political support without trying to maneuver around the issue. Bobby Kennedy was in the middle. Patterson wanted to assist President Kennedy without political risk to himself at home. Obviously decisive action from politicians was, at best, tentative.

Kennedy sent a force of 600 federal officials, spearheaded by federal marshals, to Maxwell Air Force base. After the Montgomery bus station beatings, 200 marshals were committed to the protection of the Freedom Riders, at the hospital and their new gathering place, Rev. Ralph Abernathy's First Baptist Church.

Martin Luther King flew to Montgomery to encourage the Freedom Riders and a mass meeting was called at Abernathy's church for 8 p.m. By nightfall, 1,500 blacks were jammed inside the building and twice that many whites were outside held back by marshals with nightsticks and yellow arm bands with "U.S. Marshal" stenciled on the side. Shuttlesworth arrived from Birmingham and with CORE's James Farmer in tow, made his way through the mob to the church.

The mob got progressively more violent. Automobiles were burned and the mob surged forward to throw rocks and bottles at marshals and break windows in the church. The marshals fired tear gas which drifted back into the crowded church. Kennedy committed the remainder of his Maxwell force who, unable to secure military transportation, arrived in post office mail trucks. At 3 a.m. the 1,500 blacks were still trapped in the church and the marshals were barely holding the crowd at bay. King became angry at Kennedy and Kennedy, all immediate resources exhausted, appealed to Patterson. Patterson declared martial law and sent in state police and the National Guard to disperse the mob. State police escorted King and his followers out of the church.

Two days after the church siege, 27 Freedom Riders, including James Farmer who at the last minute responded to a dramatic plea from a 17-year-old woman rider, left for Jackson, Mississippi, in two buses with a heavy state police convoy. They were met at the Mississippi line with an even larger convoy of Mississippi lawmen who escorted them to Jackson where they were arrested and jailed. The Mississippi judge gave them 60 days. And civil rights workers in the South got a new title — Freedom Riders. Their courage had captured the imagination and awe of blacks throughout the South.

Bombingham

Birmingham was infamous for the Mother's Day, 1961 mob attack on the Freedom Riders and the holiday vacation Police Commissioner, Bull Connor, gave his policemen. Also, between 1957 and 1963, 18 unsolved bombings in black neighborhoods yielded the city the infamous designation, "Bombingham." So when the Student Nonviolent Coordinating Committee (SNCC) had difficulty getting dramatic action from Albany, Georgia efforts with accompanying national media attention, Rev. Fred Shuttlesworth of Birmingham convinced them that Bombingham and Bull Connor wouldn't let them down. Shuttlesworth's home had been bombed to ruins in 1956 and he had been chain whipped when he tried to enroll his children at Phillips High School in 1957. Montgomery native and singer, Nat "King" Cole, had been beaten on stage during a 1956 performance. While raising nearly $75,000 preparing for the Birmingham demonstrations, Dr. King told the 28 audiences in 16 cities: "As Birmingham goes, so goes the South." To be launched against downtown businesses in March 1963, the plan was called Project "C" — C for "confrontation." The object was to desegregate lunch counters in downtown stores.

The Birmingham business community was not enthusiastic Connor supporters. The year before, some businesses who had about 80 percent black customers responded to a student boycott by taking down "Colored Only" signs and hiring some black clerks. The signs went back up after Connor cited them for building code violations. Connor was subsequently defeated for mayor by moderate white segregationist Albert Boutwell. On the other hand, in January 1963, new Governor George Wallace gave his

Grady's Gift: 1950s Black-White Relations in Segregated Birmingham

Photo courtesy of the New York Times

Howell Raines of Birmingham, editorial page editor, The New York Times

Birmingham native Howell Raines won a Pulitzer Prize for his 1991 article on "Grady's Gift," a personal memory of his family's maid, Grady Hutchinson, a cousin of Congressman Earl Hilliard. Raines was 7 when Grady, a recent graduate of Parker High, came to the Raines' household at age 16. Seven years later she left to seek a better life in New York City. In those 1951-1957 years, Grady shared her perspective on segregated Birmingham — what it was like to be poor and black, the routine brutality of the Birmingham police, widespread black support of the NAACP, and the suppressed rage of Grady towards the injustices. She told of "Dog Day," the one day blacks could attend the State Fair, and of the 1955 tragic lynching of Emmett Till in Mississippi, a story which brought tears to the eyes of young Howell. She taught Howell to see Birmingham as it was and that blacks were not happy with that reality. Grady also introduced Howell to Ernest Hemingway by reading **The Old Man and the Sea** to him when he had the mumps at age 8. Despite her own father's having committed suicide over job discrimination or her being denied a cherished dream of becoming a registered nurse because of segregation, she was still favorable to the Raines family. She was generous to Howell through his insecure youth by helping him develop confidence in his personal appearance, saying, on one occasion, "you look positively raping" (which she quickly changed to "ravishing").

Howell realized as an adult how much Grady had helped him make the adult choice of moderation and racial tolerance over that of segregation and racism. Although his hill country parents passed on their independence and identification with the downtrodden, he saw Grady as the one who "opened a door in his childhood to let the future in." On reflection, after a 1989 reunion between Grady and the Raines family, a mature Howell realized that Grady was the real inspiration behind his book that made him proudest — **My Soul Is Rested,** based on oral interviews with civil rights participants. More importantly, he identified Grady's special and personal gift to him in his youth — "the gift of a free and unhateful heart."

Source: Howell Raines, 'Grady's Gift,' The New York Times Magazine, December 1991, pp. 50-51, 89-90, 98-102. Now the editorial page editor of the *New York Times*, Raines is also the author of **Whiskey Man** (Viking, 1977) a novel coming out of summer visits to relatives in the hills of east Winston County, and **Fly Fishing Through the Midlife Crisis** (William Morrow, 1993).

famous inauguration speech proclaiming: "Segregation now! Segregation tomorrow! Segregation forever!"

The headquarters for the demonstrations and the place the marches downtown originated each day was the Sixteenth Street Baptist Church. Black millionaire A. G. Gaston had reservations about Project "C" but he made his Gaston Motel available to King's SCLC. The project leaders were King, his younger brother A. D., Abernathy, and Shuttlesworth. The routine of marching downtown, getting arrested, and being bailed out of jail soon exhausted the project's finances. The climax was to come with the arrest of King and Abernathy on Good Friday, April 12, 1963. They stayed in jail eight days before being released on bond. While King was in jail, a full-page ad taken out in the Birmingham News by members of the local white clergy called King a troublemaker who should have waited for the new government under Mayor Albert Boutwell to have a chance to act. He answered the call to wait for the clergymen and the world in a document now famous as the "Letter From the Birmingham Jail:"

> *... For years now I have heard the word "Wait!" It rings in the ear of every Negro with piercing familiarity. This "Wait" has almost always meant "Never." ... The nations of Asia and Africa are moving with jetlike speed toward gaining political independence, but we still creep at horse-and-buggy pace toward gaining a cup of coffee at a lunch counter ... when you see the vast majority of your twenty million Negro brothers smothering in an airtight cage of poverty in the midst of an affluent society; when you suddenly find your tongue twisted and your speech stammering as you seek to explain to your six-year-old daughter why she can't go to the public amusement park that has just been advertised on television, and see tears welling up in her eyes when she is told that Funtown is closed to colored children, and see ominous clouds of inferiority beginning to distort her personality by developing an unconscious bitterness toward white people; when you have to concoct an answer for a five-year-old son who is asking, "Daddy, why do white people treat colored people so mean?"; when you take a cross-country drive and find it necessary to sleep night after night in the uncomfortable corners of your automobile because no motel will accept you; when you are humiliated day in and day out by nagging signs reading "white" and "colored"; when your first name becomes "nigger," your middle name becomes "boy" (however old you are) and your wife and mother are never given the respected title "Mrs."; when you are harried by day and haunted by night by the fact that you are a Negro ... when you are forever fighting a degenerating sense of "nobodiness" — then you will understand why we find it difficult to wait. There comes a time when the cup of endurance runs over, and men are no longer willing to be plunged into the abyss of despair. I hope, sirs, you can understand our legitimate and unavoidable impatience ....* **(20th Century Alabama,** pp. 276-277.)

When King was out of jail, Project "C" entered a new phase, using Birmingham's black school children as demonstrators. Such use put less economic hardship on black families because the parents stayed on the job. The first group marched May 2 and 959 children, ages 6 to 18, were jailed.

The next day, as more than a thousand children gathered at the Sixteenth Street Baptist Church to march, Bull Connor brought in police dogs and firefighters with water hoses. With 100 pounds of pressure per square inch, the water hit with enough force to rip bark off trees. When the water hoses were turned on, A.G. Gaston was on the phone with attorney David Vann, the representative of the downtown stores. He was basically agreeing with Vann and the essence of the local white clergy's arguments. Vann recalled Gaston's words: "But Lawyer Vann, they've turned the fire hoses on a black girl. They're rolling that little girl right down the middle of the street. I can't talk to you no more."

Vann later noted that with Connor's attack on the children "in the twinkling of an eye the whole black community instantaneously consolidated ... behind Dr. King." Within three days, more than 2,000 demonstrators were jailed, some in a temporary prison at the Alabama state fairgrounds. Across the nation, millions watched television to see children blasted with water hoses and chased by police dogs. Governor Wallace sent in 500 state troopers. The world's eyes were on Birmingham.

Fearing damage to downtown stores, and conscious of Birmingham's worldwide negative image, the merchants were ready to negotiate. After a day's truce to clear the streets, the Senior Citizens Committee, representing 70 percent of Birmingham's businesses, agreed to desegregate the lunch counters and hire black workers in clerical and sales positions.

But the fight was not over. By radio, Connor called on whites to boycott the stores that agreed to integrate. And Robert Shelton, the Grand Dragon of the KKK, called for a rally outside the city. Shortly after the KKK meeting, bombs exploded at the Gaston Motel and the home of A.D. King. Crowds of blacks assembled at both sites. Connor's police and state troopers moved in and rioting erupted. Thirty-five blacks and five whites were injured. Seven stores were in flames.

President Kennedy dispatched soldiers to Fort McClellan. He stated he would not allow the agreement between the businessmen and the SCLC to be "sabotaged by a few extremists." Pledging to uphold the law of the land, he observed that "those who labored so hard to achieve the peaceful, constructive settlement of last week can feel nothing but dismay at the efforts of those who would replace conciliation and good will with violence and hate." The President's works and resolve quieted the city. The new mayor, Albert Boutwell, honored the negotiated settlement. *The Birmingham News* headline the day Mayor Boutwell was elected seemed even more appropriate now: "A New Day Dawns for Birmingham."

The Stand in the Schoolhouse Door

Even Bull Connor seemed to have seen the error of his ways, in a modest, tactical sense. At the request of Governor Wallace, Connor addressed a White Citizens Council's meeting in Tuscaloosa on the eve of an attempted integration of the University of Alabama. He told the council members to stay away from the University as a confrontation would play into the hands of the Kennedys — "that little old Bobby-soxer and his brother the president." The crowd saw no irony in his final statement: "If we don't have any trouble, we can beat 'em at their own game."

On June 11, 1963, Wallace honored a campaign pledge by literally standing in the schoolhouse door to stop two black students, James Hood and Vivian Malone, from registering. Journalist Wayne Greenhaw, author of the recent **Montgomery: The Biography of a City,** noted it was a "well-orchestrated show of defiance, where even the spot where he stood just under the eave of the front doorway to Foster Auditorium had been marked in white chalk." On cue, Wallace spoke out against "The unwelcomed, unwanted, unwarranted, and force-induced intrusion." Deputy Attorney General Nicholas Katzenbach left with the two students. Shortly thereafter "as had been planned by the federal government and Wallace," six trucks of federalized National Guard pulled into the parking lot. Alabama National Guard General Henry Graham, backed by federal marshals, asked Wallace to step aside. After a statement of opposition, the Governor complied. The Governor's approach served his political needs yet integrated the University of Alabama without violence. And Wallace became the recognized Southern leader of massive resistance.

The Sixteenth Street Baptist Church Bombing

The night after Governor Wallace stood in the schoolhouse door, President John Kennedy spoke on national television proposing legislation giving all Americans the right to be served in all public facilities. Assassinated in Dallas, President Kennedy didn't see the passage of the Civil Rights Act of 1964, his and President Johnson's answer to the letter from the Birmingham Jail.

It was a violent time. In the fall of 1963, Birmingham faced a court order to admit the first black students to public schools. At West End High, white cheerleaders and football players organized a movement to support integrated classes. Other students marched and threw rocks to enforce a segregationist school strike.

And Sunday, September 15, 1963, was the annual Youth Day at the Sixteenth Street Baptist Church. Four young girls in the basement ladies' room, dressed in white from head to toe, were making final preparation for their big day with other church youths to run the main service for the adults at 11 o'clock. Maxine McNair, a schoolteacher and the mother of the youngest girl of the four, Denise, age 11, was engaged in a Sunday school class titled "The Love That Forgives." Suddenly a loud explosion shook the entire church and the class was showered with plaster. The stairs to the basement were blocked and the large stone staircase outside had vanished. McNair, searching desperately for her only child, came upon her father sobbing and she screamed at him "Daddy, I can't find Denise!" The man helplessly replied, "She's dead, baby. I've got one of her shoes." He held out a girl's white dress shoe. Chris McNair traveled from his own Lutheran Church to the Sixteenth Street Baptist and finally to the hospital where he found his wife, Maxine, and her father. He soon went back downtown to accumulate the items the family would need for the funeral. Everywhere he went white sales clerks who had seen him on television burst into tears. McNair had confused emotions. He was sure white people had just killed his daughter in church but the same afternoon dignified, overwrought white

Associated Press Photo

Face of Christ blown out of Sixteenth Street Baptist Church stained glass window (framed by the crossed shotguns of Birmingham policemen).

strangers knocked at his door to express their condolences. Some arrived in cars bearing Confederate license plates.

It was a confusing time. Two Eagle Scouts, leaving a preacher-led segregationist rally, fired their new pistol at two black youths riding double on a bicycle, killing the 13-year-old on the handlebars. On Dynamite Hill hired bodyguards protected the homes of wealthy blacks against follow-up bombers.

And a young white lawyer, Charles Morgan, passionately addressed the Young Men's Business Club of Birmingham:

> *Those four little girls were human beings. They had lived their fourteen years in a leaderless city; a city where no one accepts responsibility, where everyone wants to blame somebody else .... Birmingham is a city in which the major industry, operating from Pittsburgh, never tried to solve the problem. It is a city where four little Negro girls can be born into a second-class school system, live a segregated life, ghettoed in their own little neighborhoods, restricted to Negro churches, destined to ride in Negro ambulances to Negro wards of hospitals or to a Negro cemetery. Local papers, on their front and editorial pages, call for order and then exclude their names from obituary columns. And who is really guilty? Each of us. Each citizen who has not consciously attempted to bring about peaceful compliance with the decisions of the Supreme Court of the United States .... Every person in this community who has in any way contributed during the past several years to the popularity of hatred is*

Associated Press Photo

The large crater was dug by the explosive thrown into the Sixteenth Street Baptist Church basement, killing four young black girls. The powerful blast blew out the windows of the building across the street.

Alabama Bureau of Travel and Tourism

Stained glass window donated by the people of Wales, United Kingdom, to the Sixteenth Street Baptist Church in Birmingham.

at least as guilty, or more so, than the demented fool who threw the bomb.
20th Century Alabama, pp. 282-283.

On Wednesday, September 18, 8,000 braved the vigilantes and jeep patrols to attend the giant funeral by Dr. King for three of the four young girls. Among the mourners were 800 Birmingham area pastors of both races, making it by far the largest interracial gathering of clergy in the city's history.

Following up on Charles Morgan's speech, attorneys from the Young Men's Business Club successfully petitioned to have the city's commission form of government replaced by a mayor-council form. Thus Bull Connor was removed from office. One new white commission member, George G. Seibels, won black support with fairness and, with it, the mayor's office in 1967. Civil rights attorney Arthur Shores became the first black councilman the same year followed four years later by the second — current mayor of Birmingham Richard Arrington. In 1973, 10 years after his daughter was killed in the Sixteenth Street Baptist Church bombing, Chris McNair was elected as one of the Jefferson County representatives to the state legislature. Today, across the street from the church, is a modern facility housing the Birmingham Civil Rights Institute. Admission is free and the featured attraction is a self-directed chronological tour of exhibits depicting the major events of the Civil Rights Movement.

The Selma March

Less than a year after the Birmingham demonstration, M.L. King and the SCLC were in Selma. A 54-mile, four-day march to Montgomery was planned to dramatize the need for a Voters Rights Act to expedite black voter registration in the south. Joe Smitherman was the Mayor and Wilson Baker was in charge of the Selma police but the "Bull Connor" of Selma was the sheriff of Dallas County, Jim Clark. Smitherman reflected: "They picked Selma just like a movie producer would pick a set. You had the right ingredients. Clark, in his day, had a helmet liner like General Patton, an Eisenhower jacket, and a swagger stick ...."

Selma was ripe for voter registration. Although blacks made up about one-half the voting-age population of Dallas County, only 1 percent were registered to vote, compared to 65 percent of whites. In Selma, only 156 of the city's 15,000 voting-age blacks were on the rolls. The registration office was open only on the first and third Mondays of each month, and 100 people would stand in line on a given day with only 10 getting registered to vote. In King's not-as-well-known "Letter from a Selma Jail," he asks, "Have you ever been required to answer 100 questions on government, some abstruse even to a political science specialist, merely to vote? ... This is Selma, Alabama, where there are more Negroes in jail with me than there are on the voting rolls."

Two months of piecemeal registrations preceded partial marches toward Montgomery. Early media high points were photographs of Sheriff Clark violently pushing one black woman down the street with a billy club and whacking another in the head as three deputies held her down. It was not Clark's best day, as just before the photograph, the woman, Annie Lee Cooper, had punched him not once, but three times — knocking the bulky

Alabama Bureau of Travel and Tourism

Edmund Pettus Bridge, scene of "Bloody Sunday," March 7, 1965, and launching point for the four-day Selma-to-Montgomery march two weeks later.

lawman to the ground! The local reaction took a turn for the worse with the police killing a black demonstrator, Jimmie Lee Jackson, in nearby Marion, Alabama.

Then on "Bloody Sunday," March 7, 1965, Hosea Williams and John Lewis led marchers on the first scheduled march to Montgomery. They were met at Edmund Pettus Bridge over the Alabama River by Alabama state troopers commanded by Major John Cloud. The Major gave the marchers two minutes to disperse then ordered "Troopers, Advance." Tear gas was fired and the lawmen on horseback charged into the protestors. Mayor Smitherman recalled, "When that beating happened at the foot of the bridge, it looked like war ... (and) the wrath of the nation came down on us."

From Atlanta King sent telegrams to prominent clergymen across the nation to join him in Selma Tuesday, March 9, for a minister's march to Montgomery. Faced by Federal Judge Frank M. Johnson's injunction not to march until after a hearing on the matter, King led 1,500 marchers to the bridge, asked Rev. Ralph Abernathy to lead a prayer, then withdrew. Some of the marchers had come a long way to Selma and were disappointed. King asked them to stay a few days longer. That night, three white Unitarian ministers were attacked by whites outside a black restaurant, Walker's Cafe, and one, Rev. James Reeb, died. The killing of the white minister stirred a nation unmoved by the earlier killing of Jackson.

The Montgomery Advertiser

Three Alabama veterans of the Civil Rights Movement: Ralph Abernathy, Rosa Parks, and Coretta Scott King.

In the Montgomery hearing, Judge Johnson ruled the protesters had the legal and constitutional right to march. President L.B. Johnson federalized the Alabama National Guard and ordered 1,800 to watch over the march. He also dispatched 2,000 Army troops, 100 FBI agents, and 100 federal marshals. On Sunday, March 21, the Selma-to-Montgomery march finally got under way. Eight thousand began the march but on the final leg of the four-day sojourn, 25,000 people moved on the capitol. As they passed Dexter Baptist Church, Coretta King reflected back 10 years to the boycott days when only blacks were in the movement. Now blacks and whites marched together. And the movement's leaders were out in force — Rosa Parks, Roy Wilkins of the NAACP, Whitney Young of the National Urban League, A. Philip Randolph of the Brotherhood of Sleeping Car Porters, and John Lewis of SNCC.

Dr. King walked up the steps to the front of the capitol and turned to address the crowd and the world. He recalled Sister Pollard's boycott comment on being asked if she was tired of walking: "My feets is tired, but my soul is rested" (**My Soul Is Rested** is the title of a book of civil rights interviews by Howell Raines.) He commented that even with the anticipated passage of the Voters Rights bill, voter registration would be a long, hard

THE JUDGE WHO CHANGED CIVIL RIGHTS: Jack Bass on Judge Frank M. Johnson Jr.

Judge Frank Minis Johnson Jr.'s landmark decisions in voting rights and desegregation cases in Alabama 30 years ago made him one of the most hated men in the South — now he is revered for his courage. Today, Johnson is a senior judge on the 11th U.S. Circuit Court of Appeals. The violence that tried to deny what Civil War-era constitutional amendments had promised is history. The hopes of the Civil Rights Act of 1964 and the Voting Rights Act of 1965 are now 30-year legacies.

But when President Dwight Eisenhower appointed Johnson in 1955 to the district court bench in Montgomery, the struggle had only begun. He would receive death threats and require constant protection from federal marshals. He would become the legal conscience in the heart of Old Dixie.

In 1961 Johnson enjoined the Ku Klux Klan from further violence after a planned assault at the Greyhound bus station in Montgomery bloodied "freedom riders" who had arrived from Northern states. The hearings exposed Ku Klux Klan secrets, including a bitter rivalry between leaders, and evidence revealed a conspiracy in attacks on freedom riders in Montgomery, Anniston and Birmingham.

When a voting rights march in 1965 from Selma to Montgomery ended in nationally televised assaults by state lawmen, Johnson issued an injunction to halt a second march until he could hold hearings. He privately warned lawyers for Martin Luther King, Jr., that he would jail the civil rights leader if he violated the order and marched anyway. After four days of hearings that recorded widespread abuse and officially sanctioned violence against blacks attempting to register to vote, Johnson issued an order that he said reached the outer limits of what is constitutionally allowed. Johnson's approach applied to constitutional wrongs the same measure of proportionality used in civil and criminal law — the greater the wrong, the greater the penalty. Or in this case, remedy. "It seems basic to our constitutional principles that the extent of the right to assemble, demonstrate and march peaceably along the highways and streets in an orderly manner should be commensurate with the enormity of the wrongs that are being protested and petitioned against," Johnson said. "In this case, the wrongs are enormous. The extent of the right to demonstrate against these wrongs should be determined accordingly."

In an early voting rights case, Judge Johnson noted that Alabama officials had routinely ignored state literacy requirements to register whites to vote, but enforced them zealously against blacks. His remedy: The least restrictive qualifications for whites would be the standard for blacks as well.

Lyndon Johnson once said that he would not have to be president if his name were Frank Johnson. "What he was saying," Bill Moyers, who worked for Lyndon Johnson in the White House, explained, was that

Judge Frank Johnson had been able, by a series of decisions, to bring the moral force and legal force of the U.S. government behind the kind of changes that we were trying to bring about in Washington. It was a recognition of Johnson's ability to accomplish justice through the courts in a less tortuous path than through Congress." During 24 years as a trial judge, Johnson fashioned relief that transformed the law in school desegregation, voting rights, jury selection, First Amendment issues, gender discrimination, and treatment of mental patients and prison inmates.

Johnson took on critics who charged that judicial activism was fundamentally at odds with neutral principles of law. "In my view, the doctrine of neutral principles robs the Constitution of its vitality. It freezes constitutional thinking in the interest of theoretical purity. The framers were pragmatic men and the Constitution is a practical blueprint. Its genius lies in its generality. Perfect logical consistency has always given way to practical distinction, as well it should."

To Judge Johnson, one principle guided him as a federal judge — the supremacy of law. "It is the obligation of every judge to see that justice is done within the framework of the law. I have attempted to fulfill that obligation by applying the rule of law to the facts before me ... I am confident that my faithful adherence to the rule of law has yielded true justice," he said.

As to right and wrong, Judge Johnson received inspiration from a quote from Lincoln kept under a glass paperweight on his desk: "I'll do the very best I know how — the very best I can; and I mean to keep doing so until the end. If the end brings me out all right, what is said against me won't amount to anything. If the end brings me out wrong, ten angels swearing I was right would make no difference."

In the end his most severe critic, former Governor George C. Wallace, stated he had been wrong and Judge Johnson right. And the Alabama House of Representatives, which once urged Congress to impeach Johnson, in 1992 voted unanimous praise for the naming of the Montgomery Federal Courthouse in his honor.

Excerpted from Jack Bass' "The Judge who Changed Civil Rights," ABA Journal. December, 1994. Bass is the author of **Taming the Storm: The Life and Times of Judge Frank M. Johnson Jr. and the South's Fight Over Civil Rights,** (N.Y.: Doubleday, 1993).

road but, in perspective, not long. "How long? Not long. Because you shall reap what you sow. How long? Not long ... because the arc of the moral universe is long, but it bends toward justice. How long? Not long. Because mine eyes have seen the glory of the coming of the Lord."

On August 6, 1965, President Johnson signed into law the Voters Rights Act in the presence of Rosa Parks and Dr. Martin Luther King, Jr. A year later, 9,000 blacks had registered to vote in Dallas County. Sheriff Jim Clark was voted out of office.

The tragedy was not over. As volunteers drove marchers back to Selma, three Bessemer Ku Klux Klansmen shot and killed a Detroit housewife, Mrs. Viola Liuzzo. Acquitted of murder by an all-white Lowndes County jury, they were sentenced a maximum of 10 years by U.S. District Judge Frank M. Johnson for violating Mrs. Liuzzo's civil rights. And in 1968, in Memphis, Tennessee, Dr. Martin Luther King, Jr. was killed while supporting a sanitation workers' strike.

From the Montgomery Bus Boycott of 1955-56 to the assassination of Dr. King was what Wayne Greenhaw called "A powerful time." It featured more social change, more court decisions, and more civil rights legislation than any decade in United States history. And a major setting for these momentous events was the state of Alabama. The tragedies are many and they are immortalized in marble in Maya Lin's Civil Rights Memorial less than a block from where it all started, the Dexter Avenue Baptist Church.

From Big Jim to Little Jim: Alabama Politics Since World War II

In 1946, "Big Jim" Folsom (6-feet-8 and 245 pounds), accompanied by a hillbilly band, the "Strawberry Pickers," made more than 300 "turnip greens and corn bread" type speeches throughout Alabama. His homespun campaign rhetoric included promises for teacher raises, old-age pensions, rural roads, constitutional revision to reapportion the legislature and repeal the poll tax, and getting tough with the "Big Mules" (the interests). Although he faced a hostile legislature after his election, Folsom got bills for a teacher raise, a nine-month school term, a small old-age pension, and an anti-masking law against the KKK. His administration built 3,000 miles of farm-to-market roads. Folsom's second administration featured another teacher's raise, a $110 million bond amendment for school buildings, a Competitive Bid Act, $250 million expenditures on farm-to-market roads, a general anti-segregation stand, an increased rate of industrialization, and an expansion of the State Docks. A considerable welfare program included legislation to get federal funds for hospitals under the Hill-Burton Act, the establishment of the Pensions and Security Department, and additional services for the mentally ill, the deaf, and the blind.

The governor between the two Folsom terms, Gordon Persons (1951-1955), secured bills to raise teachers' salaries, establish the first statewide educational television network in the nation, fulfilled a campaign pledge to reduce the cost of auto tags to $3, appropriate $1 million for health and welfare, and float bond issues of $25 million for roads and $100 million for school construction. Poor health prevented his participation in the 1958 election. (A homespun perspective on the Folsom-Persons years and rural socio-economic life in the 1950s is in the sidebar on "Uncle Ben.")

As no candidate received a majority in the 1958 Democratic primary, a runoff was held between Attorney General John Patterson and Circuit Court Judge George Wallace. Patterson's father, Albert J., had been murdered in 1954 by Phenix City criminals after being nominated for Attorney General on a platform to clean up "Sin City." John subsequently secured the nomination and, as Attorney General, pursued the "clean-up of Phenix City" with Governor Persons and a special circuit judge, Walter B. Jones of Montgomery. Attorney General Patterson also acquired a segregation image fostered by shrewd use of early TV "news" releases for his opposition to the

The Montgomery Advertiser

Morris Dees and the Southern Poverty Law Center: Dees grew up in rural Montgomery County near Mount Meigs and graduated from the University of Alabama Law School. Early developing a knack for making money, he combined his business skills with a concern for the rights of the downtrodden to found the Southern Poverty Law Center, now on Washington Avenue, one block south of Dexter Baptist Church. Fronted by an impressive marble Civil Rights Memorial by Vietnam Memorial designer Maya Lin, the Center, through effective direct mail solicitations, is one of the best-financed non-profit organizations in the United States. The Center's 1990s focus is on fostering racial toleration and combating terrorist activities of white supremacist hate groups such as the Ku Klux Klan. Source: Wayne Greenhaw, ***Montgomery: The Biography of a City*** *(Montgomery: The Advertiser Company, 1993), 109-110.*

'Uncle Ben': Preacher, Peddler and Politician (1893-1962)

Uncle Ben Dodd was one of the more picturesque characters ever to come out of the North Alabama hill country. "Bent over" from a coalmining accident, he used his handicap to good advantage in business, politics, and everyday life. To his unique appearance he added a flair for the colorful, a comical wit, and the ability to entertain. He loved life and really liked people.

An ordained Missionary Baptist preacher for 41 years, Uncle Ben, as did most ministers of his day, preached on Sundays but worked during the week — mainly in the coal mines of Walker County. After a broken back in the coal mines and rheumatism crippled him with a crooked back, he pursued less strenuous occupations. He did some farming, worked as a salesman, and operated a store and post office at Manchester.

Roy Rose, son-in-law of Uncle Ben, recalled a part of Ben's tenure as the Republican Postmaster at Manchester before the "New Deal." One day Uncle Ben walked into his store to find a number of his Democratic friends. He mournfully complained, "What is the world coming to?" "What's wrong?" chorused his audience. "Some Republican broke into my smokehouse and stole half my meat." "How did you know it was a Republican?" asked the group. Uncle Ben smugly replied, "Because if it had been a Democrat, he would have stolen all the meat." Later, when he was about to give up his position as postmaster, some of the same folk asked when he was going to move out. "Soon as they can find a Democrat who can read and write," Uncle Ben joyfully reported.

After being replaced as postmaster by a literate Democrat, Ben moved his family to Haleyville. Uncle Ben soon became the local insurance agent for James E. Folsom's Cullman agency. "Big Jim" occasionally spent the night at the Dodd house, a large yellow house with a front porch facing a long sidewalk leading down to the eastern entrance of Haleyville's main street. Uncle Ben's wife, Alta, recalled "Big Jim" being so tall she had to put a chair at the foot of the bed to hold his feet. She also remembers being embarrassed by his risque ribbings. Once a group of people gathered around Big Jim's car on main street as he and Uncle Ben were about to depart on an insurance foray to surrounding towns. Alta watched from the porch. Just before leaving, Big Jim paused and tipped his hat toward the porch and to the amusement of the crowd and chagrin of Alta, shouted in a loud voice, "Missus Dodd, I shore did enjoy spending the night with you."

Uncle Ben recalled Big Jim's patterning himself after Huey P. Long, the "Kingfish" of Louisiana. "Every man a king but no one wears a crown." While driving through a small town one day, Jim pointed to a bank and said "Ben, when I'm governor, I'm going to break up all of these banks and give the money to the people." Ben briefly explained the banking process and thought to himself that no one so naive could ever be governor! Uncle Ben and Big Jim later had a falling out over an insurance matter and Ben felt wronged. Perhaps a bit unknowledgeable about the intricacies of business, but with a big heart and reconciling nature, Big Jim, on becoming governor, called Uncle Ben. Stating he knew they had their grievances and wanted to make it up to him, Jim invited Ben to come to Montgomery and he would find Ben a good job. Hillbilly to the core, with always more pride than possessions, Uncle Ben told the generous governor, "Jim, you don't have anything I want!"

After his insurance experience, Uncle Ben ran routes as a wholesaler to country stores. He initially operated out of his car but by the late 1940s Dodd Sales Company of Haleyville, Alabama, had 10 trucks on the road selling cigarettes, cigars, candy, dry goods, and drug sundries (patent medicines, including their own "D & D" Cough Syrup) to the country and small town stores of Northwest Alabama. Although Uncle Ben spent a lot of time at the home office in Haleyville where, among other things, he hosted numerous checker games and secured a local reputation as a hard man to beat, he was most "at home" on the road — preferring a haphazard route, chosen seemingly by the vehicle, to a systematic route on a regular schedule. His intermittent visits to the small country stores in Winston, Walker, Cullman, Lawrence, Franklin, Marion, and Fayette counties were highlights of the daily social life centered around the crossroads store because Uncle Ben could be counted on for spicy comments and jokes on politics, religion, or any aspect of contemporary affairs. He would, upon request, do a buck dance, tell a joke, or linger around a pot-bellied stove playing checkers for hours with the local champions — joining them in chewing tobacco (Red Ox Twist and Brown Mule chewed together were his favorites because they "made a good team") and spitting in the ashes around the stove with an occasional well-placed squirt into the white-hot section of the stove for a spectacular zinging-sizzling sound. If the store owner was persistent, Uncle Ben would also ramble out to his vehicle and come back with an armful of "specials," often to the protest of the merchant who wanted something he bought "last time" — white cotton sox, nylon hose, a box of Stanback sold under cost, or whatever. After one or two specials were purchased, the item initially requested would be sought — a burrowing operation into the center of the pile of goods, which to the amazement of everyone except Uncle Ben, would sometimes actually yield the desired object.

All the while he would continue a stream of homespun witticisms:

Merchant: "Uncle Ben, do you have any samples?" Uncle Ben: "Didn't you hear?" Merchant: "Hear what?" Uncle Ben: (with a slap on his knee and a hardy laugh) — "The sample end of our factory burned out last week."

Merchant: "Hey, I need this, what's it sell for?" Uncle Ben: "Two dollars." Merchant: "Two dollars! So and so only gets a dollar and half!" Uncle Ben: "Why didn't you buy it from him?" Merchant: "He was out." Uncle Ben: "Oh, that's different. When we're out, we sell it for a dollar."

Companions of these sojourns, often sons Bobby or Don, heard some of the same lines over and over, but Ben generally did not repeat a story at the same store, and he was also careful to gear his approach to the particular buyer's personality. He would admonish his sons:

"You can mention religion here because Brother Smith is a good Missionary Baptist, but don't mention politics because he is the most pig-headed Democrat I have ever seen."

"Don't try to sell him any knives, about half of the last batch he bought were stolen."

"Don't mention Christmas goods, he still has jewelry and fireworks left over from last year."

"Don't ask him if he is any kin to the guy who runs the store down the road. They are brothers but they hate each other."

"Look around the store and see what he is out of or about out of and go bring it in while I talk to him about religion. Don't mention specials or he won't buy anything."

"Carry in the buttons, thread, and nylon hose samples for Mrs. Jones while I sell Mr. Jones some auto accessories. If she looks our way, ask about her health. She'll tell you about her operation. Listen sympathetically but if she starts our way act as if you're going to take the buttons back to the truck. If we don't keep them apart we won't sell either one of them anything."

"This guy's one of them smart-alecky Yankees who thinks he's the world's greatest buyer. If you say something is $2.00, he'll say, 'give you $1.50.' If he asks the price of anything, add 50 percent to the regular price and don't go down a cent. I'll go down some but not to the standard price. He's a pain in the neck but it's been a slow day today and we'll stop."

"This guy's a compulsive thief. He'll steal something before we leave. If you see what he gets let me know but don't say anything to him, I'll add it to the cost of something he buys. Don't get mad at him, he's one of the best customers we have."

"This is the crabbiest person I know. Don't offer to shake hands with him because he will refuse. Don't say anything. We will drink a Dr. Pepper, pay for it, and start to leave. If he wants anything he'll tell us on our way out."

"Mrs. Johnson's a good ole lady but her checks always bounce. She won't buy anything without writing a check. It will bounce but she'll pay us the next time we're around. It's sort of like a consignment."

"Uncle Joe is a bootlegger but a pretty good fellow otherwise. Don't look shocked when he pays the entire bill in quarters and half-dollars."

Of course most of the customers were normal, cordial, accommodating, thrifty, and the sort of individuals one likes to be around — typical hill country merchants. They were respected community leaders who paid for their purchases with cash and wanted a reasonable price — nothing more and nothing less. They were solid, hard-working, citizens and their stores were the cultural centers of the community life of rural Alabama.

Uncle Ben's once-a-month expeditions throughout Northwest Alabama carried him to such interesting and quaint communities as Wolf Creek, Wren, Needmore, Helican, Belgreen, Glen Allen, Cordova,

Corona, Townley, Detroit, Boston, Kansas, Texas, Sipsey, Bug Tussle, Slick Lizard, Arkadelphia, and Rabbittown.

But casual management takes its toll and Dodd Sales Company went under. Refusing to bankrupt, Uncle Ben liquidated all assets to pay debts and moved to a 15-acre farm with an outdoor toilet and a dug well on the back porch. Buying a '37 Chevy coupe on credit for $375, he ran for the legislature and beat Judge Frank M. Johnson's brother by nine votes.

He was the only Republican legislator in the Gordon Persons' administration and later the only Republican sheriff in Alabama. As the lone Republican in the House of Representatives, his speeches were often prefaced with the comment that the House had heard the majority point of view on the issue at hand and as the head of the minority party in the House he would present the minority report. On leaving the House Chamber on one occasion someone asked him where he was going. "To caucus" was Uncle Ben's reply.

Not only an amusing House member, Uncle Ben was also effective. His timely speech in favor of the Persons Administration's "Three-Dollar Tag Bill" helped pass the measure. Governor Persons asked him what he could do for him and Uncle Ben instantly replied, "a state highway between Jasper and Haleyville." He got it. He also secured local legislation including bills which made it possible to have local bond issues for Winston County factories; to permit a branch bank in Double Springs; to outlaw "Scrip" payments for jury duty which courthouse bankers bought at a discount; and a bill to place Winston County highways under the State Highway Department as a "captive county." As a consistent supporter of administration measures, he also successfully supported the state employment applications of many Northwest Alabama residents, especially as state troopers.

For his uniqueness as a Republican officeholder, even before the Ike years, he was dubbed "Mr. Republican" by some Alabama journalists. To friends and relatives, however, he was just plain ole "Uncle Ben" who dabbled a little in politics. Some said if he were a Democrat he might have been governor. To Uncle Ben, that was like saying if he were a Catholic, he might have been Pope. He was a Baptist and he was a Republican, and in his words, "nuff said."

Sources: Informal conversations through the years with Ben G. and Alta Savannah Dodd,G.R. "Bobby" Dodd, Roy and Dot Rose, and Lanta Sims.

NAACP, desegregated public schools, and the black boycotts of buses in Montgomery and stores in Tuskegee. Wallace, a former legislator and Folsom supporter before becoming circuit judge, shared a segregationist position with Patterson, but his position was not so widely publicized. Patterson "outsegged" Wallace 315,353 to 250,451.

Patterson's administration secured a $100 million bond issue for classroom construction, a $60 million bond amendment for roads, a

The Montgomery Advertiser

Big Jim to Little Jim: Immediate post-World War II Governor "Big Jim" Folsom gives a big bear hug to a 5-year-old "Little Jim." Big Jim's two administration likewise responded to the little folks. And, as things turned out, Big Jim passed on more than a hug — the political leadership of the state — as Little Jim became governor in 1993.

$7 million bond issue for inland dock construction in the Tennessee Valley, and a 10 percent tax on whiskey to be divided between mental health and old-age assistance.

Wallace won the 1962 election in a runoff with Ryan DeGraffenried of Tuscaloosa and dominated Alabama politics for a quarter of a century ... until he retired in 1986. In his inaugural speech from the brass star that marks the spot Jefferson Davis became President of the Confederacy in 1861, Wallace, a century later, again appealed to Southern nationalism and the pursuit of yct another lost cause: "In the name of the greatest people that have ever trod this earth, I draw the line in the dust and toss the gauntlet before the feet of tyranny ... and say ... segregation now, segregation tomorrow, segregation forever." Besides being pro-segregation, the Wallace administrations supported education, highways, and aid to the handicapped. In his first term, Wallace obtained an additional annual appropriation of $44 million for education. In 1965 he added a $116 million bond issue for education and launched a statewide program of post-high school educational facilities yielding 12 junior colleges and 18 vocational schools. He also secured free textbooks through the 12th grade and a $110 million bond issue for highway construction.

The Montgomery Advertiser

"Big Jim" in a suspender pose reminiscent of classic ones by Huey P. Long, the 'Kingfish' of Louisiana, after whom Big Jim patterned his political career.

When a 1966 constitutional amendment allowing him to succeed himself in office was defeated in the Senate, Wallace ran his wife Lurleen. The 1966 gubernatorial race, one of the last ones to feature comprehensive statewide stump-speaking campaigns, made the most of a grand "last hurrah." When Wallace announced Lurleen would be his stand-in candidate, Shorty Price, the perennial candidate who persistently dogged the campaigns of his fellow Barbour Countian Wallace, announced he was running his wife. Ryan DeGraffenried, considered Lurleen's major

The Montgomery Advertiser

Governor Lurleen Wallace and the Wallace family — Pictured in the Executive Mansion in Montgomery are: (left to right) Peggy Sue, George Jr., Lee, Gov. George C. Wallace, Gov. Lurleen B. Wallace, and Mrs. Jim (Bobbi Jo) Parsons.

opposition, was killed early in the race when his private plane crashed into a mountain in North Alabama. Attorney General Richmond Flowers campaigned almost exclusively for black voters and got them, for a second place finish. Carl Elliott, a special target of Kluxer-type vandalism for his congressional support of the Kennedy Administration, still had some Wallace-size crowds (aided by Hank Williams, Jr., and Audrey Williams appearing with him) and came in third. Ex-Governor Patterson had long since been upstaged by Wallace on the segregation issue and had a negative image from school teachers still smarting from proration. Another candidate was perhaps a dab too risque, by trying to get a gathering around a go-go girl, and still another underfinanced candidate sold tickets on a motorboat to finance his travels. It was a carnival atmosphere in the best spirit of Alabama circus politics. But when the music stopped and the hoopla was over, Lurleen had more votes than all the others combined! She, unlike husband George four years before and four years after, won without a runoff.

Carl Elliott: Alabama's Education Congressman

Born the son of a Franklin County tenant farmer just before World War I, Carl Elliott read from the Bible at age 4 and two books a week by grade school. Finishing high school when 16, he went to the University of Alabama with $2.80 cash and initially lived in an abandoned building. Before he graduated, he was the student body president. He began practicing law in 1936 and in 1948 served the first of his 16 years in Congress. Although a busy congressman, he maintained his goal of reading one book a week and co-authored the Library Services Act (1956) which built libraries and carried books to rural youths via "Library-on-Wheels" bookmobiles. In 1958 Elliott pushed through Congress his crowning achievement, the National Defense Education Act (NDEA) providing college scholarships and loans to lower-income students. Appointed to the powerful Rules Committee by the Kennedy Administration, he was one of the most influential and respected members of Congress ... at the apex of a distinguished career.

Meanwhile, back in Alabama, Alabamians followed the Southern nationalistic leadership of George Wallace to pursue another lost cause — public school segregation. But it was the rage of the day and Wallace rode the whirlwind. The chief loser was Elliott, whom Wallace singled out for defeat in the 1964 statewide congressional race. Elliott followed the loss by putting his total financial resources into a 1966 losing gubernatorial effort against Lurleen Wallace.

For the quarter century after 1966 ex-congressman Elliott represented black-lung claimants from his home and office in Jasper, where he worked to pay off his campaign debts and pursued his love of northwest Alabama history. His **Annals of Northwest Alabama** was extended to five volumes, he assisted several local authors in publishing pamphlets on hill history, and also accumulated interviews with elderly citizens of the Red Bay area for a history of that city (with 22 historical sidebars expounding on the information given by the interviewees). His work was interrupted in a most favorable way in 1990 by his being selected as the first recipient of the John F. Kennedy Profiles in Courage Award. Encouraged by Doubleday editor Jacqueline Onassis, and with the assistance of Michael D'Orse, Elliott turned out his autobiography, **The Cost of Courage** (1992). Meanwhile, some 20 million students received NDEA aid due to the efforts of the former Congressman from Jasper ... Alabama and the nation's most outstanding education-focused congressman.

Source: **Twentieth Century Alabama,** 266.

Mrs. Wallace's administration continued the Wallace program and strengthened the mental health program. Lieutenant Governor Albert Brewer became governor on Lurleen's death in 1968, but was defeated by Wallace two years later in a very close runoff.

In addition to serving as governor of the state, Wallace was actively engaged in national politics. Alabamians had shown a tendency to buck the

"Solid South" tag of constant support for the Democratic Party on a number of occasions: in 1928, Hoover lacked only 7,072 votes of carrying the State (attributable to a protest vote against Democrat Al Smith — a Catholic, a wet, and a product of the sidewalks of New York); in 1948, the state was carried by the Dixiecrat slate of Senator Strom Thurmond of South Carolina and Governor Fielding Wright of Mississippi (a reaction to the strong civil rights plank in Truman's platform); and in 1964, the state supported Republican conservative Barry Goldwater and elected five Republicans in their U.S. House delegation of seven.

Republicans capitalized on some of the anti-National Democratic Party sentiment by electing mayors in Mobile and Birmingham and Congressmen in the Mobile, Montgomery, and Birmingham districts. The "urban Republicanism," first appearing during the Eisenhower years, was weakened by post-1948 Democratic Party actions such as the Vice-Presidential nomination going to Alabama U.S. Senator John Sparkman in 1952.

The major "Dixiecrat-type" revolt of the 1960s, however, was captured by Governor Wallace. Wallace entered Presidential primaries in 1964 and received more than 30 percent of the vote in Wisconsin and Indiana and 42 percent of the vote in Maryland. Known for his 1963 "stand in the schoolhouse door" at the University of Alabama, Wallace hoped, by a favorable showing in the primaries, to defeat the Civil Rights Act of 1964. The Act passed and, following the Selma March of 1965, a Civil Rights Act of 1965 was also passed. In 1968, Wallace entered the Presidential race as a third-party candidate and carried five states (Arkansas, Louisiana, Mississippi, Alabama, and Georgia). A third national effort, in the Presidential race of 1972, was cut short by the near-assassination of Governor Wallace following a speech in Maryland.

Lieutenant Governor Jere Beasley of Barbour County assumed the governor's duties while Wallace recuperated. As Wallace was not constitutionally able to succeed himself as governor in 1978, political pundits predicted a "3 B's" Democratic primary — Beasley, Baxley, and Brewer. Not! Former Auburn football star Fob James, an engineer earlier known for advocating long-range non-political planning for highway construction, and owner of a very successful sports equipment company in Opelika, Diversified Products, pulled off an upset of 17-16 proportions. Through modern public relations techniques emphasizing television marketing, James projected an image of a non-political businessman who could bring economy to government. Campaigning in a yellow school bus he declared "War on Illiteracy" stressing efficiency in education rather than more tax dollars. Baxley, trying to effect a New Deal-type coalition of state workers, educators, labor, and blacks, lost a close runoff election to James' popular reform-without-cost campaign. Though new to the state political process, James, as governor, did implement periodic student testing to identify areas of educational need. In a more direct way of executing reform, the James administration built new prisons in Jefferson, St. Clair, and Limestone counties to try to make possible citizen desires to keep more criminals behind bars. As had governors before and after, James failed in his attempt to overhaul Alabama's outdated and over-amended 1901 constitution.

In the 1982 elections, George Wallace was elected to a fourth term as governor, Bill Baxley became the lieutenant governor and Charlie Graddick of Mobile was reelected attorney general. When Wallace retired in 1986, Baxley and Graddick vied for the Democratic nomination for governor. Initial results of the runoff election showed Graddick the winner by 8,000 votes. But as Graddick violated a Democratic Party Executive Committee rule by encouraging Republican primary voters to "crossover" to vote in the Democratic runoff, the committee declared Baxley the Democratic primary winner. Graddick appealed the ruling through the court system but lost. The Democratic Party dissension cost them the November general election as an alienated citizenry elected the Republican Guy Hunt, a Holly Pond farmer, Primitive Baptist preacher, and former Probate Judge of Cullman County. Hunt was reelected in 1990 and served until convicted of a felony (misuse of inaugural funds) and removed from office in 1993. He was replaced by Lieutenant Governor Jim Folsom, Jr. Newcomers to the state political process like the James administration before them, Hunt's administration did not have good relations with the legislature and is known primarily for executive actions promoting business and industry. To be elected governor in Alabama, unless you are George Wallace, apparently means you must achieve high name recognition without being tainted by being another one of those politicians in Montgomery. Aspiring governors-to-be must answer the question: "How does one acquire the political experience necessary to be a successful governor while maintaining a fresh, non-political political image?" Obviously political inexperience should not be a cardinal virtue for would-be officeholders. Perhaps newly elected Governor Fob James, the only Alabama governor to be elected as a Democrat and a Republican, has the answer — serve one term, take a low profile for a while until your opposition is labeled as the candidate of the Capital City powerbrokers, then resurrect as a relatively fresh face.

On the senatorial level, John Sparkman of Huntsville moved from the House to the Senate in 1946 to join Lister Hill of Montgomery. Sparkman, born on a tenant farm in 1899, graduated from the University of Alabama, became a Huntsville lawyer, and was elected to the House of Representatives in 1936. He was the unsuccessful Democratic candidate for Vice President in 1952 running with Adlai Stevenson of Illinois. In the Senate, Sparkman was the Chairman of the Foreign Relations Committee and the Banking, Housing, and Urban Development Committee. He sponsored legislation favoring labor, TVA, and middle-income housing. He retired in 1978 after 42 years of Congressional service and was succeeded by former Chief Justice of the Alabama Supreme Court, Howell Heflin. Lister Hill retired in 1968 and was replaced by former Lieutenant Governor Jim Allen who died of a heart attack in 1978. His widow served the remainder of his term after which Vietnam POW and Naval retiree Jeremiah Denton, Jr., the first Republican Senator since Reconstruction, served for one term. Democrat Richard Shelby of Tuscaloosa won Denton's seat in 1986 as the junior senator to Howell Heflin. Shelby withstood a challenge from Birmingham state

U.S. Space & Rocket Center

Rocket Park, U.S. Space and Rocket Center, Huntsville. The world's largest exhibit of space technology and home of the Space Camp. In the display are the first rocket to launch a U.S. space satellite, the first to put a U.S. astronaut into space, and Saturn V, the largest rocket ever built.

legislator Chris McNair in 1992. After the Republican rout in the 1994 elections, Shelby switched to the Republican Party, as Strom Thurmond of South Carolina had shifted after the Barry Goldwater-inspired gains in the South in 1964.

In the House, Alabama's post-World War II Congressional delegation of nine was reduced to seven by reapportionment resulting in the loss of two senior congressmen via statewide balloting in the 1960s — Frank Boykin of Mobile and Carl Elliott of Jasper. In 1992 the newly drawn black 7th district yielded the first black Congressman in 116 years, State Senator Earl Hilliard of Birmingham. Farther south, in the 2nd district, Republican Bill Dickinson retired after 28 years in the House and was replaced by fellow Republican Terry Everett, an Enterprise realtor, farmer, and former newspaperman, who defeated Democrat George Wallace, Jr., for the seat.

The other five 1992 Alabama Congressmen were Sonny Callahan, (1st District Republican), Glenn Browder (3rd District Democrat), Tom Bevill (4th District Democrat), Bud Cramer (5th District Democrat), and Spencer Bachus (6th District Republican).

Sonny Callahan, a corporate executive before a decade in the state legislature, has been in Congress since 1984. Glenn Browder, a former political science professor at Jacksonville State University, served one term

Photo by Don Newton, Jr., Birmingham Chamber of Commerce

Daylight view of Birmingham skyline

in the state legislature and as secretary of state before his election to Congress in 1989. A Jasper attorney, Tom Bevill, the dean of the Alabama Congressional delegation with continual service since 1967, became a major supporter of the Tennessee-Tombigbee Waterway and of funding buildings for state universities. Bud Cramer, former Madison County district attorney and a national advocate for children's rights, entered Congress in 1990. Spencer Bachus represented Jefferson County in the state legislature and served as the state chairman of the Republican Party before his election to Congress in 1992.

Twin Themes: Diversification and Democratization

As early as 1930, Birmingham was the state's leader in population, per capita income, and industrial production. The Tennessee Valley supplanted the Black Belt as the leading cotton producing area. The Black Belt still led

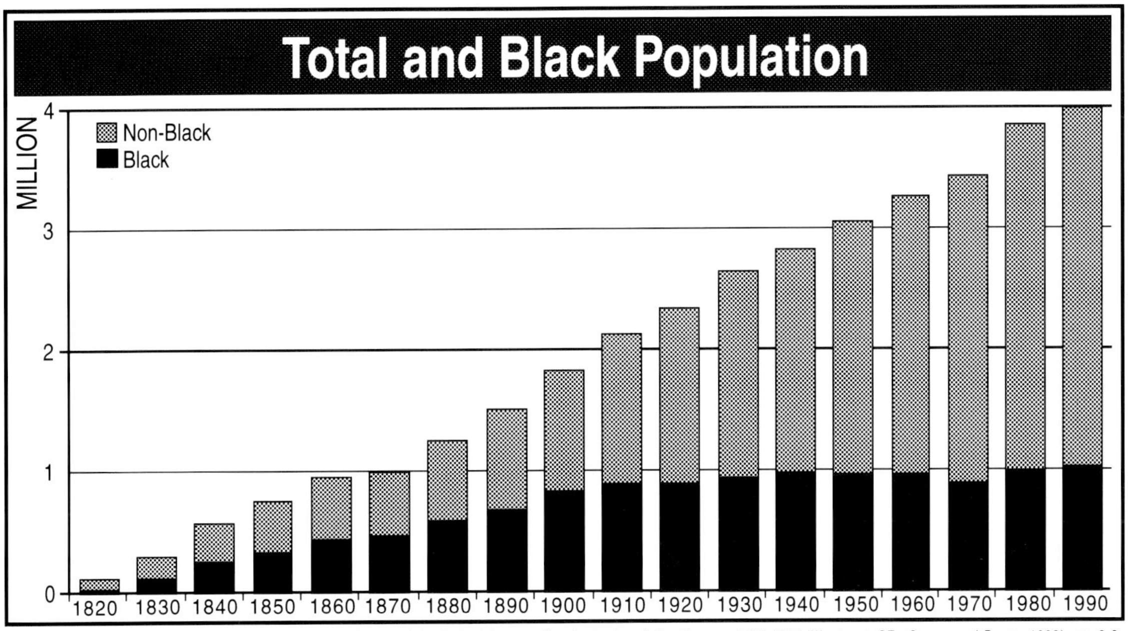

Source: Donald B. Dodd, *Historical Statistics of the States of the United States: Two Centuries of the Census, 1790-1990* (Westport, CT: Greenwood Press, 1993), pp. 2-3.

in the number of black residents, the highest percent of blacks in the total population, and the highest percent of illiteracy. Birmingham, Montgomery, and Mobile were the only three cities of 75,000 or more but urban complexes of 45,000-75,000 emerged in Dothan, Selma, Tuscaloosa, Huntsville-Decatur, and Gadsden-Anniston. The Birmingham to Tuscaloosa area experienced a marked population increase from 1930 to 1940. These demographic trends continued for the next half-century.

In 1960 Alabama became an urban state — that is, more people living in places of 2,500 or more than in those of less than 2,500. (The United States as a whole reached this status in 1920.) A great 1950-1970 surge in the Huntsville-Decatur area resulted in Huntsville's replacing Montgomery as the third largest city for one census year, 1970.

By 1970, one-half of the state's population resided in north-central Alabama inside the industrial area bordered by the urban sprawls of Tuscaloosa, Decatur, Huntsville, Gadsden, Anniston, and Birmingham. In the percent of total population living in towns of 2,500 or more there was also, by 1970, a southeastern urban center bordered by Dothan, Ozark, Montgomery, Opelika, and the Georgia line.

The black population continued to shift to the cities, especially to Birmingham, Mobile, and Montgomery. The Black Belt still led in the percent of blacks in the total population which yielded large numbers of black officeholders. The most significant black population statistic, however, was the number of blacks leaving the state. In 1880 blacks constituted almost one-half of Alabama's population, declining to 36 percent in 1930, and 30 percent in 1960. In 1990, Alabama's total population of four million included slightly more than one million blacks (about 25 percent of the total population). See the accompanying graph for relative ratios of black and white populations through the years.

Cotton production nose-dived even more than the black population. Alabama's annual production hovered around one million bales from 1860 to 1930, but, by 1963, this was cut in half. In 1990, it was down to 383,000 bales. Alabama was the "Cotton State" in 1860 and "Cotton Tom" Heflin could still proclaim it so in the 1930s — but not anymore. Marijuana may now be the greatest cash crop (estimated over $300 million) and peanuts topped cotton $157 million to $119 million in 1989. Soybeans yielded $67 million. The Alabama of the 1990s features diversified agriculture and rapid industrialization-urbanization.

One standard industrial measure, value added by manufacturing, showed a statewide annual increase from 258 million dollars in 1930 to 2,325 million in 1963, and to 20,583 million by 1990 — about a tenfold gain from 1930 to 1963 and again 1963 to 1990. The market centers were north-central Alabama — the Tuscaloosa-Huntsville-Anniston triangle — and Mobile.

Before the 19th century, transportation hubs became urban centers with the Tennessee River, Alabama-Tombigbee Rivers, and Chattahoochee River as major arteries. Birmingham's iron ore, coal, and limestone resources attracted railroads by the late 19th century and the resulting industrial-urban concentration, in turn, made Birmingham the center of post-World War II airline activity. In the 19th and 20th centuries industrialization became almost synonymous with urbanization. But as we move toward the 21st century, the service sector (government, health care, education, and wholesale-retail trade) becomes more significant. The space industry remains the major force for Huntsville, and the State Docks for Mobile, but the major employer in Birmingham after the 1980s was not U. S. Steel (or rather USX) but the UAB Medical Complex. South Central Bell was number two. In 1990, wholesale/retail trade employed 111,000, government 77,000, and mining, iron and steel, and fabricated metal a total of 19,000. Montgomery's primary economic producer is governmental — the state capitol and Maxwell and Gunter Air Force bases — and second is wholesale-retail trade. The No. 1 expenditure of state government is education and educational institutions play a major role in the economics of cities from Athens to Auburn and all the larger cities. Russell Corporation (sportswear) is the major employer in Alexander City. Alabama led the nation in auto tire production in 1990 with Goodyear in Gadsden, Michelin in Dothan, Uniroyal Goodrich in Tuscaloosa and Opelika (both Michelin-owned), and Dunlop (Sumitomo-owned) in Huntsville.

Extractive industries declined. Woodward Iron Company closed Alabama's last iron ore mine in the 1970s yielding to a lighter grade of Venezuelan ore available via Mobile and the Tombigbee-Warrior River barges. The largest coal producers, Jim Walter Resources and Drummond, mined enough low-sulphur coal for Alabama to be ranked No. 12 nationally but, in the 1980s, employment in the industry dropped 40 percent. Birmingham turned a lemon into lemonade by converting a rusty iron mill, Sloss Furnace, into an industrial park. With the Tannehill complex near Bessemer and Red Mountain Cut, the Vulcan, and other industrial preservation efforts documented in the spring 1994 Alabama Heritage, one can see Birmingham is a national center for industrial preservation.

Unfortunately much of Alabama's historical efforts to attract industry — low taxes, tax exemptions, state bonds for factory construction, anti-union policies, and cheap labor — contributed to the development of a low-skill manufacturing economy. Smokestack-chasing strangulated Alabama's tax base. The results were 1988 rankings of 50th in expenditures for elementary and secondary education and in spending for public welfare.

Fortunately recent efforts to attract industry have yielded higher quality manufacturers. The Alabama Development Office (ADO) notes that 53 companies have taken advantage of the new incentives for attracting industries provided by the Folsom administration's Alabama Act 93-851 representing a total investment of about $2 billion and more than 7,000 jobs. The most recent, by Packard Electric Division of General Motors, is a million-square-foot facility in Gadsden to produce wiring assemblies for mid-size mini-vans. Slated for a mid-1995 opening, it will have an initial workforce of 300 with an eventual projected expansion to 1,200.

The most publicized coup of the Folsom plan was the $300 million 1.2 million-square-foot Mercedes-Benz plant to build four-wheel drive sports utilities vehicles at Vance in Tuscaloosa County. Set to open in 1997, the plant will employ about 1,500 workers. To land the plant, Alabama gave a $253 million financial incentive package which essentially waived immediate benefits such as property and employment tax revenues in return for anticipated long-term benefits — sales and income tax revenues. The facility is anticipated to create an ancillary job growth of 10,000 jobs in 5 years and 15,000 in 20 years and an economic impact of $500 million annually and more than $7 billion in 20 years. The Mercedes development hopefully will anchor a large research and development, industrial/business park in the 55-mile interstate corridor between Tuscaloosa and Birmingham, patterned after the Research Triangle Park in Raleigh-Durham-Chapel Hill, North Carolina, as envisioned by former University of Alabama President Joab Thomas. Thomas helped recruit the high-tech Japanese firm JVC to the corridor in 1986.

A particular clean industry showing great growth the past two decades is tourism. According to Wayne Greenhaw, director, Alabama Bureau of Tourism and Travel, tourists spent almost $4 billion in Alabama in 1993 and tourism-related industries yielded more than $350 million in state revenue. At the current growth rate, it could be the number one industry in the state by the early 21st century. The top four "admission-charging" attractions in 1993 were Huntsville's Space and Rocket Center (427,000), the Birmingham Zoo (360,180), the Montgomery Zoo (299,478), and Mobile's USS Alabama Battleship Park (298,568). The Alabama Shakespeare Festival (Montgomery), Birmingham Children's Theatre, and Creek Bingo Palace (Atmore) each had about 200,000 admissions. The top "natural destinations" were the Alabama State Parks with Gulf State Park Resort (Gulf Shores) with 2,280,926 guests and Joe Wheeler State Park (Rogersville) with 797,974 leading the 1993 list. Oak Mountain State Park (Pelham) and Eufaula Wildlife Refuge each attracted more than 500,000 visitors. A recent project destined to attract golfers to the state is Alabama's Robert Trent Jones Golf Trail which offers 100 miles of golf on seven facilities — 54-hole complexes in Huntsville, Birmingham, Auburn-Opelika, and Mobile, and 36-hole facilities in Calhoun County, Greenville, and Dothan.

Photos by Dan Brothers, Alabama Bureau of Tourism and Travel, of posters in the office of Michael Boyer, director of the Alabama Film Office

Posters of nine movies made in or about Alabama

One of the more dramatic new industries is filmmaking. More than 50 movies have been made in Alabama from "The Phenix City Story" in 1955 to "Cobb," partially filmed at the nation's oldest baseball park, Rickwood Field in Birmingham. Based on the success of Steven Spielberg's "Close Encounters of the Third Kind" in stimulating the economy in the Mobile area, Governor Wallace created the Alabama Film Office. Mobile's USS Alabama battleship has been the setting for several movies including "War and Remembrance," "Mission of the Shark," and "Under Siege," which the Mobile Department of Tourism estimated as having an economic impact of $12.5 million in 6 months. Mobile's filmmaking frequency and an expanding technical crew base influenced filmmakers David Prior and Patrick Gallagher to locate a $2.5 million filmmaking facility, Southern Star Studios, on 10 acres outside the port city. Southern Star hopes to tap the product demand created by more and more cable channels, perhaps up to 500 channels within a half-decade. See the accompanying photographs of posters of movies made in Alabama and the sidebar by Wayne Greenhaw on a personal experience with 1970s Alabama filmmaking.

Democratization

When the four young girls were killed in the 16th Street Baptist Church bombing in 1963, there was not a single black elected official in Alabama. Ten years later when one of the girls' father, Chris McNair, was elected to the state legislature from Jefferson County, he joined more than 100 other black elected officials in Alabama. Lucius Amerson of Tuskegee (Macon County) became the first black sheriff in the South in 1968 and Johnny Ford was elected mayor of Tuskegee 4 years later — the same year Jay Cooper was elected mayor of Prichard, a suburb of Mobile. The Birmingham list included new City Council members attorney Arthur Shores and Miles College professor Richard Arrington. In 1979, Arrington, a Ph.D. in biology from the University of Oklahoma and son of a Fairfield steelworker, won the mayor's race in Birmingham by 2,000 votes (of 87,000 votes cast). After his 1983 reelection, he formed the Alabama New South Coalition. With Senator Hank Sanders and his wife Rose, J. L. Chestnut, Jr., all of Selma, and Michael Figures of Mobile, he challenged Joe Reed's Alabama Democratic Conference (ADC) for statewide black political leadership. After successful mayoral races in 1987 and 1991, Arrington led the New South Coalition into endorsing incumbent Governor Jim Folsom, Jr. in the 1994 Democratic primary. Reed's ADC backed his Alabama Educational Association (AEA) colleague Paul Hubbert, long time executive director of the AEA. Birmingham newspaperman Ted Bryant sees Reed and ADC as the major losers in the campaign because Reed lost his hold on his Black Belt power base. In view of the Republican sweep in the November general election, it appears the Democrats may have been weakened by these internal power alignments.

Despite internal divisions, blacks have made great political advances since the massive black registrations following the Voters Rights Act of 1965. Black women have shared in these gains, especially in Jefferson County. In the last two decades black women have been elected to the Birmingham City Council and to represent Jefferson County in both the

Drawing by Tom Sangster, The Lavender Agency, Bay Minette, Alabama

E.O. Hall & Son's Store at Cecil near Montgomery. Hall's store is typical of the Alabama crossroads stores so much a part of the rural landscape in the living memories of the "Baby Boomer" generation (and older folks). It is as Southern as country churches, dusty roads, barn roofs printed with "See Rock City," and all-day-singings-with dinner-on-the-ground. But it was also a setting for a Truman Capote TV special. (See the Wayne Greehaw sidebar.)

State House of Representatives and the State Senate. Odessa Woolfolk, a black woman and former administrator at UAB, has been mentioned as a potential successor to Mayor Arrington. When American historians selected the most distinguished women of the 20th century, an Alabama black woman, Rosa Parks, was ranked No. 3 (Helen Keller of Tuscumbia was No. 9). A recent book by Jo Ann Robinson on the Montgomery Bus Boycott was subtitled "And the Women Who Started It" honoring their widespread initiation and continued support of the boycott.

Women in general have made progress in politics, dramatized by State Senator Ann Bedsole's unsuccessful 1994 gubernatorial campaign, but less so than their neighbors — 5.7 percent of Alabama state legislators being

Personal Memories of the Filming of Truman Capote Short Stories near Montgomery

By WAYNE GREENHAW, director, Alabama Bureau of Tourism and Travel

During the shooting of Truman Capote's "A Christmas Memory" at John Hall's Store in the crook of State Highway 110 at Cecil, actress Geraldine Page and the young actor playing her cousin pushed an ancient wicker baby-buggy filled with their goods to make fruitcake. As they moved out of the store and down the road, a train was heard in the distance. Director Frank Perry, who was famous at the time for his prize-winning film "David and Lisa," whispered, "Keep on rolling." The train rumbled past, disappearing into the distance, then cinematographer Conrad Hall said, "If this was being made by David Lean, it would have cost a half million for the train." Everybody on the set broke up.

Several years later, Frank Perry called me and asked if I would find locations for a sequel to be called "The Thanksgiving Visitor." I was sent a list of location descriptions and found most of them straightaway. But the main location, a house from the early part of the century, could not be found. Every time I discovered a new old house, I sent photos to New York, but none hit Frank Perry just right. Finally, after looking every day for more than six weeks, I came upon an old house on Mount Meigs Road being used as a goat house. That evening I called Frank and told him about the house, and he immediately said it sounded perfect.

He flew down Friday. I met him and we drove out. Traipsing through the mud and manure, Frank explained excitedly how this was fantastic.

That November, Frank's wife, Eleanor, the screenwriter, wrote a part in the Truman Capote for me. I was Cousin Wayne.

During the shooting Capote and Princess Lee Radziwill visited the set. We had a huge picnic on the grounds of Woody Bartlett's farm and that evening Frank and Eleanor hosted a party at the Governor's House Motel for the distinguished guests.

women in 1991 compared to a nationwide 17 percent. Only Kentucky and Louisiana had less. Books such as Paul Gaston's **Women of Fair Hope** and Virginia Hamilton's **Alabama** have publicized educational and other non-political contributions of Alabama women.

Although males still dominate Alabama politics and society, many Alabamians share a cultural appreciation of obstacles overcome by economically oppressed males not unlike that others have had for more clearly identifiable "minorities." In Wayne Flynt's concluding chapter, "Gender, 'Jocks,' and Shakespeare: Alabama Society and Culture, 1970-1993," he cites a 1989 Alabama poll asking, "What Alabamian, living or dead, do you admire the most? George Wallace and Bear Bryant won handily with Bo Jackson and Hank Aaron named next. Flynt follows with descriptions of the Bear's childhood, the youngest of 11 children of a semi-invalid father, his playing football for the Fordyce (Arkansas) High School

The Montgomery Advertiser

The Bear: Even from the stands, his presence on the field was striking. His pregame pose leaning on a goalpost is as legendary as his winning record and was sometimes awesome. At Clemson in "Death Valley" during the Snake Stabler days of the 1960s, a significant portion of the student body lined the homeschool's entrance to the field and as kickoff time approached, began to make one hell of a racket. Suddenly in wave-like fashion, a deadly silence progressed from the students through the stands to the goalpost on the other end of the field. It was like the final scene from "Close Encounters of the Third Kind" or almost a "Second Coming." Or more, it was the Bear!

Red Bugs, and the Bear's motivating fear of going back to plowing mules and chopping cotton for 50 cents an hour. After playing "the other end" across from Don Hutson at Alabama, Bryant (1913-1983) capped an outstanding coaching career with a 1958-1981 Capstone tenure encompassing six national championships, three national coach of the year awards, culminating in his becoming college football's winningest coach with 315 victories. Meanwhile Auburn football, baseball, and basketball player Ralph "Lefty" Jordan (1910- 1980) became Coach "Shug" Jordan and in the 1951-1975 years won 175 games (24 consecutive ones, 1956-58, with a national championship in 1957) went to 12 bowls, and coached 20 All-Americans including Heisman Trophy winner Pat Sullivan. As football was a way out of poverty for Bryant so was it for a black 262-pound Alabama nose guard who grew up like Bryant — but more than a half-century later. Willie Wyatt's house at the end of a dirt road near Gardendale did not have running water, indoor plumbing, or central heat. Bare light bulbs hung from exposed rafters. Flynt cited Wyatt's "incentive":

I'm not ashamed to say I had it rough growing up. But having it rough is not always bad. What I've learned and what I've seen, I'll never forget. Those are vital experiences in my life that helped set my values. I didn't have the things a lot of others take for granted. But maybe that's the reason I worked so hard. (p. 620)

Football is no doubt overemphasized in Alabama society but, as Flynt notes and Andy Doyle demonstrates herein, as a cultural focus, it provides a vehicle for one to analyze the culture's values. It also, with other Alabama traditions like racial conflict and poverty, contributes to a tenacious folk culture and, for some, a strong work ethic and a sense of individual responsibility. Though plagued by racial polarization, lack of political vision, and short-sighted leadership, Alabamians face the 21st century with the possibility of greater contributions from women, blacks, and maybe from some folks who just grew up rough, a visionary young business community, and a "physical environment incredibly beautiful and diverse, even if often neglected and polluted." (Flynt, p. 622). Sometimes Pogo's assertion, "We have met the enemy and he is us" seems appropriate. But Alabamians are a proud, independent, individualistic lot. And they will not forever tolerate political leadership by good ole boys who are primarily good to themselves and a state legislature who, through political pragmatism, irresponsibly leaves politically tough decisions like reapportionment and the funding of state services (mental health, prisons, education) to the federal, and recently, even state, courts. General discontent with the way things have been run was reflected in the 1994 general election. Hopefully, the new leadership sees this as a mandate for a government that responds to the general welfare of the whole rather than the special interests of the few ... and not of one set of special interests over another. Pogo's dictum is a haunting one. But so is the cliche on fooling folks ... all of the people some of the time, some all of the time, but not all all of the time.

Alabamians have overcome a lot in the last half of the 20th century. Rapid changes threatened traditional ways. Industrialization and urbanization converted our agricultural and rural world from a self-directed way of life to one focused on organization. While recognizing the need to conform to organizations and institutions in a complex world, Alabamians sought to maintain values and a way of life from simpler and more serene times. It has not been easy. A white and male-dominated society was challenged by blacks, and then women, who also wanted the opportunity to pursue their dreams. The 1960s were especially turbulent.

Our roots are in a small-town past ... strong on families, communities, and rural values. Nurturing these roots can fortify us to solve the problems of the present. We will muddle through. Utilizing the talents of all our people, united and stronger, we have the opportunity to do more. If individuals develop the self-esteem, self-reliance, and courage to fulfill their potential, and our leadership marshals these human resources in pursuit of worthy and attainable goals, the 21st century promises a better quality of life for all our citizens.

Photo by Dan Brothers, Alabama Bureau of Tourism and Travel

Then and Now: The 285-foot, 44-ton paddlewheeler Delta Queen going through the locks at Wheeler Dam near the Route 101 bridge. From 1929 until World War II, Delta Queen was a luxury overnight ferry on the Sacramento River, transporting passengers between Sacramento and San Francisco. She now regularly visits Florence, Decatur, and Huntsville on the Tennessee River. The Delta Queen is the only authentic, fully restored, overnight steamboat in the world. Source: "Alabama Travelgram," fall 1993, 4-5.

Index